INSIGHT GUIDES

BRITTANY

Edited and Produced by Brian Bell

A P A

PUBLICATIONS

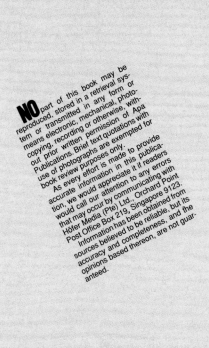
BRITTANY

First Edition
Printed in Singapore by Höfer Press Pte Ltd

ABOUT THIS BOOK

Insight Guide: Brittany, following hard on the heels of Insight Guides to Ireland, Scotland and Wales, is the fourth title examining one of Europe's Celtic fringes to be produced by project editor **Brian Bell**. Born in Northern Ireland, whose political turmoil compels all its citizens to examine their allegiances, he well understands the debates about national identity that have occupied a small region such as Brittany.

As a London-based journalist with wide experience in newspapers and magazines, Bell was first attracted by Apa's approach to travel guides because it combined detailed reporting about what makes a place tick with a bold, photojournalistic style of illustration. In a crowded publishing market, he believes, too many guidebooks content themselves with anodyne prose and picture-postcard photography; yet a country's warts can often be as interesting as its beauty spots and usually make it more enticing to the adventurous traveller.

Definitive Study

A journalistic perspective dominates this book, therefore. For an account of Brittany's history and for insights into such cultural activities as *pardons*, Bell turned to **Ward Rutherford**, a newspaper and television journalist and author of 16 books, including *The Druids* and *The Ally*, a definitive study of the Russian Army in World War I. Rutherford, a Jerseyman, now lives in Brighton, in England, but growing up in the Channel Islands gave him close contacts with nearby Brittany, especially the Côte d'Emeraude. At

that time many Bretons would come to work on Jersey's farms.

Rutherford sees parallels between Brittany and Wales, partly in the clannishness of the people, in their friendly yet reserved personalities, and partly in the fact that so much of the tourist industry is run by people from outside the region. Yet, despite the recent drive to attract new industries, he doesn't think the rural community has changed very much in the past quarter of a century. "There's a tendency to think more touristically, perhaps," he says. "Churches, even remote ones in small towns, tend to be floodlit, for instance."

Jill Adam, another confirmed francophile since schooldays, took on the daunting task of documenting such touristic facts for the Travel Tips section. Having edited the *French Farm and Village Holiday Guide* for some years and, more recently, acted as deputy editor for the *Good Beer Guide* published by Britain's Campaign for Real Ale, Adam is no stranger to marshalling large quantities of information. Renovating an old bakery in France has given her the excuse for many summer sallies across the English Channel and working on this guide enabled her to "snatch an out-of-season trip to Brittany which reinforced my opinion that the best of France can be enjoyed when the holiday crowds have gone home—although I didn't spend much time on the beach."

Robin Neillands, a familiar byline in British newspapers, is the indefatigable author of 40 books (including some with "Brittany" in the title), but is certainly no armchair travel writer. He regularly walks, cycles or canoes distances that would exhaust Concorde and his contributions to the Places section of this book took the customary heavy

Bell

Rutherford

Adam

Thomas

toll of shoe leather and bicycle tyres.

Roger Thomas, another contributor to the Places section, is also an author and a walker. Most of his books are about his native Wales and he draws the inevitable parallels between it and Brittany. "You can still find a genuine sense of community and comradeship. They're both stunningly beautiful—and the countryside really is countryside, not some clogged, pale green, pseudo-rural imitation."

Patricia Fenn, as the author of eight "eating, drinking, sleeping and viewing guides" to France, found it hard to choose which area of Brittany to write about for this book. "Family sailing holdiays along the north coast and St-Malo? Trips down the River Rance to Dinan? Short breaks in the Cancale peninsula? Further west, the pink Granite Coast is unbeatable. But then Finistère, especially in the south around Bénodet, has such wonderful scenery, climate and restaurants." Finally, she settled on the unique Gulf of Morbihan. "*Sans pareil*," as she says.

Peter Forde, a freelance agricultural journalist, living in Cornwall, first visited Brittany 20 years ago to look at cauliflower production, just as the area was about to explode with economic and social development. "Going back two or three times a year at least, I have seen the transformation of a backward and forgotten people into a vibrant region," he says. "What draws me back is the warmth of the people and the way of life handed down through so many generations."

Philippe Barbour, half-Breton and half-British, trained his mind in that most traditional bastion of English education, Oxford University, but lets Brittany's sea air clear it again each summer. He is currently an editor with a London-based publishing company specialising in books on wine.

Rob Shipley is a Jerseyman who turned from teaching to journalism, with a stint as a professional fisherman in between, skippering a crabbing vessel. Though he now earns his living as managing editor in a Channel Islands publishing company, he is still much involved with the sea, enthusiastic about scuba diving, underwater photography and anything to do with boats.

Mike Mockler, who has written about birdwatching and flora and fauna for several Insight Guides, is a British-based writer, photographer and teacher. For him, travel is an opportunity to seek out beautiful countryside, interesting animals and exotic birds.

Visual Splendour

The visual standard of *Insight Guide: Brittany* owes much to the work of such regular Apa photographers as **Lyle Lawson**, **Catherine Karnow** and **Alain Le Garsmeur**. And the excellence of the **Brittany Ferries Photo Library** proved that the Bretons' drive to attract business to their province has been thorough. The maps were drawn by **Kaj Berndtson Associates**.

The book's smooth progress into print depended on the help given by Brittany Ferries' **Toby Oliver**, and on the skills of typists **Janet Langley** and **Valerie Holder**, proof-reader and indexer **Rosemary Jackson Hunter** and computer tamers **Audrey Simon** and **Karen Goh**.

Fenn

Forde

Barbour

Shipley

HISTORY AND PEOPLE

PLACES

FEATURES

MAPS

TRAVEL TIPS

"The people of Lower Brittany are as lively as broomsticks," claimed an old Breton song. It was most heartily sung, no doubt, by the people of Upper Brittany, the eastern part of the province which, being geographically closer to the rest of France, was less immersed in Celtic culture.

As far as the rest of France was concerned, however, both Basse-Bretagne and Haute-Bretagne might as well have been on another continent. Armorica, the "land by the sea" as the early Celts called it in the sixth century, had always been a world apart, an isolated granite peninsula whose fishermen fought hostile seas and whose farmers struggled to coax crops from the thin soil.

For centuries, indeed, France had been an unfriendly neighbour. After 1532, when Brittany at last came under the control of the French monarchy, the chief enemy lay to the north: England.

The Celtic inheritance: England's enmity was shared with other Celtic groups, in particular the Irish, the Scots and the Welsh, all of whom retain cultural links with Brittany. In terms of personality, Bretons seem closest to the Welsh. Both have maintained as great a degree of independence as they reasonably could from an often insensitive ruling power to the east, and both peoples, though warm and welcoming, appear on first acquaintance to be reserved, even distrustful.

This trait was noted by Eugene Fodor's pioneering 1936 guidebook, *On The Continent*, which advised: "It is absolutely futile to try to have a conversation with a Breton peasant who does not want one. Your efforts will come to nothing. On the other hand, once he has confidence, the Breton will prove a joyous companion glad to render service, and very hospitable."

Since, historically, most visitors to Brittany had been invaders, such confidence was not won easily. Few casual travellers were attracted to such a seemingly backward place and, in any case, a jagged coastline and

windswept uplands made parts of the province virtually inaccessible until the railways came in the late 19th century.

All that has changed, but the centuries of relative isolation served to preserve a distinctive way of life. As in other Celtic regions, tales of myth and magic were passed from generation from generation, populating the misty landscape with magicians and dragons, fairies and devils.

And—another Celtic trait—religious observance did not become diluted, as it did

in much of western Europe. Bretons cherished their army of saints, most of them democratically elected by the local population rather than authorised by the Pope in Rome.

To express their devotion, the people provided lasting monuments to their saints in the form of churches and cathedrals; few areas one-third the size of Scotland could boast nine cathedrals. Today's *pardons*, though they are an undoubted tourist attraction, remain a sincere expression of Breton piety as villagers parade through the streets with banners, candles and statues to ask forgiveness of their local saint.

Preceding pages: item in Nantes Museum; rural transport; tractor in Cornouaille; farmers; at Audierne; family near Quimper. **Left,** confrères in Cornouaille. **Above,** girl at Concarneau.

Grave concerns: Death has always held a particular fascination, even by Celtic standards, for Bretons. The cemetery lay at the heart of the old villages; it was a playground for children, a meeting-place for lovers and a convenient spot to sit and gossip. As a cemetery became crowded with corpses, space for new arrivals would be created by removing old bones to ossuaries. "We live with our dead," a Breton would explain. "If we bury them away from the village, they will hear neither the singing nor the services."

Religious belief was tailored, from earliest times, to fit the Breton character. Some experts believe, for example, that the

mysterious *menhirs* which dot the landscape of the south were meant to represent God but that, because their long forgotten creators did not know His shape, they left Brittany's grey granite rocks untouched by the chisel as the most appropriate expression of the eternal. Later, the 16th and 17th-century sculptors who carved intricate calvaries depicting Christ's Passion and Crucifiction introduced a host of anachronisms from everyday life: in one calvary, for instance, Christ enters Jerusalem on a donkey accompanied by musicians wearing traditional Breton breeches and playing tambourines and bagpipes.

Happily, the Bretons' cultural heritage has not been relegated, as has been the case in so many countries, to the sterility of the folk museum. Young people have been pumping new life into old dances and folk music—even developing a form of Breton pop music. Many have been trying to revive the Breton language.

But cultural integrity does not feed and clothe families. Sensing that the priorities of the authorities in Paris lay elsewhere, Bretons have turned their traditional energy and self-sufficiency to good use, nominating themselves architects of their own economic reconstruction.

In the 1960s the province's farmers, angered by the unfair farm prices set by middle-men, formed cooperatives to take control of their own marketing and distribution. Their success was spectacular; their confidence grew, and soon they even set up their own shipping company, Brittany Ferries, which has become a major force in the English Channel.

As employment in commercial fishing continued to decline, the Bretons set out to attract light industry to the area. Again, they succeeded; companies realised that the availability of willing labour more than compensated for the region's relative remoteness—and even that problem of distance began to vanish as new roads were built and the service of the TGV express train was extended to Brest.

It's appropriate that Brittany's greatest hero is Bertrand du Guesclin. He was born in the early 14th century with few advantages, an ugly and neglected child, the eldest of 10; but, by his courage and determination, he rose to be commander-in-chief of the French army.

In the same way, Bretons have turned their geographical disadvantages into opportunities and, in doing so, have not allowed the temptations of 20th-century consumerism to corrupt their values. That's why, once you have broken through their initial reticence, they make such delightful companions. The virtues captured by the artistic imagination of Paul Gauguin and the other painters who flocked to Pont-Aven in the late 19th century have now been perceived by the rest of the world.

Above, boy at Quimper. Right, café society.

GENESIS OF A PEOPLE

Certain places can give you the feeling of being caught in a time-warp. Athens, overlooked by the Acropolis and the Parthenon, can still seem to bask in its classical heyday. There are sections of Paris which carry you back to the *fin de siècle*. Over many British towns the spirit of the 19th century lingers like the mists of autumn.

In Brittany, and especially in the old parts of towns like Quimper, Lamballe or Dol, it is the Middle Ages. Indeed, what now serves as a market-place, such as the Place du Guesclin at Dinan, was the spot where once stood the lists, the arenas in which the knights played out their tourneys, observed from the overlooking windows by their ladies.

Yet the basic ingredients of the Breton racial mix has been blended over many epochs. The first to be recorded were those settlers who journeyed northward up the seaboard of Europe in the Late Neolithic Period, that is to say some 4,000 to 5,000 years ago. The waymarks of their progress were the stone constructions, the megaliths, of which Brittany has such a profusion. These testify, of course, to a genius for large-scale organisation, but apart from this and the fact that their builders grew wheat, barley, lentils and a small apple possibly used for cider, we know little about them.

The second ingredient came from the people known to archaeology on account of the shape of their pottery as the Bell-Beaker Folk who began to arrive about 2000 B.C. bringing with them the knowledge of gold, copper and bronze working.

A new name: The last and perhaps most enduring ingredient was added in the late Bronze Age by the Celts from Central Europe who overran the area which the classical writers came to call Gaul and is now France, from which they spread across the Channel to Britain. Those who settled on the most westerly peninsula of Gaul gave their new homeland the first name known to history: Armor, Land of the Sea.

Preceding pages, traditional folk costume. Left, Brittany's ancient rocks (detail from Octave Pinguilly-l'Haridon's *Les petites mouettes*). Right, an early visitor, Julius Caesar.

Excellent farmers and stock-breeders though they were, the Celts' almost insatiable appetite for war led them constantly into rash adventures such as their expeditions against Rome in 387 B.C. and Greece in 279 B.C. As a consequence they came to be seen as a menace to be neutralised. The task fell largely to Julius Caesar but was made easier by his enemies' inability to sink tribal differences and consolidate themselves into a single nation. From the middle of the first century B.C., partly by military

Jules César.

action, partly by diplomacy, Caesar began picking off the Celtic tribal territories one by one until gradually almost the whole of Gaul was subjugated.

Among the exceptions was Armor where the most powerful of its tribes, the seagoing Veneti, inhabited an area round the Gulf of Morbihan. With the other Armorican tribes, they had, in fact, handed over hostages to Rome as pledges of peaceful intent. Then, in 55 B.C., they seemed to have had second thoughts and seized two Roman envoys sent to Vannes, their capital, by Publius Crassus, the local commander, in the hope of exchanging them for their hostages.

THE MYSTERY
OF THE MENHIRS

One does not have to travel far in Brittany before encountering those huge upright stones the locals call "menhirs". But where did they come from?

The belief that they were the work of the Druids, the Celtic caste of wise-men having long been discredited, the most widely held theory is that their builders were an unknown seafaring race of the late Neolithic and Early Bronze Ages (roughly 5000 to 3000 B.C.). Travelling up the Spanish and Portuguese coasts, possibly from North Africa, the so-called "Megalith builders" marked their progress with a trail of stone stretching as far as Scandinavia.

The one certainty is that organising ability of high order, as well as enormous resources of manpower and formidable engineering skill were necessary for their building. Some stones weigh as much as 350 tons, greater than many used in the Pyramids.

Not surprisingly, size and extreme antiquity has led to their acquiring a heavy layer of folklore. They are said to be petrified giants who return to carnate form at certain times of year to drink or bathe in the nearest river—and woe betide those who see them! The custom of anointing the menhirs with honey, wax and oil survived down to the beginning of this century and probably still continues in remote places. Naturally, the Church frowned on such heathen practices and, where it failed to extirpate them, instead Christianized the stones by incising crosses on them, placing them on their summits or by inventing stories which linked them with the lives of the saints.

Broadly, the megaliths fall into three groups, *menhirs*, *dolmens* and *alignements*. Strictly speaking, the *menhirs*, (from *men*, "stone" and *hir*, "long"), are single stones. Of these there are at least 20 higher than 20 ft in Brittany with the largest (64 ft) at Locmariaquer. Some are the sole survivors of larger groupings; others must always have stood in isolation. Many are set at a precarious angle, at one time assumed to be the work of time. It is now realized that they were actually erected in this way and the phallic character this suggests is confirmed in folk custom. Girls would slide down them, as W. Branch Johnson puts it, "after removing a portion of their clothing"; barren women rubbed their naked bodies against them that they might become fertile; childless couples even mated under their shadow.

The oldest of the megaliths are undoubtedly the *dolmens* (Breton *dol*, "flat", and *men*, "stone"), among which is "The Merchants' Table" also at Locmariaquer. This consists of three large, flat stones erected horizontally to form a sort of three sided box and topped by an even larger flat stone as a lid. Originally they were covered with earth to form burial-mounds or tumuli and those now visible are ones which time and the elements have scoured clean. This is not always the case. In some the covering has survived erosion and a few, such as those at Ile de Gavrinis, have stone-lined corridors leading to the burial chamber and are known as passage-graves. The stones of the Gavrinis passage are richly decorated with carvings.

More recent are the round tumuli, such as that of St Michel at Carnac. Most dramatic of all are the *alignements*, vast arrays of menhirs, as at Carnac, where more than 3,000 of them, a petrified army, stretch away to the horizon.

The incredible effort involved in the erection of the *alignements* and the obvious care taken in their arrangement has always posed the question of their purpose. In 1963, the astronomer Professor Gerald Hawkins advanced the theory that they were Neolithic astronomical computers. That his ideas aroused bitter and sustained controversy has not stopped his findings—which he related specifically to Stonehenge—being applied to other sites. One of these was Carnac, exhaustively investigated by Professor Alexander Thom, an advocate of the astronomical observatory hypothesis. He claimed to have discovered two such observatories. Thom's work, like that of Hawkins, has been criticised rigorously and often immoderately. Nonetheless, the application of the computer to the growing mass of measurements taken at the sites is beginning to shift opinion in favour of the observatory-hypothesis—at least for the moment.

It was a provocation Caesar could not ignore, but to humble the Veneti he had first to break their naval power, a formidable enterprise as they had numerical superiority and were equipped with sailing ships, while the slower Roman galleys were propelled by oars. However, in an engagement which took place off the south east coast of Brittany—according to tradition, watched by Caesar himself from a nearby hill—the Romans were favoured by the weather. A flat calm left the Gaulish ships stranded and, taking advantage of the mobility given him by his oarsmen, the Roman admiral manoeuvred his vessels close enough for his sailors to hurl grapnels attached to ropes into

gions. Their departure left both countries defenceless against the savage Viking raiders and Britain was soon to experience something more permanant than passing forays. It was overrun by Angles and Saxons from across the North Sea. While one part of the British population retreated westward, another sought refuge in Armorica.

Little and large: The fugitives poured in for the next two centuries. Though of the same basic Celtic stock as the indigenous population from whom some had actually originated, their coming was totally to transform the character of the region. To distinguish it from their original land, *Grande* (or Greater) *Bretagne*, Armorica was rechristened *Petite*

the enemies' rigging. As his ships rowed away, the masts and sails of the Venetian ships were dragged down while other galleys attacked and boarded them.

Their fleet destroyed, the Veneti were impotent. Caesar occupied their country, had their leaders executed and the rest of the population sold into slavery.

In the next century the Pax Romana embracing Gaul was extended to Britain and lasted until the crises of Rome in the early fifth century forced a withdrawal of the le-

Left, the mysterious *alignments* at Carnac. Above, a druids' sacrifice.

Bretagne (Lesser Britain), a name later shortened to Bretagne.

The five old Amorican tribes, including the once powerful Veneti, were swamped by two new groupings, the Dumnonii, from Devon, who had occupied the coastal strip from the River Couesnon to the Atlantic coast, and the Cornovii, from Cornwall, who gave their name to Cornouaille. (Those who lived outside these two areas were lumped together as "Bretons".)

The changes extended to linguistics. The newcomers spoke a Celtic language; that of Armorica had been fundamentally modified by borrowings from the Low Latin of the legionaries, yielding the basis for what came to be known as French.

It may have been late migrants from Britain who brought with them tales of a brief heroic age under a king they called Arthur, though it is also possible, as the stories themselves assert, that before the usurpation of Mordred, Arthur had indeed ruled both *Grande* and *Petite Bretagne*. Soon the mythology had taken such deep roots among the Bretons that they came to see it as the site of many of its major incidents. What is now the Forest of Paimpont was equated with Broceliande and a dolmen near Trébeurden came to be regarded as Arthur's tomb. Competing claims are, of course, made by

places as widely separated as Sicily and Edinburgh, to say nothing of Glastonbury.

But what must have wrought the greatest change was another of their imports, Christianity, introduced by British missionary saints like Guénolé, Jacut, Gildas, Brioc, Malo, the centenarian St Pol-de-Léon (the name is a corruption of St Paul Aurelian) and, particularly, Samson. If their efforts failed entirely to eradicate all traces of the gods and practices of heathenism, the magnitude and permanence of their achievement is manifest in the churches and cathedrals of Brittany and in the deep piety which Bretons retain and into which they have incorporated customs whose origins may well go back to the megalith-builders.

The spiritual benefits which might be claimed for the new faith were not, for the average Breton of the period, accompanied by material ones. Tyrannical overlords often imposed taxes so extortionate that many could pay only by stealing. It was a road to anarchy but it continued to be followed until, in A.D.799, Charlemagne conquered Brittany and reformed its administration.

Bald facts: The policy was pursued by Charlemagne's son, Louis the Pious, who in 826 made Brittany into a duchy, appointing a local man, Nominoé, as its first duke. But Nominoé, unable to envisage a future as liege-man to a foreign potentate, planned instead to make himself king of an independent Brittany, an ambition which, in 840, the quarrels over the Carolingian succession after Louis's death enabled him to realise. By 845, when one of Louis' sons, Charles the Bald, woke up to the situation and attempted to reassert his authority, the new king had already united Brittany under his rule. Charles's army was defeated at Redon, near Rennes.

The royal house Nominoé founded lasted for over a century. By the time he died in 851, when his eldest son Erispoë acceded, the boundaries of Brittany had been established. Except for the brief incorporation of Anjou and Cotentin during the reign of Salomon, they were to remain fixed until the French Revolution in 1789.

Salomon (or Salaun), nephew of King Nominoé, seized the throne in 857 after killing Erispoë but gave it up in 872 and, as penance for the manner in which he had acquired it, retired to a hermitage in the Forest of Brocéliande. Here, two years later, he and his son were murdered while at prayer by partisans of his cousin.

The leadership crisis thus precipitated was temporarily obscured by another. From the time of Nominoé the Bretons had suffered so greatly from the depredations of the Vikings that special measures had had to be taken to try to prevent them. Then, in 911, Charles the Simple, king of France, purchased peace for his own people by granting lands and the title of duke to the raider-chieftain, the 80-year-old Rollo. The enemies from the north were now poised on Brittany's borders, ready to cross when the mood took them.

Eight years later, greedy for yet more land, they did so, overrunning most of the duchy. The occupation was mercifully short for, in 939, the Breton king, Alain Barbe-Torte, having taken refuge in England, returned, rallied his forces and expelled them.

This incursion had interrupted, but not ended, the struggle for power. At Alain's death in 952, it broke out anew, to be complicated by an event which was to link Brittany with the destinies of both Normandy and England: the Norman Conquest of 1066.

Breton participation in this was considerable. Many of its aristocrats saw in it the chance, if not of regaining territories their ancestors had abandoned to the German

of gaining English backing in his quarrel with his stepfather, Eudo, during the continuing struggle for succession.

Such advantages could be ephemeral or illusory. When Conan abdicated in 1166, Henry II treated Brittany as a personal fief, finally arousing the people of Brittany to open revolt by ravishing Eudo's daughter, Alix. Already contending with the rebellion of his sons who were trying to establish independent dominions in France, Henry employed maximum savagery to crush the latest threat. When he died in 1189 this repression was continued by his son Richard I.

With England already bloodily embroiled in Breton affairs, it was now the turn of

invaders, at any rate of compensating themselves with others. Typical was Brient de Penthièvre who was rewarded by William for his support with vast Saxon estates in Richmond, Yorkshire.

The prolonged contact between Breton and English noble houses which now came about inevitably led to unions of convenience between them. Thus the marriage of Constance, daughter of Conan IV of Brittany to Geoffrey Plantagenet, the son of Henry II of England, was used by Conan as the means

Left, a 14th-century tournament at Rennes. Above, the Combat des Trente.

France to join in. Since the death of its last king, Alain Barbe-Torte, Brittany had reverted to being a duchy. In 1341, the reigning duke, Jean III, died without issue. To the fury of his nephew, the English-backed Jean de Montfort, who regarded himself as next in line, Jean bequeathed his rights to his niece, a descendant of Brient de Penthièvre and wife of Charles de Blois, nephew of Philippe V of France. In 1351, the contenders mobilised their vassals and plunged Brittany into a civil war compounded by the Hundred Years' War which, since 1337, had been raging between France and England.

In one of the first encounters, the de Blois

forces captured Jean de Montfort. He was rescued by the efforts of his wife, Jeanne de Flandres, who persuaded the English king to intervene and, in one battle, donned armour and fought like a tigress herself.

The Blois forces were also victorious in the battle known as the "*Combat des Trente*", The Battle of the Thirty (the spot is now marked by a stone pyramid), one of those formalised chivalric engagements which characterised the age. The two commanders, Beaumanoir, captain of the castle of Josselin, representing Blois, and the English commander, Bemborough, meeting under flag of truce, decided that the outcome should be settled by 30 picked knights from

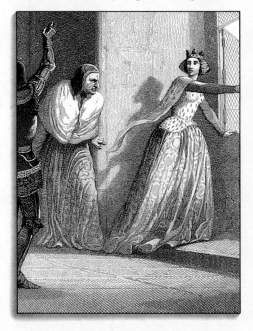

each camp fighting on foot. They met at the mid-point between Josselin and the castle of Ploërmel, held by the English. From early morning 60 men hacked at one another with swords, daggers, battle-axes and pikes until, by nightfall, Bemborough and eight of his men were dead and the rest had surrendered.

The outcome of the Battle of Auray which ended the War of Succession, 13 years later, was less fortunate for Charles de Blois. He now had in his retinue one of Brittany's and France's greatest soldiers, Bertrand du Guesclin, but ignoring his warning that the Montfort army held the dominant terrain, he attacked it and was beaten and slain.

New hope: Under the rule of the Montfort dukes the country, devastated by the war, was not only restored, but saw the dawning of the most brilliant period in its history. Yet not all the portents were good. Economically and militarily Brittany had been far outstripped by its neighbours France and England. Victory in the War of Succession had been gained at the cost of a significant increase in the influence of the latter, guaranteed through astute dynastic marriages as a result of which English royal and Breton ducal houses were now interrelated. Some of the aristocracy even maintained garrisons of English troops at their châteaux.

A people fiercely jealous of its independence could see such developments only as menacing it, and successive dukes sought to reduce the English hold. The need to ensure that this did not give an advantage to the neighbour across their borders meant having to walk a tightrope. None did this more skilfully than Duke Jean V, nicknamed the Wise, who from 1399 until his death in 1442, kept both England and France at bay and, in the process, spared his subjects the worst horrors of the Hundred Years' War.

But the war was actually having the effect of bringing Brittany into a closer relationship with France. There were strong feelings of sympathy among the populace in general for the sufferings imposed by the English invaders. What was more, Breton soldiers had served on the French side. One of the most famous, Bertrand du Guesclin, had been commander-in-chief, and was succeeded by a fellow-countryman, Olivier de Clisson, dubbed "The Butcher of the English". The link was strengthened in 1457 when Arthur de Richmont (his title came from the Penthièvre estates in Richmond, Yorkshire), a companion in arms to Joan of Arc, succeeded his brother as duke.

In any case, the Montfort's unequivocal support for England earlier—combined with Brittany's strategic position and its possession of a port at St-Malo ideal for troops landing from across the Channel—caused some unease. France drew one compelling conclusion: that Brittany represented a potential threat which could be eliminated only by its incorporation.

Above, Jeanne de Montfort. Right, du Guesclin remembered today.

34

BERTRAND DU GUESCLIN

Like many a medieval dynastic marriage, that of Jeanne de Penthièvre and Charles de Blois at Rennes in 1338 was celebrated with an extravagant tournament. Though the contestants included some of France's finest knights, interest quickly centred on an unknown who unhorsed challenger after challenger. It was not until someone knocked off his helmet that the 17-year-old Bertrand du Guesclin's bullet head, snub nose and swarthy countenance was revealed.

To many, he was already notorious as the tearaway ringleader of a peasant gang. His parents, minor Breton nobility from La Motte-Broons, near Dinan, were said to have despaired of Bertrand, the eldest of their 10 children.

But opportunities for his talents were soon to present themselves. The previous year the English invasion of France had started the Hundred Years' War. By 1341 when Jean III, Duke of Brittany, died, the Duchy found itself embroiled in a struggle for succession between Jeanne de Penthièvre's husband and his English-backed cousin, Jean de Montfort. Now 21, du Guesclin threw himself in on the side of de Blois, harrying the de Montfort lines with a private army of cut-throats, allegedly financed with money and jewellery stolen from his mother.

Soon their daring and the boldness of their leader had made them such a local legend that, when Charles de Blois was captured by the English in 1347, Bertrand was sent to negotiate his ransom.

By 1359, after he had held Dinan against the Duke of Lancaster, his fame reached Paris and he was awarded a royal pension.

At the siege he had shown he had lost none of the skill in single combat he had shown at Rennes. When his brother, Olivier, was taken prisoner by Sir Thomas of Canterbury in violation of a truce, Bertrand challenged the captor to a duel in Dinan marketplace and was supported by the English commander. After splintering lance and sword, Bertrand ended the struggle with a crashing blow to his opponent's face with his mailed-fist.

The incident had been witnessed by a pretty 24-year-old Dinan girl, Typhaine Raguenel. After a brief wooing, the untutored soldier—he never learned to read or write—married the girl who studied the occult and read philosophy in the classical languages. Evidence suggests they remained genuinely fond of one another.

By May 1364, Bertrand was earning further laurels by defeating Charles II of Navarre, ally of the English, at Cocherel in Normandy.

That same year the mailed-fist which had vanquished Thomas of Canterbury was again in use at the Battle of Auray, this time less successfully. The Blois forces, attacking against Bertrand's wishes, were not only beaten but Charles was slain, thereby ending the War of Succession. Bertrand fought like a demon. The English commander, seeing him flailing at his enemies with his fists, told him: "The day is not yours Messire Bertrand; you will be luckier on another." He shrugged—and surrendered. Such was his value that the French were prepared to pay a ransom of 100,000 crowns.

In 1370 he was promoted to Constable of France—effectively commander-in-chief.

His final battles, however, were to leave his reputation permanently stained in the eyes of Breton nationalists. In 1373 he was ordered by Charles V to subdue Brittany's Montfort duke, Jean IV. The Duchy taken, Charles tried to annex it to France. The Bretons prepared to resist the threat to their independence, but the expected French onslaught never came. The Breton mercenaries who made up the majority of Bertrand's army refused to fight their own kin and deserted en masse. Their commander offered to return his Constable's sword.

Instead his king sent him to fight in the Massif Central. Here, at the age of 60, he deployed his siege machines for the last time. He was, as ever, victorious. Death, on 13 July 1380, prevented his knowing the outcome, but acknowledgment that the day was his was posthumously accorded to him by the surrendering English commander who put the town's keys in the dead warrior's fingers.

His body was laid in the church of St Denis in Paris, burial place of French kings. His heart, however, reposes in the church of St Sauveur in his beloved Dinan.

ANNE DE BRE

THE BATTLES FOR BRITTANY

In 1461, Charles VII of France died. He was succeeded by Louis XI and in 1483 by the weakly 13-year-old Charles VIII, who gave the impression of possessing neither the aptitude nor the intelligence for his role. These were characteristics readily exploited by his sister, the ambitious and scheming Anne de Beaujeu who made herself head of an unofficial Council of Regency.

Almost from the time of the king's accession her powerful enmity had forced many to flee court and country and take refuge in Brittany. In 1487 they were joined by the Duc d'Orléans. This group of dissident expatriates were soon planning Anne's overthrow, for which they succeeded in gaining the support of the Duke, François.

France's fear of Brittany had been increased by the betrothal in 1486 of the Duke's 11-year-old daughter Anne to the Hapsburg prince Maximilian. By his election as King of the Romans, this formidable soldier and statesman had become heir to the Holy Roman Empire on the death on his father, Frederick III. Maximilian's previous marriage to Mary of Burgundy, who had died four years earlier, had made him master of her dominions on France's eastern border as well as extensive Burgundian possessions in the Netherlands.

Survivors massacred: In the spring of the following year, Anne de Beaujeu decided to forestall what now seemed inevitable, the addition of Brittany to his other territories. The duchy was invaded by a 15,000-strong French army which, being repulsed, was followed the next year by an even larger one. At the Battle of Saint Aubin du Cormier in July 1488, the Duc d'Orléans was captured and most of those Bretons who survived the day were massacred.

Three weeks later, Duke François was compelled to sign the humiliating Treaty of Verger agreeing, *inter alia*, that his daughters would marry only with the consent of France. Within a fortnight he was dead, largely it was said of a broken heart. He was

Left, Anne of Brittany, forever stained in Dinan. Above, Anne and Louis d'Orléans in Rennes in 1491.

succeeded by the 12-year-old Anne, who was to become one of the most beloved figures in Breton history, recalled in some form in almost every one of its towns.

With her accession the French king, prompted by his sister, saw an opportunity. Margaret, Maximilian's daughter, to whom he had been betrothed in 1482, was packed off back to her father and Charles transferred his suit to the young Breton duchess, making clear that he would brook no refusal. She and her advisers were now in a dilemma: consent

would compromise the duchy's independence; the alternative could unleash another disastrous war.

But there were other important factors even in marriages of political necessity. In spite of a stained glass window in the church of St-Malo in Dinan which shows her as a pretty young girl, there is no reason to question the accuracy of Jean Bourdichon's representation of her as a rather plain, if pleasant-faced, young woman and contemporary accounts speak of her as small, thin and handicapped with a limp. But these disadvantages were amply compensated for by her charm, vivacity and intelligence. In addition, she was well educated, knew Latin and Greek, and throughout her life was a patron of artists and writers and an endower of churches. By contrast, Charles, besides his reputation for stupidity, was short, thick-lipped, had pale, myopic eyes and a great hook of a nose. To a girl, imbued with a strong sense of her own worth and already engaged to a king who would one day be Holy Roman Emperor, he must have possessed few recommendations.

And it was this engagement which now seemed to offer a way of saving both Anne and her duchy. In defiance of the terms of the Treaty of Verger, Anne married Maximilian in 1490 in such haste that the religious cere-

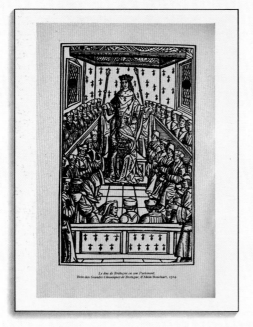

Le duc de Bretagne en son Parlement.
Bois des Grandes Chroniques de Bretagne, d'Alain Bouchart, 1514.

mony was conducted by proxy.

Marriage or no marriage, the French stuck to the letter of the treaty and Charles continued his demands with accompanying threats. In August 1491, after she had refused him, he laid siege to Rennes. Anne stood firm in the belief that Maximilian would come to her aid, but as the weeks turned into months with the blockade of the city tightening, he remained incomprehensibly passive.

At the end of three months of siege a delegation of city elders, nobles and church leaders presented themselves to her and described the hardships her subjects were enduring. Moved by their account and reluc-

tantly forced to accept there was to be no succour from her husband, she set aside her own wishes in the interests of her people, and in a gesture which was to earn their perpetual gratitude, agreed to marry Charles.

Before this could be done, however, her marriage to Maximilian had to be ended. This was referred to the Vatican, which agreed to an annulment. The wedding took place in the royal castle of Langeais, in the Loire valley, on 6 December 1491.

Though Anne was said to have averted her face as she gave Charles her hand, there is little doubt that his feelings for her went far beyond political expediency. Throughout their married life he showed her the greatest affection, nicknaming her "*ma petite Brette*" and Anne, herself warm-hearted, early responded to his manifest love.

Shrewd woman: Anne was now, of course, Queen of France. A more important effect of the marriage was to bring her own duchy into a closer relationship with its neighbour. She had, however, been shrewd enough to ensure that the marriage settlement safeguarded her position as sovereign duchess of an independent Brittany. After Charles's accidental death in 1499, when she re-married, this time to his successor, Louis XII—thus again becoming Queen of France—she ensured that this clause was retained.

In 1514, at the age of 37, Anne died at the Château de Blois. As she left no male issue the duchy went to her daughter Claude, who in the spring of that year had married François d'Angoulême, the king's cousin, and heir presumptive to the throne. On New Year's Day 1515, at the death of Louis XII, he acceded as François I.

Claude, like her mother, was now Queen of France and, also like her, kept the title of Duchess of Brittany. François had other ideas and successfully persuaded her to will it to their son, the Dauphin, thereby linking it to the French crown.

After Queen Claude's death in 1524 he went still further. He paid a personal visit to the Breton parliament, the States of Brittany, and, while arguing that its interests and those of France coincided, left the parliamentarians in no doubt what would happen if they wilfully persisted in following the course of independence. During the ensuing debate, some favoured defiance, but François had already gained a formidable reputation as a soldier by defeating Massimiliano Sforza's allegedly invincible Swiss troops at the Battle of Marignano, a circumstance which dictated prudence rather than valour.

After a session at Vannes in August 1532, the States unanimously requested union with France. It was a petition the French king had no hesitation in granting.

At Nantes, that same month, "the perpetual union of the Country and Duchy of Brittany with the Kingdom and Crown of France" was formally proclaimed. Under the terms of the Final Act, the rights and privileges of the Duchy were to be upheld: it could maintain an army and all taxation would require the approval of the States,

The period saw the flowering of the Flamboyant style in architecture in which Brittany itself participated with the building of châteaux and churches like Notre Dame de Lamballe. It also benefited from the reforming zeal of a monarch who, summer and winter, rode the length and breadth of his kingdom, smelling out abuse, dismissing corrupt judges and emptying the prisons of those languishing under injustice.

Then, in 1534, a Breton was responsible for enhancing the renown of France by increasing its territory. Jacques Cartier sailed from his native St-Malo in search of the apocryphal Northwest Passage. Instead he discovered the mouth of the St Lawrence

which would also retain its position as high court of justice.

It could well have appeared to be the best of both worlds and, to many Bretons, a good time for their nation to have plighted its troth with France. The new king's court became the resort of wit and beauty and the rendezvous of the most gifted men of Europe. Even Leonardo da Vinci was able to pursue his art unfettered by financial constraints, thanks to the pension granted him by François.

Left, the Duke of Brittany and his parliament in 1514. Above, power players await the next move.

where Indians he met told him stories of gold, silver and copper mines and abundant spices further west. Cartier took possession of the land on behalf of his king, calling it by a name he had heard the natives use, *Canada*, actually the Huron Indian word for "village".

The French, on the other hand, might have been forgiven if experience tempered their initial enthusiasm for the new province. In the 12th and 13th centuries France had been torn apart by the religious wars in which the heretical Cathars had been suppressed with unparalleled savagery. Emergence of another heresy in the form of Protestantism in the mid-16th century clearly spelled trouble.

Henri II, François's son, an ardent Catholic, met the challenge by systematic persecution and, for a time, this policy was pursued by his successor, Henri III. However, in 1576 financial pressures forced him to make concessions to the Huguenots, the main French Protestant sect. The Catholics formed the militant Holy League to oppose what they saw as a surrender to heresy.

Nowhere was Catholicism more deeply entrenched than in Brittany where, in 1582, a 24-year-old local nobleman, the Duc de Mercoeur, had been appointed governor. Seven years later, when Henri III was assassinated and succeeded by Henri de Navarre, the Huguenot leader, Mercoeur rallied

Catholic opinion against him, establishing his own court and naming his son, Philippe, "prince and duke of Brittany". When the Spanish king backed him with 7,000 Catholic troops and Protestant England countered with troops and ships, his revolt looked set to plunge France into civil war.

The contending forces collided at Craon in Anjou in 1592. Mercoeur emerged victorious. However, in 1592 Henri demolished the foundations of the rebellious duke's case by converting to Catholicism with the famous

Above, wolves were a menace in the 16th century. Right, a calvary at Pleyben.

40

comment, "Paris is worth a Mass". The following year Mercoeur submitted, married his daughter Françoise off to Henri's bastard son and went to fight the Turks in Hungary in the army of the Holy Roman Emperor. There, he died of fever.

Although nationwide insurrection might have been averted, Brittany itself was thrown into chaos. One cause was the degeneration of what had started out as religion-motivated guerrillas into gangs of brigands whose sole concern was to "pluck the goose where it was fat," as a local saying put it.

Among the most notoriously cruel of these was La Fontelle. He ravaged the countryside from a lair on the island in the Pouldavid estuary to which he added fortifications by the simple expedient of demolishing and purloining those of Douarnenez.

It was against such men as La Fontelle that, in 1597, States of Brittany petitioned Henry IV for aid in restoring order. The king came in person in August 1598 and was so stunned by the wealth and power of the Breton dukes he saw manifested in their great castles that he is said to have stood before one of them and whistled in admiration, exclaiming, "God's teeth, they're no small beer, these Dukes of Brittany!"

It was at Nantes on this same royal visit that he signed the famous Edict, whose 92 articles were supposed to settle the religious question permanently.

Axes fall: The policies of Louis XIII's chief minister, Cardinal Richelieu, if beneficial to France at large, had been less so for Brittany. As part of his planned enlargement of the navy he established a huge naval dockyard at Brest. As an employer of labour it was welcome. But, as the keels of the first ships were laid down, the axes began to ring in the Breton forests, denuding the area of an important resource.

Jealousy of the chief minister's almost absolute power had already provoked several conspiracies against him, and feeling was bound to be further exacerbated by acts of this kind. Twenty-eight years after Henri's visit, the then Duke of Brittany, César of Vendôme, the king's illegitimate son by his mistress Gabrielle d'Estrées, joined his mother in yet another. Like the rest, it miscarried and its chief architect, the Comte de Chalais, was executed, while César was stripped of titles and office.

Ludovico Magno

The rebellious spirit of the Breton was to continue to be a thorn in the flesh of Paris. In 1642 Richelieu and his king died within six months of each other and Louis XIII's throne was occupied by his four-year-old son, Louis XIV. Like his father, he had as his chief minister a cardinal, Jules Mazarin, a Sicilian recommended by Richelieu, but, in 1661, when Mazarin died, the king, though only 23, announced his intention of arrogating all executive functions to himself.

Among his first acts was to commission the building of a huge and magnificent palace to serve as a royal pleasure-dome, and as the means of impressing his own absolutism on his subjects and the grandeur of France on the world at large. It called for enormous sums of money and the responsibility for finding it fell to Jean-Baptiste Colbert who, as Comptroller-General of Finance, was already trying to raise funds to continue Richelieu's work of building up the French navy.

Vigilant for potential sources, in 1675 he decreed that to have any legal status, all contracts and similar acts must be recorded on specially stamped paper. The cost of the stamps involved would go into the royal coffers.

The uprising which broke out in Brittany soon afterwards, called the "Stamped Paper Revolt", was caused by Colbert's fiscal measures, and was compounded by an unrelated peasants' revolt against their feudal overlords.

Resentment smoulders: The majority of those inhabiting Brittany's extensive coastline were seafarers and heavy smokers. To safeguard them from the price rises caused by periodic increases in central government's duties, some few years earlier the States of Brittany had purchased immunity for the extortionate sum of two million livres. Without compensation or even consultation Colbert highhandedly re-imposed the tax. Such acts helped to reinforce the

belief, born of Richelieu's ruthless exploitation of the forests, that Brittany was regarded in Paris as a colony to be milked whenever the need arose. More practically, the government's imposts and the sum already spent on immunity from the tobacco tax had brought the duchy to the brink of bankruptcy.

Yet it was at another port that the spark of rebellion first kindled. Bordeaux was seized by insurgents who held it for three days in March 1675. Then, in April, the inhabitants of Rennes followed their example, attacking

government buildings. Only the mass drunkenness which followed an attack on the excise office responsible for collecting the duties on alcohol gave the authorities the opportunity to regain control. This didn't stop the riots from spreading to Nantes. The unrest was prevented from reaching St-Malo by a timely decision to let the crews of ships about to sail to the Newfoundland fisheries buy their tobacco duty-free.

At Versailles Louis, determined to curb this challenge, cast round for someone to restore his centralist authority. His eye fell on the Duc de Chaulnes, a former governor of Brittany, who was marched back at the

Preceding pages, Camille Corot's *Bretonnes à la Fontaine de Batz-sur-mer* (*circa* **1855**). **Left, Louis XIV, the Sun King. Above, Cardinal Richelieu.**

head of an army. A few salutary hangings subdued Nantes and Rennes through June, but the truce was ended by two further Colbertian measures: a duty on grain and a proposal to introduce a salt *gabelle*.

The *gabelle* was a state monopoly in a particular commodity which at the same time stipulated the minimum quantity each family, irrespective of need, had to buy. Thus the government had it both ways. In July, there were further riots in which mobs attacked the stamped paper offices at Rennes, as well as others at Châteaulin, Quimper and Guincamp.

But in Basse-Bretagne, roughly the area west of a line from St-Brieuc to the Gulf of

to free labour, which local aristocracy levied on the peasants. Now they became the target of attacks which, at first minor, quickly developed into a mass movement as, with the church bells ringing the call to arms, revolts broke out in 40 parishes and their inhabitants marched on the local châteaux—in at least one instance with their priest heading them.

Soon a *Code Paysan*, a "Peasants' Code", was circulating. With its proposals for the administration of the law through locally elected justices, the abolition of clergy tithes, of labour for the landowners and of all social distinctions, it read, in many ways, like a Digger or Leveller pamphlet. More specific to local grievances were its propos-

Morbihan, events took on a different complexion.

In Britain the Civil War which broke out in 1642 had spawned a plethora of egalitarian movements, among them the Diggers, who set up agrarian communes, and the Levellers, who advocated universal suffrage and equality for all before the law. Now these ideas seemed to have crossed the Channel. Armed bodies of peasants, who came to be called the *Bonnets Rouges*, began turning on another enemy.

Since the Middle Ages there had been smouldering resentment at the often intolerably onerous exactions, including the right

als that anyone trying to administer the *gabelle* should be shot "like a mad dog" and that tobacco should be distributed free at Sunday Mass.

New leader: What the *Bonnets Rouges* had so far lacked was a leader of the calibre of the Leveller's John Lilburne. They believed they had found one in Sébastien Le Balp, a Carhaix lawyer. Under him the flame of rebellion spread from Carhaix and its surrounding villages to Pontivy, with even the historic château of Josselin coming under threat. But Le Balp was also planning a general uprising which was to be run like a military operation. He even had in mind a soldier to lead it: the Marquis de Montgaillard who, with his brother, had shown some sympathy with the peasants' cause.

But de Chaulnes had not been idle either and, having pacified Rennes, was able to shift his attention to Basse-Bretagne. His first tactic was to offer pardons to all who laid down their arms. He was assisted by the seminarians from the big Jesuit colleges in the duchy who portrayed the proposals of the Code Paysan as heretical, if not downright anti-Christian. Such arguments were highly successful with the devoutly Catholic peasantry, drastically eroding Le Balp's forces. Even more alarming, the inference to be drawn from the amnesty offer was that, in the

Rouges from embarking on an attempt on Morlaix they invented the story that 6,000 of de Chaulnes troops were stationed there.

Shorn of what was to have been its crucial element, the uprising still went ahead and, on 3 September, 30,000 *Bonnets Rouges* put Carhaix to the torch. The next objective was to have been Quimper where the Duc de Chaulnes now had his headquarters. On the way Le Balp halted at the Mongaillard château where he told the brothers of the plan and offered them the choice of participating or facing the wrath of the mob outside. The Marquis's response was to run Le Balp through with his sword. There was a moment or two of tension as reactions were awaited.

event of his failure, a terrible price was going to be exacted from those who had not taken advantage of it.

He saw that he needed allies and in desperation began looking to France's enemies. With the Dutch fleet in the Channel, he hatched a scheme to seize Morlaix and offer it to De Ruyter, their admiral. The plan might have succeeded but for the Montgaillards; they already had misgivings about Le Balp's conduct, and were horrified by this treasonable proposal. To dissuade his *Bonnets*

Then, leaderless, the mob drifted disconsolately away. The Great Uprising was over.

And now came the reprisals. A few, the better off and those who had the right connections, managed to reach the Dutch ships or escape to the Channel Islands. Those caught and regarded as ringleaders were hanged or broken on the wheel. Many more were sentenced to death on the mere suspicion of complicity. The luckiest were two men sent to rot in the galleys and one whose only punishment was banishment.

One horrified observer of these barbarities from her château at Les Rochers, near Vitré was Mme de Sévigné. In letters to her

Left, St Malo's ramparts in the 15th century. Above, the port of Concarneau.

THE BRETON COSTUME

If one thing typifies Brittany it must surely be costume: men in black wideawakes, broad-lapelled jackets and gilt-buttoned waistcoats; women in black dress and apron, topped by their precarious-looking *coiffes* have figured and still figure on thousands of postcards, guides, and boxes of Breton crêpes, biscuits and sweets.

The sad truth is that, unless you make a point of attending a *pardon* or one of the great festivals like the *Fêtes de Cornuaille* in July, such representations are all that you are likely to see.

Even in traditionalist areas like Morbihan or Finistère the *coiffe* has become a rarity, and long vanished are those old ladies once seen on every market-day selling produce from the family smallholding or peddling handmade articles such as lace gloves. Inquiries at a *Syndicat d'Initiative* will evoke only the suggestion that one visits the town museum. It is often easier to see living examples in the cities and bigger towns outside the duchy where youths and girls dress up to promote tourism.

It seems ironic that the Bretons, whose culture has survived centuries of suppression, should find their highly distinctive costume in danger of extinction—or surviving only as a folkloric curiosity—in today's more tolerant climate.

In the past every Breton man was expected to outfit himself with at least one complete suit and its accessories. A girl might expect to have an entire wardrobe of clothes, from silver lace-embroidered for occasions like weddings to sombre black for funerals.

Even though some of this might be handed down through her family or acquired as part of a trousseau, the cost was enormous and there is no doubt that costume was a means of displaying family wealth. The many-tiered skirts of the women of the "Bigouden country" of the Penmarch Peninsula actually provided a ready-reckoner by which it could be assessed.

And cost is certainly one of the factors which has contributed to decline. To assemble even a minimal outfit would cost a small fortune at to-

day's prices. Associated with cost is the loss of traditional skills. The dressmaker, the hatter and the bespoke tailor have been displaced by the fashion *boutique* and the off-the-peg departments of the large stores. The women of the household, once content to pass winter evenings with their lace bobbins, have now, like their sisters worldwide, been seduced by *le télé*.

The term "Breton costume" is of course misleading. There isn't a single one, but many costumes, each identifying the wearer's area. The dress of the Bigouden men was distinguished by long, embroidered waistcoats worn under short jackets of dark cloth. Besides tiered skirts, their women wore richly embroidered silk bodices. On the other hand, at nearby Quimper, the men's jacket was pale blue, while the women's dresses included multi-coloured and highly intricate embroidery and on this account was regarded as the finest in the duchy. Elsewhere one might have come across men in the baggy, homespun breeches known as *bragoubras*.

However, two items of the women's apparel were of special significance. The first was the apron, usually of satin or velvet, brocaded or embroidered and edged with lace, the richness of decoration revealing the family status. As with the rest of the costume, aprons also varied from place to place. Those of Cornouaille were brightly coloured and had flowing ribbons. The Pont-Aven apron was small. That of Quimper had no bib. In Lorient, by contrast, the bib came up to the shoulders.

But above all, there was the *coiffe* varying widely in size and complexity. That of Douarnenez, for instance, was no more than an adornment for a bun at the back of the head; that of Cornouaille, a little cap on the top of the head. In Huelgoat it was a net over the hair; in Plougastel a simple white linen cap, often with lace used only as an edging.

The Auray *coiffe* partly hid the forehead; the Quimper one resembled the Spanish *mantilla*. The two most elaborate were that of Pont-Aven with upturned wings to its wide, starched collar and, perhaps most famous of all, the Pont l'Abbé *coiffe*, a veritable tower intended to represent a menhir, usually with a lace streamer behind.

daughter which have been preserved she writes of the frightened peasants throwing themselves on the mercy of French troops, soon to find themselves standing on the scaffold asking only for a drink and quick death.

Having taught Basse-Bretagne its lesson, de Chaulnes decided to punish Rennes. Whole suburbs were emptied of their inhabitants and burnt down. As final acts of vengeance for its recalcitrance, the duchy was fined three million livres and 10,000 French troops were billeted on private homes throughout the winter. They conducted themselves like the hordes of a barbarian conqueror, raping, looting and committing

And soon Brittany was to release another straw into the wind.

Pirate power: However, the ensuing years were to show that there was an obverse to the coin—a group of Bretons who were not only unquestionably loyal to France but whose careers enhanced its reputation. These were the privateers, Breton sailors who, armed with "Letters of Marque" which legalised their activities, turned their vessels into men-of-war, preying on enemy—which was to say British—warships or merchantmen.

Greatest of these, though there were many others, were Duguay-Trouin (1673-1736) and Surcouf (1773-1827). René Duguay-Trouin, intended for the priesthood, had

murder, unchecked. It was not until the following summer that the people of Brittany were judged to have been chastised enough and life began to return to normal.

The government's victory had been total and crushing, but by the light of hindsight it is easy to see the "Stamped Paper Revolt" as the foreshadowing of events to engulf the entire nation just over a century later. Even the Phrygian caps adopted by the *Bonnets Rouges* were to be copied by the mobs who stormed the Bastille, Versailles and the Tuileries.

Above, waiting for the fruits of a wreck.

disappointed his father, a St-Malo shipowner, by a dissolute youth. In the end the sea was perceived as the only means of curing him. He quickly became a legendary figure. Captured by the British in 1694, he escaped disguised as a Swedish skipper. Three years later, still only 24, he was promoted to commander and at 32 given a peerage. He was to go on to still greater things, for in 1711 he seized Rio de Janeiro from the Portuguese. Though, in the event, it was to be held only briefly it was a considerable achievement celebrated with unbounded patriotic joy in France.

The life of Robert Surcouf, born 100 years

after Duguay-Trouin, was no less distinguished. He too came from a St-Malo shipowning family and was originally destined to be a priest, but, expelled from a religious school at the age of 10, he was packed off to sea. Given his first command at 20, his first major coup was the seizure of the 26-gun HMS Triton with its crew of 150 by the 18 men of his own vessel.

This was overshadowed by a later achievement. In 1800, in *Confiance*, a privateer of his own design, he surprised an armed East Indiaman, the *Kent,* in the Bay of Bengal. In spite of heavy fire from the Kent's 38 guns, Surcouf managed to edge close enough to board. The British crew had been supplemented by 437 soldiers but in a desperate struggle the combined defences were gradually forced back. When the Kent's commander, Captain Rivington, was killed, they gave in.

After his retirement in 1809, Surcouf, enriched by his privateering activities, continued to amass wealth as a shipowner and slave-trader. Ever-jealous of his country's honour, in 1817, a plump 44-year-old, he fought duels with 12 Prussian officers who had insulted it in a St-Malo restaurant. After killing 11, he spared the last to carry the story back to Germany.

The privateering careers of Duguay-Trouin and Surcouf had been possible only because their lives straddled a period of continual wars between France and Britain. In June 1758, during one of these, the Seven Years' War, a 14,000-strong British task-force was assigned to capture St-Malo. It landed at Cancale, to the east, reached St-Servan just outside St-Malo but, unable to advance further, destroyed the town and re-embarked.

In early September another attempt on St-Malo was made, this time with the troops landing to the west, at St-Briac. From the first this had no better luck than the previous one. The British naval ships, instead of giving covering fire, had to sail westward to St-Cast to escape unseasonal gales. Alarmed at this loss of support, the army commander wheeled his men about and marched off in the same direction.

On the way they ran into a small blocking force and were held up long enough to give the French commander-in-chief, the Duc d'Aiguillon, time to regroup. On 11 September he defeated the British at St-Cast and they were again forced to leave Brittany. The victory is commemorated by a column on a promontory overlooking the sea, on the summit of which the rusting iron Breton greyhound mauls an equally rusty British lion.

Jesuit power: Hero of the Battle of St-Cast though the Duc d'Aiguillon may have been, he was to find himself viewed in a less favourable light in his other role, that of governor of Brittany, when he became embroiled in a dispute with the powerful Society of Jesus. This, like the "Stamped Paper Revolt", was an omen for the future.

As their behaviour then had shown, the Jesuits did not have any scruples about using their power for political ends. At a time when Enlightenment thought was penetrating even into remote Brittany, this could only aggravate hostility to what was seen as their religious dogmatism.

In 1760, the duchy's Public Prosecutor, La Chalotais, wrote a highly critical report which was soon a national best-seller. Even Voltaire, from his eyrie at Ferney, was moved to comment that it was "the only work of philosophy ever to come from the Bar". On the basis of the report, La Chalotais induced the States of Brittany to vote for the order's expulsion.

As the king's representative, the Duc d'Aiguillon sought to have the vote reversed. When the States were immovable, Louis XV intervened and, finding himself faced with continuing obduracy, exiled three of its members and sent La Chalotais to jail. As a method of trying to secure compliance it was a spectacular failure, having precisely the opposite effect.

The Paris Parliament came out in support of their Rennes colleagues and there was evidence that many of the other provincial Parliaments would do the same. Louis, who had not bargained for confrontation on this scale, found himself in the embarrassing position of having to back down.

The two great revolts had taken place within less than a century. In one case, the people had risen up against both the exactions of central government and their feudal masters. In the other, royal absolutism had been humbled by the Parliaments.

Right, a "man of the coast" in Finistère.

The meaning of these omens became clear in 1789 with the French Revolution. Its promise of release from the ancient tyrannies was bound to make it welcome to the Bretons and they celebrated the Fall of the Bastille on 14 July of that year as enthusiastically as anyone in France.

Yet disillusionment had already begun to set in by the autumn when the government turned on the church, to the Bretons an act of sacrilege. There were heavier blows to come. In the following year a reorganisation of the administration deprived the province, not only of the liberties accorded by France in 1532 but of its very identity. It became five prosaically-named *départements* tagged on to the rest of France. What was more, the revolutionary government, determined to hammer the nation into a single, monolithic unity, began the attacks on the language and the persecution of its speakers to be continued by its successors.

Divining the pattern of events, the Marquis de la Rouërie, initially a supporter of the Revolution, founded a resistance movement, the *Association Bretonne*, to strive to recover Brittany's lost rights. A strong impetus was given to it by the execution of Louis XVI in January 1793, because Brittany's liberties had always to some extent been linked with the crown.

In March the Terror reached Rennes in the person of Jean-Baptiste Carrier, a Convention deputy for the Cantal. Though its mayor, Leperdit, did his best to temper his efforts, the guillotine's blade was soon falling remorselessly in the Breton cities.

Brutal treatment: Everything combined to give a people, for whom the rest of France was alien anyway, the feeling of being under a particularly brutal occupation, an impression reinforced by the ruthless requisitioning of foodstuffs from the countryside, causing severe hardship, and by the introduction of conscription, a measure compared by later

historians with the Nazi compulsory labour laws.

During this time the Association Bretonne had suffered a series of setbacks. Overwork combined, many said, with the shock of the king's execution, had caused the death of the Marquis de la Rouërie. Then it was betrayed by an informer and 12 of its leading members were guillotined.

Yet, damaged as it had been, the Association's survival was ensured by the Convention's conduct and, insensed by this, Breton

youth was soon flocking to join. It had even found a new leader, Georges Cadoudal, the 22-year-old son of a Morbihan farmer who had fought in the Vendée, the coastal region between La Rochelle and the Loire estuary already in open revolt. He had been captured by Convention troops and had escaped. Under his captaincy the Association, to become better known by its nickname of the *Chouans* (from the cry of the screech owl used as an identifying signal) would carry out its most daring operations.

The centre of counter-revolutionary activity was Nantes and in October Carrier was moved there to purge it of "all rotten matter".

Preceding pages, Jean Baptiste Jules Trayer's *Le Marché aux Chiffons* (1886). Left, 19th-century Nantes style to rival anything in Paris. Above, François Talay dit Talec's *L'Aumône* (1845).

He arrested so many that, with the prisons already overflowing, the question of accommodation arose. His ingenious solution was to load his prisoners on barges which were sunk in the Loire, piling horror on horror by such embellishments as his *mariages républicains* whereby condemned couples were tied together naked before being consigned to the waters.

When these stories reached Paris they were too much even for the Convention's normally robust stomach. Carrier was dismissed, tried and guillotined.

But terror having acted as spur rather than deterrent, Cadoudal's *Chouans* were maintaining such a campaign of harassment that

Louis-Lazare Hoche, ablest of the Revolutionary generals, was sent to end it.

By 1795, however, Cadoudal had become party to an ambitious plan hatched by exiles in Germany and Britain. A 100,000-strong expeditionary force was to land on the Quiberon peninsula, where it was to link up with the *Chouans* to launch a counter-revolution. By boasting of their intentions, the exile-conspirators warned Hoche's spies well in advance.

When the army, a mere tenth of the number envisaged, landed on 27 June, a dispute arose with Cadoudal. It was made clear to him that no-one was interested in re-estab-

lishing Breton liberty, that they had come with the sole purpose of restoring the *ancien régime*—the very one which had incited the *Bonnets Rouges* to revolt.

By the time the advance began, Hoche had laid his trap at the upper, narrowest end of the peninsula and the combined The *Chouan* and royalist forces marched straight into it. Many of the exiles had brought their families with them, so that the fighting troops found themselves caught in a confusion of screaming women and children. All were forced, pell-mell, down the peninsula. Here attempts to re-embark were frustrated by a heavy swell which kept the transports provided by the Royal Navy on the roads,

though a few managed to reach them.

The remnant was mustered into a thin defensive line. On 20 July Hoche attacked and broke through. Only surrender remained and by the end of the day 900 prisoners were in his hands. After summary trials, all were sentenced to death and, in spite of Hoche's appeals, shot, some at Quiberon, others at Auray and Vannes so that as many as possible might witness what happened to those who opposed the Will of the People. (A somewhat idealised portrayal of the executions is shown in an oil painting at Dinan Museum.)

If it was the last organised attempt at a

royalist counter-revolution, it was not quite the end of the *Chouans*. Most, it was true, had either melted away after the Quiberon disaster or accepted the amnesties offered by Hoche, but Cadoudal himself had escaped. In 1799, believing that Napoleon, who had just been appointed first consul, was as unlikely as anyone else to restore Breton freedom, he reconstituted his *Chouans*.

Special mobile columns were created to flush them out and these, uniting with the surge of nationwide patriotism which greeted Napoleon's victories at Hohenlinden and Marengo, brought the rebellion to an end. Cadoudal again managed to escape before he could be taken, this time by fish-

XVI's ultra-reactionary brother as Charles X. In 1830, when his repressive decrees had finally provoked revolution, Louis-Philippe acceded.

As always with sudden changes of ruler there were those left aggrieved. One was the widowed Duchesse de Berry. Since her late husband had been the son of Charles X, in her view the heir was her son, the Comte de Chambord. Her intriguing resulted in banishment to Italy, but in 1832, disguised as a peasant, she crossed the border and made her way to Brittany. Recalling its royalist sympathies during the Revolution, she had convinced herself that its people yearned for nothing so much as government by their

ing-boat to Britain. From here, in 1804 he made his final bid: a plot to kidnap Napoleon. It failed. He was arrested, sentenced to death and executed and, as a posthumous insult, his body was handed over to anatomy students.

Chouannerie was to raise its head once more—this time to the derision of the whole nation. After Napoleon's defeat in 1815, the throne had briefly been occupied by Louis

Left, Vannes Cathedral as it was, and the Château de la Bourbansais, Pleugueneuc. Above, Olivier Perrin's *Le Champ de Foire à Quimper* (1810).

legitimate sovereign.

Her attempts to raise the flag of revolt, though unsuccessful, brought her to the attention of the police who burst into the house in Nantes where she was hiding. It was apparently deserted, but they decided to wait, nonetheless, and when it grew cold tried to get a fire going. After several vain attempts, the reason revealed itself: with an enormous commotion four blackened, spluttering figures landed in an undignified pile on the hearth. It was the Duchess and three of her most loyal followers emerging after 16 hours up the chimney.

Some saw in the Duchesse de Berry's discomfiture the last gasp of *Chouannerie* and for many years it looked as if they had been right. Then, after nearly four decades, the objective which they had embodied—the freedom of Brittany—was shown to be far from at its last gasp.

In 1911 the first Breton separatist party, Strollad Broadel Breiz, was established, its first public gesture a demonstration at the unveiling of a monument to the 1532 union of Brittany and France. A local court showed its sympathies by fining the ringleader, Camille Le Mercier d'Erm, a derisory two francs. The monument continued to be an irritant until it was actually blown up 21 years later on the 400th anniversary of the

taking its name from the colours of the Breton flag, which was responsible for the bombing of the monument to the union.

The next few years saw many, less dramatic *manifestations*, some the work of Gwenn ha Du, some that of its rivals. But then, once again, external events supervened: by the autumn of 1939 France, with Britain, found itself once more at war with Germany.

During the early months there was every reason to suppose that, as in World War I, the front line would be many kilometres from the peninsula. But after May 1940, as Holland and Belgium fell and then the Allied armies fought hopeless rearguard actions

union, never to be replaced.

The 1914-18 War put a temporary brake on nationalist activity and the scale of Brittany's contribution is testified by the long lists of the slaughtered on its memorials. After the war, the separatists were quick to point out that these sacrifices had been made on behalf of the power which had filched Brittany's autonomy and done its utmost to suppress language and culture.

Secret society: Among the new, more militant nationalist bodies which came into existence was a Breton "army", Bezenn Perrot, which was to eject the French, and a secret society, the Gwenn ha Du, White and Black,

across France, the struggle came remorselessly closer.

There was one point, when the fall of the rest of France seemed imminent, that a plan to maintain Brittany as a bridgehead, the so-called "Fortress Brittany Plan", was seriously canvassed. It was made obsolete before it could be implemented by the tempo of the German armoured advance.

By mid-June it had become obvious that France must seek an armistice at once or accept unconditional surrender later. Over the ensuing days the German occupying troops began arriving in Brittany. During the 1930s some of the separatist groups, among them Gwenn ha Du, had forged links with the Nazis and there was, of course, full knowledge of the Bezenn Perrot in Germany.

In consequence they expected to be welcomed with open arms and were prepared to respond by treating the Bretons with unusual leniency. Prisoners-of-war who had been members of the separatist organisations were released; others were kept in local camps within reach of their families; the Breton language was introduced into schools' curricula; and a separatist newspaper, *L'Heure Bretonne*, allowed to publish subject only to German military censorship.

None of these concessions endeared them

to a people unwilling to exchange one conqueror for another and more oppressive one. The Germans' stripping of the land to supply the Reich inspired the general public to christen them *les doryphores* after the Colorado beetles which could destroy whole fields of potatoes.

But opposition was not limited to name-calling. Indeed, Breton attitudes had been made plain even before the Germans' arrival. On 18 June, 24 hours after he had

Left, typical workers in the 1930s. Above, a Breton peasant welcomes the liberating troops in 1945.

reached London, General de Gaulle broadcast to the nation his intention of continuing the fight and appealed to all loyal Frenchmen to join him. Among the first to respond were 130 sailors and fishermen from Ile de Sein, the youngest of them a lad of 14. The Germans found it inhabited only by women, children and old men.

Throughout Brittany hundreds were to slip across the Channel over the ensuing years, while those who remained behind were soon involved in a resistance movement modelled on Cadoudal's Chouans. One of its activities was the operation of an escape network. An inscription on a monument at Plouha records how 135 Allied airmen were sent back to England in the first eight months of 1944.

Smoking ruins: But the Resistance was also responsible for countless acts of sabotage. These activities reached a climax in the days immediately preceding the D-Day landings in Normandy. Scores of troop and munition trains were derailed and hundreds of telephone and power cables cut. Ambushes were set and often turned into open battles, inflicting hundreds of casualties.

By D-Day itself almost 20,000 were under arms. Within a month the number had swollen to over 30,000 and, on 3 August 1944, when the liberation of Brittany began, the *résistants* mobilised through a coded BBC message, fought shoulder-to-shoulder with units of George Patton's US VIII Corps. Among their achievements was the capture of Vannes airfield.

Nonetheless, the struggle was a hard and bloody one lasting over six weeks. By the time victory had been gained several Breton towns, among them St-Malo, lay in smoking ruins.

This was far from the greatest cost it had to bear, as the monuments marking places of mass-execution bear witness. Such acts as this were known of at the time from the posters announcing the executions, which for purposes of deterrence, the Germans plastered over every town and village. But many of the most hideous atrocities perpetrated not only by the Gestapo, but by its creatures, the Vichy secret police and the Cossacks, only came to light after the war. An example is Port Louis, where the bodies of 69 men, tortured and mutilated to death, were found tossed in ditches.

BRITTANY'S RESURRECTION

In the first 20 years of peace after 1945, the regular visitor to Brittany would have witnessed the rebuilding of those cities and towns which had been destroyed or severely damaged during the six years of war. But the timelessness and the "away from it all" atmosphere still remained.

The roads were glorified lanes. The small fields produced their seasonal crops of cauliflowers, artichokes, early potatoes and onions, or were home to small herds of cattle, pigs and horses. The tourist industry languished as a highly seasonal operation in coastal towns and villages, and the humorous picture presented by Jacques Tati's *Monsieur Hulot's Holiday* was not inaccurate. But throughout the region an air of despondency was growing into a black storm-cloud.

To arms over artichokes: For a region whose history was punctuated by the Great Norman Invasion, the Battle of the Thirty, the War of Succession and the Stamped Paper Revolt, it was not surprising that the early 1960s would be dominated by the Artichoke War, an event historians will pinpoint as the birth of Brittany's renaissance in economic and social development.

At that time, Brittany relied too heavily on its indigenous agriculture and horticulture. Nearly 80 percent of the population looked directly or indirectly to the land for livelihoods, and the prospects were bleak. Nor were they any brighter for the naval ports of Brest and Lorient or for the fishing industry centred on South Finistère. With France an all-important member of the European Community, then consisting of six nations, Paris looked eastwards to the rest of the Community, leaving Brittany to feel isolated and neglected.

Despite the dramatic exodus of young people from the region to seek their fortunes elsewhere, there remained in Brittany those who had faith in the region but knew that their destiny rested with them rather than with the politicians in Paris.

Many of these young farmers—like Alexis Gourvennec, of Taule, near St-Pol-de-Léon—were inheriting the family small-holdings and found that their produce of cauliflowers and artichokes was at the mercy of 80 or so dealers.

There was no structured marketing, little or no market intelligence and the dealers easily played off the 7,000 or so growers against each other in setting prices. The traditional independence of the older growers made them too proud to confide in one another about the prices they were getting; so, in the absence of any unified bargaining, the dealers were easily able to talk down the market.

In the summer of 1960, and at the height of the growing season, the price of artichokes in Finistère collapsed. But, rather than retire and mutter about the money received, the growers, under the influence of Gourvennec, took their lorries loaded with artichokes to Paris and sold the produce directly in the streets. The growers were angry that, although the Government had urged them to produce more and more, the politicians had done nothing to amend the outmoded marketing system.

During that autumn and winter Gourvennec, then 24 and a leading militant member of the Young Farmers' Movement, set about changing the marketing structure so that the growers themselves could sell from a position of strength. Within a tightly-knit area of North Finistère, a total of 1,800 tightly organised meetings persuaded the growers to form a co-operative.

The type of co-operative envisaged, however, was opposed by the French Government. The dealers were predictably antagonistic towards the concept, and many were reluctant to risk their independence in the marketplace.

But, in the late winter of 1961, SICA St-Pol-de-Léon (Société d'Intérêt Collectif Agricole) came into being with Gourvennec at the helm as president. The organisation was still unrecognised as the only market for vegetables and one major battle was still to come.

At the end of May, a seasonal glut knocked the bottom out of the potato and vegetable markets. At Pont l'Abbé in South Finistère, farmers set fire to ballot boxes in local elections and, to the delight of the media, filled the streets with tons of potatoes. Ten days later, 4,000 young farmers invaded Morlaix in North Finistère with their tractors, seized the sub-prefecture and held it for several hours. Gourvennec and a colleague were arrested, but sympathy riots flared throughout France's western seaboard, with roadblocks and demonstrations in the Pyrenees and in Languedoc.

It was rumoured at the time that Gourvennec had been encouraged to get himself arrested because of the pressure coming from influential friends in the French Minis-

first move was to establish a pension fund to encourage old farmers to retire, allowing their holdings to pass to the young. Most importantly, he gave official blessing for farmers to form groups for both marketing and production.

The example set by the SICA St- Pol-de-Léon was quickly followed by others in Brittany's various *départements*. All were linked to Gourvennec's group.

Wider ambitions: But Gourvennec wanted more than stability and viability for agriculture. He recognised that agriculture wouldn't prosper if the economy of the region as a whole was not thriving. There was a close interdependence between agricul-

try of Agriculture to bring matters to a head. The Breton demonstrations were not like others which punctuated the history of rural life in France. The protestors and demonstrators were not middle-aged or older farmers resisting change to their work and life styles. Instead, the voice of youth was demanding change. It was a voice that would be heard again seven years later during the 1968 student riots in Paris.

Sensing that Government action was needed, President Charles de Gaulle replaced the mild, liberal-conservative of the old school, Henri Rochereau, with Edgard Pisani as Minister of Agriculture. Pisani's

ture, the food processing industry, industry in general, tourism and every other form of economic activity.

At that time no meeting point existed between the various sectors. Also, despite agriculture's importance, the industry tended to be ignored by the other sectors, even in rural environments.

Gourvennec, with the power and growing influence of the co-operatives behind him, set about convincing the rest of the region of

Above, market days power the Breton economy. Right, Britain's Prince Charles meets Brittany's Alexis Gourvennec.

THE MAN WHO MADE MODERN BRITTANY

The setting was a market hall in Northern Brittany, packed with 4,000 angry pig farmers. They were meeting to oppose Common Market arrangements which allowed heavily subsidised pig meat and pork products into France from Holland, Belgium and Denmark. On the platform strode the stocky figure of Alexis Gourvennec, wearing a grey suit and open-necked shirt.

The heavily amplified sound system boomed out his message: "Bretons wounded and humiliated become very angry. It was because we did not want to become Parisians that we made Brittany the premier agricultural region in France. We want to be able to stay that way. We *will* stay that way."

With which voice was Alexis delivering his message? Not in his capacity as France's largest individual pig farmer; nor as president of a giant vegetable co-operative; nor as chairman of the region's economic expansion committee; nor as chairman of Brittany Ferries. On this occasion, his role was that of regional chairman of Crédit Agricole, the farmers' bank.

Within the audience there were many who had heard similar sentiments more than 20 years previously when, as a brash 24-year-old just taking over the family's seven rented hectares of cauliflowers and artichokes, Gourvennec began his crusade to free the region's farmers and growers from the shackles of an archaic marketing system over which the producers had little or no control. His mission was to improve the livelihoods of farmers and to transform the region from a backward and despondent province into a virile, forward-looking Brittany.

Two major demonstrations, one arrest, and 1,800 meetings later, the first stage was accomplished in 1961 with the setting up of a co-operative to handle the marketing of horticultural produce. Throughout the region there was a snowball effect as more and more co-operatives became established. The next step was for Gourvennec to expand his vision for the future by persuading local mayors, chambers of commerce, industrial interests and the tourist industry to unite to present a regional voice, a voice which transcended party politics and produced the plan that became the cornerstone for the economic renaissance of Brittany.

Today, he recalls the basic philosophy of those days. "We were poor enough to want to do something about it but we were not poor enough not to be able to do anything," he says. When farmers in other underdeveloped area of the world ask him whether his achievements could be repeated in their countries, his reply seldom varies: "Are you hungry enough? We were and we did something about it. Can you say the same?"

As a Celt, Gourvennec wanted to see a Celtic economic and trading alliance stretching down the entire Atlantic coastline of Europe, from the northwest of Scotland, through Ireland, Wales, southwest England and the west coast of France. But he was aware of the physical, political and philosophical problems standing in the way of progress. For instance: "Where is the one man in the British Isles who can speak for all the Celts and to whom I can talk?"

Despite his many positions which go far beyond his farm gate—politics have not really interested him on the basis that "there is a permanency about the jobs I do here and in French politics one can be in and out very quickly without having achieved anything"—Alexis Gourvennec still sees himself as essentially a farmer. The family smallholding has grown to 250 hectares (620 acres) and in addition to the pigs there are other interests including fish farming.

The fire in his belly still burns fiercely, although age has slightly mellowed the militant young farmer. Gourvennec has moved away from rabble-rousing and accepts that an economic analysis can achieve the same objectives. When the marketing committee needed a brand name for the region's produce, they settled on "Prince de Bretagne" and there were few within the region who did not couple Gourvennec's name with that choice.

Indeed, when Britain's Prince Charles visited Finistère in 1988, the local media headlined the event as "Prince of Wales at the home of the Prince of Brittany" with a photograph of the two men greeting each other.

the need for a unified economic voice. An economic expansion committee was created involving the local authorities, the chambers of commerce, industrial and other interests and, with Gourvennec as chairman, set about an analysis of the type of economic growth needed 20 years hence. This culminated in the regional structure plan.

That plan, a massive document, contained more than 200 proposals and plans for action. Realism dictated that such a document would be warmly welcomed in Paris but that action would be taken only on minor points, with the Government avoiding any major reforms.

A "hatchet committee", headed by Gour-

vennec, reduced the demands to just five which were felt to be the basic conditions of development. The prerequisite for development was based on the principle that it was not the State's business but something which could be achieved within the region, provided the State removed the barriers to that development.

The five fundamental proposals called for: a modern road network to reduce the distance between the region and Paris and the heart of Europe; the equipping of the region with an ultra-modern telecommunications system to allow it to trade efficiently throughout Europe and the rest of the world;

a strengthening of the educational system, particularly Brest University; improving general industrial development in Brest; and the construction of a deep-water port at Roscoff on the north coast.

Faced with the strength of Breton determination and with the small number of proposals, the French Government gave the go-ahead in October, 1968.

Meanwhile, another group had been beavering away. This was made up of various co-operatives forming a Regional Economic Committee to concentrate on the promotion and marketing of the region's produce. With Gourvennec as chairman, this committee also took an important role in the planning of the overall economic development, and one of its first actions was to create a brand name for all the region's produce which passed strict quality controls. With those controls in force and with continual improvements being made to the crops, *Prince de Bretagne* is now a powerful name and brand leader in world markets.

Putting down routes: The visitor to Brittany in 1970 and in the following years could see many physical changes taking place. While the Paris-Brest highway moved westwards from Rennes, so the western seaboard highway from Brest to Quimper and other points south cut a swathe through the rolling countryside. The railway from Paris to the west was improved to meet the challenges posed by the new road.

During the construction of the Roscoff deep-water port, efforts were made to find suitable cross-channel operators. All existing ferry companies in France, Britain and in the rest of Europe were highly sceptical of such a venture across what would be the longest stretch of the Channel: Roscoff to Plymouth. Gourvennec persuaded the vegetable growers through the co-operatives to invest in a new scheme and, with other support coming from local chambers of commerce, Brittany Ferries started operating in January 1973 with a second-hand freight carrier.

Within 12 months, the first custom-built ferry came into service and the line now has a fleet of 10 ships with a new "jumbo" ferry under construction at St-Nazaire. As trade and traffic increased, new routes were opened: Portsmouth to St-Malo in 1976; Plymouth to Santander in Spain in 1978;

Roscoff to Cork in Ireland, also in 1978; a joint venture in 1985 between Portsmouth and the Channel Islands; and, 1986, services between Poole and Cherbourg, Portsmouth and Caen. Today the company, still controlled by the farmers, is carrying more than 1.25 million passengers, 275,000 cars and other vehicles, and 113,000 freight lorries.

Brittany's most persistent problem was more difficult to crack: how to halt the drift of the young away from Brittany to Paris and other industrial centres, particularly the young from farming backgrounds. To a large extent, this was solved by instituting subsidised cheap loans to the young farmers and those involved in related businesses, includ-

nowhere better than in Brittany during the 1970s. The disastrous winter of 1962-63 with its snow (almost unheard-of in Brittany) and frosts was the co-operatives' biggest challenge.

At St-Pol-de-Léon the response was an active programme of diversification into other cash-producing crops, including nursery stock, cut flowers and bulbs. New salad and vegetable crops were planted, and dairy and other livestock farmers found they had the cash and the ability to expand their herds and output.

Such developments were not possible because new markets had been identified but in many cases, Brittany's growth was at the

ing commercial fishing. With land prices still high, these funds were used to buy "extra acres" in the shape of buildings to be used for the keeping of pigs, poultry and other livestock.

There was also the general awareness within agriculture that the industry could not flourish tied as it had been to a handful of vegetable crops. Through the SICA came the message and know-how to diversify. The European Community's cry of "Produce, Produce and Produce" was perhaps heeded

Left, Brest was revived as a major naval base. Above, farmer at Rimou.

expense of other regions within France. Shallot growers in the Loire Valley, for example, woke up to find that their northern cousins were not only producing more of the crop than they were, but also that they had collared their traditional markets. Dairy farmers in Normandy, for long France's main milk region, found themselves in second place as the Bretons unleashed a flood of milk and dairy products into the marketplace.

On the Breton farms, the new buildings were quickly filled with pigs and poultry, either for meat or eggs. From a backwardness and social deprivation which seemed destined to sink still further, the region exploded into an area of undreamt-of production.

Today, Brittany is still France's biggest producer of field vegetables; it provides half of the country's pig and pork needs; it is the largest producer of eggs and chicken (and has one company which is the world's largest exporter of chicken meat); it has consolidated its position as the leading milk producing region; and it provides more beef and veal than any other French region.

The revolution extended beyond the primary producers. Large food processing plants have been built, and the marketing, thanks to the influence of the regional eco-

the homes in the town, villages and depths of the countryside, but it became evident very quickly that the real answer lay in building new houses.

Thus started a boom period for the region's construction industry as new homes, with every modern convenience, started appearing throughout the countryside. The design and size of these homes varies considerably but they all obey one major planning regulation, reminiscent of Henry Ford's dictum about his model T: that you can have any colour of roof provided it is black.

An even more basic change came with the alteration of Brittany's very shape. The Government in Paris re-drew regional

nomic committee, is aggressive and very successful.

An associated revolution was taking place in the social environment. The traditional Breton home, beloved of artists and photographers—particularly if an elderly woman in local costume happened to be standing at the door—was in reality a cheerless place. If running water existed, it was confined to one cold-water tap in the kitchen and all other facilities were basic and primitive.

Mindful of the "palaces" being built for livestock and other agricultural purposes, the authorities turned their attention to housing. Schemes were launched to modernise

boundaries as part of the national plan to give the regions greater autonomy in their lives and in events generally, and the Département of Loire-Atlantique suddenly found itself taken out of Brittany.

At a stroke, this removed from administrative control such places as St-Nazaire, Nantes and the "Jewel of Brittany", La Baule. However, while no longer officially part of the Breton environment, the people still regard themselves as Bretons and align themselves to the areas to the north rather than to the official south.

The story of Brittany's renaissance in economic terms is not one of total success.

The one admitted partial failure concerns the industrial development of Brest. Apart from the national and international fluctuations in industrial terms which had their effect in Brittany, as they did elsewhere in France, it was acknowledged with hindsight that the move to bring industry to the major seaport was premature.

Industrial development was not linked to an equally fast developing infrastructure during the years of economic growth and, although new industries have settled in the area, there is still a high dependence in the overall economy on agriculture and food. The days when 80 percent of the population looked to agriculture for a living may have

seen thousands more people from Britain centre their vacations on the coast or, in increasing numbers, inland. The building of new homes released old houses and barns which have now been converted into *gîtes*, self-catering accommodation for families of varying sizes. The region enjoys a good reputation for the short-break holiday and the days when a Brittany ferry could cross the Channel with a handful of passengers, several cars and a small number of lorries are fast becoming a distant memory.

In the transport field, there is a regional airline, Britair, started by Morlaix Chamber of Commerce in 1973 with backing from banks, finance houses and local companies.

gone, but it is currently estimated that nearly half of the working population is directly or indirectly employed in that industry.

One sector which has benefitted over the past 20 years is tourism. It is still possible to find the quiet retreats and backwaters and it appears unlikely that the various *côtes* will ever find themselves in direct competition with the purpose-built centres in Spain or other Mediterranean countries.

But the provision of new entrances to Brittany through Roscoff and St-Malo has

Left, farm in central Brittany. Above, protest against the adoption of nuclear power.

The objective was to facilitate business-taxi flights from the region. The company has grown from three employees, 600 passengers, and an income of 600,000 francs to 220 employees, 320,000 passengers and an income of 220 million francs. Its fleet of aircraft totals 15.

If the momentum generated by the frenzy of activity in the 1970s appeared to slow down in the 1980s, it was not because the people responsible had run out of ideas. A period of consolidation and a time to draw breath had been anticipated; circumstances dictated the timing..

The next stage in continuing economic

expansion is under way. There is in the province, as in every other region within the European Community, an acknowledgement that agriculture is facing a global crisis which could be devastating to areas such as Brittany.

During 1987 work progressed by the various economic groups within Brittany on what is now known locally as the Brest Charter. Like the previous regional plan, numerous suggestions and ideas were put forward as priority issues. But, with the known success of the previous tactic of isolating only a few, two specific recommendations were finally adopted.

Essentially the two aims in the charter,

ratified by the French Government in February 1988, call for the making of western Brittany more accessible to the rest of the world and for the creation of a technical centre around the strong agri-foodstuffs and electronic sectors and technologies connected with the sea.

The accessibility factor involves the current seaport of Brest being adapted to take container traffic. The internationalisation of the city's airport calls for major development to cope with all types of aircraft and give it the capacity for all-weather landing.

The technical centre calls for the creation within the University of Western Brittany of an Institute for the Science of Agriculture and the Rural World and for a National College for Agri-Foodstuffs Engineers. In addition, there will be the creation of a research-development unit centre on electronics and the sea. The current higher education system will be strengthened; this involves the National College for Engineers, National Telecommunications College, Commercial and Business Management College.

As was the case when the first regional plan was approved, a new air of optimism pervades the region and it comes with the confidence in the region's ability to meet the challenge of 1992 and the introduction of the Single European Market.

The by-products of the Charter are certain to become a reality: the completion of road connections, the arrival of the TGV express train to Brest, new companies, a training ground for new companies, professional training for staff in those companies and a strengthening of the relationship between Brest's naval dockyard and local and regional companies so that they can make better use of the opportunity created by the construction of the Charles de Gaulle nuclear aircraft carrier.

A bridge too far: An indication of how the Breton economic leaders set about refining their requests comes with the Brest Charter. The choice lay between making the airport an international one, providing a new and much needed hospital, or constructing a new and urgently needed road bridge.

The bridge was quickly downgraded on the basis that, because the existing one would need to be replaced anyway, the Government could make that choice easily. The hospital, it was claimed, would be needed only if there was the population to justify its operation. The airport, on the other hand, would assist existing and new businesses—which in turn would lead to a stable if not growing population. This would mean that the hospital would be a requisite in the near future and that such increased commercial activity would hasten the building of the new bridge.

It is the increased sophistication of Brittany's economic thinking that bodes well for the region as the 21st century approaches.

Above, seafood in Quimper market. Right, a Breton's favoured transport.

THE LANGUAGE OF EDEN

To those familiar with French there is something alien about all those Breton place names: Trémazan and Le Minihic, Kergoat and the Russian-sounding Roscoff, port of arrival for so many visitors. Coming on names recognisably French—Fougères, Pont l'Abbé, or Petit Minou Point—is almost a relief. At least you can have the gratification of boring your fellow-travellers by explaining what they mean: respectively "Ferns", or "Abbot's Bridge" and "Kitten Point".

Of course, even if you didn't know before you arrived, you will very soon learn that the Bretons are Celts and that their language is related to Welsh and Cornish, having been brought to the French side of the Channel by fifth and sixth-century Britis fugitives fleeing the Anglo-Saxon and Jutish invaders. They rechristened what was then Armorica *Petite Bretagne*, or Little Britain, to distinguish it from their former homeland of *Grande Bretagne*. Although the British still call their country "Great Britain", no doubt because of its self-glorifying evocations, *Petite Bretagne* has been reduced to Brittany.

The Bretons insist that theirs is the language spoken by Adam and Eve before the Fall, a notion which echoes the Welsh belief in theirs as "the language of heaven". And, to be sure, many of the words enshrined in place names are common to all three languages: for instance, the suffixes *pen-*, "head" as in Penhors, Penzance and Penrhyn; *tre-*, from *treb* or *tref*, "town", as in Tresco, Trefnant and Treguier.

However, appealing as the image of Bretons, Welsh and Cornishmen conversing happily in their Celtic *lingua franca* may be, it has little substance. According to some, the foundations of the legend lie with those itinerant Breton onion-sellers once to be seen in basque-beret and fisherman's striped jersey peddling their wares from bicycles so loaded that keeping them in balance must have required the skill of an acrobat. Observers reported hearing them deep in conversation with Cornish-speakers or, crossing to Wales, Welsh ones.

Notwithstanding those cynics who suggest that they learned a phrase or two of both languages in the interests of commerce, the story actually may have a much longer ancestry. In the Middle Ages, it was said that monks from Brittany were also rumoured to be able to communicate with those from Cornwall and Wales. Such basis in reality as this might have probably arose from the fact that the monks of all three places spoke ecclesiastical Latin. Either in spite of or because of their ability to communicate, they frequently came to blows over counter-claims as to the location of events in Arthurian legend.

For all the mythology, the truth of the matter is that even Cornish and Welsh-speakers, whose languages were once the same, are forced—if reluctantly—to communicate with one another in English. And they aren't separated by the English Channel.

In any case, the language of each area has undergone its own natural evolution, besides being shaped by external influences. In Brittany there was the 20-year Norman occupation, for example, while it must also be remembered that the original inhabitants of the whole of France, the Gauls, were themselves Celts and that many Celtic words have survived in French as in English. Examples are "Alp" (*Alpe*), "briar" (*bruyère*) and "league" (*ligue*). One comes on words like "aval" (apple) "aven" (well) and "nant" (valley), still used in current Welsh, in French place names even near the shores of the Mediterranean. At the same time, the sheer proximity of a much larger nation would ensure that French loanwords penetrated Breton, as English ones have Welsh.

In fact, when some of those British refugees who had been driven out by the German invaders returned 400 years later with the armies of William the Conqueror, they already spoke a language native Welshman and Cornishmen found laughable when it wasn't incomprehensible.

The story of Breton, as of all the Celtic languages, is one of irrevocable decline, in this case from the high point achieved in the ninth century when the duchy reached its greatest territorial spread. In part, this was due to such exigencies of history as its annexation by France in the 15th century. But there have also been the attempt made by central governments, in London and Paris, to suppress the Celtic languages. Since the Revolution, whose makers were determined to unify a fragmented nation, the policy has been pursued in France with remorseless vigour. Older Bretons still recall the time when anyone caught speaking their native tongue at school was forced to wear a wooden *sabot* round his neck, a humiliating encumbrance which could be got rid of only by denouncing another Breton-speaker.

No less important as instruments of decline have been the depressed economies of the Celtic lands, especially after their annexation by larger entities, a condition in which Brittany shared. The ambitious were forced to migrate and this, of necessity, meant learning the language of their adopted homelands. Those who remained saw that the way of advance was open only through mastery of the conqueror's tongue.

The net result has been that, though Breton survived, there was an ever-dwindling—and still dwindling—band of those who couldn't understand French. The dangers besetting the language, long recognized, were articulated by the native poet Théodore Botrel in the early part of the century. "We are menaced," he said, "with a great evil. Not only is the Breton tongue threatened, but the very Breton soul itself…"

The nationalist movement tried to reverse the trend and has forced concessions in the use of the language. It is now taught at the universities of Brest and Rennes, and the latter has a chair of Celtic Language. Pressure by the Union for the Defence of the Breton Language (UDB) has secured the optional teaching of Breton in the secondary and teachers' training schools in Lower Brittany. There is also a growing clamour for an Institute of Celtic Languages.

Even now, however, Breton is effectively excluded from primary and secondary schools, while the claim that there are more Breton- than Welsh-speakers, cannot be tested because no statistics are maintained. All that is certain is that few children are now being brought up in Breton.

In reviving language, the revivalists were understandably anxious to resuscitate a literature of which all that remained from the 15th century were mystery plays and other religious material.

However, by the 1920s these endeavours were threatened by another problem. A literature required not just the spoken language Breton had become, but a written and, hence, a standard one. They found themselves faced with what had degenerated into a series of local *patois*. In the end, two standards had to be adopted. One, KLT, was named after the initials of the Breton forms of Cornuaille, Léon and Tréguier. The other was the dialect of Vannes.

Of necessity this has placed an enormous restraint on literary activity and Breton writers could only look with envy at the Welsh bardic *Gorsedddau*. Works produced in Breton have little chance of reaching a readership much in excess of 10,000 people. Obviously, this is not promising for the future and it is little wonder that

one finds the general pessimism of other Celtic-speaking lands is even deeper here. If the advocates of its tongue might find some slight encouragement in the efforts made to revive Welsh, they also have the sad example of the total disappearance of one Celtic language, Manx, in the period from the middle 19th to the early 20th centuries.

There is perhaps one compensation. The contemporary native literature may be small, though it includes Auguste Brizieux, author of *Arvor Telen*, but the duchy has undoubtedly made its contribution to French literature.

An almost endless list includes the 12th-century poet and theologian Peter Abelard; Alain-Réne Lesage, author of *Gil Blas*; François-Réne de Chateaubriand, author of *Essai sur les révolutions, Le Génie de Christianisme* and the remarkable *Mémoires d'outre-tombe*; Ernest Renan, freethinker and author of the still controversial *Vie de Jésus*; the writer of science-fiction fantasies, Jules Verne; and the idiosyncratic Tristan Corbière, whose single volume of poems *Les amours jaunes* startled the Paris literary world of the 1870s.

The list continues, down to Max Jacob who died in Drancy concentration camp in 1944 and, in our own times, Alain Robbe-Grillet, founder of the *Nouveau Roman* movement, best remembered for the script of Alain Resnais's extraordinary 1961 cult film *Last Year in Marienbad*.

Leave the Morlaix-Brest highway and you find to the north a hinterland of roads, lanes and tracks. To the untrained eye, much of it looks like a sea of artichokes in the summer or of cauliflowers in the winter. But closer inspection reveals a wide-ranging variety of crops, countless long, low farmyard buildings, and pigs and poultry by their hundreds of thousands.

Alain Kerdiles, who, with his wife and one worker, farms 100 acres (40 hectares) of land high above the village of Plouvorn, near Landivisiau in North Finistère, is typical of an ancient Breton tradition. There was never any question that he would become a farmer; generations of his family had worked on the land and he began carrying on the tradition in 1962, when he was 15.

"When I started, the upheaval in Brittany's farming scene was just beginning," he says. "Major steps were being taken to ease the drudgery that the growing of the vegetables and the trying to sell them at a fair price entailed for all the farmers in the region".

He had already seen at first hand the "Artichoke War" at the start of the 1960s. "The demonstrations were begun by the young farmers who wanted to change the old-fashioned system of the ups and downs of prices which the growers were receiving for their produce. What was needed was stability and a greater say in the marketplace by the farmers."

Choking in the streets: Although too young to join a major demonstration in Paris where artichokes were either given away to the bemused Parisians or thrown away, he was present when the growers "invaded" nearby Morlaix, submerged the streets in tons of artichokes and stormed the sub-prefecture. Contemporary history books are illustrated with scenes from this "manifestation" showing the ringleader, Alexis Gourvennec, standing up to his knee-caps in artichoke globes and leaves.

As the young Alain Kerdiles worked the fields with the still traditional crops of cauli-

flowers and artichokes, he was fired with enthusiasm for the potential promised by the growing number of new farmer co-operatives. He joined the enterprising SICA at St-Pol-de-Léon, but had six years to wait before the dream of total producer control of the market became reality.

Anticipating by 20 years the European Commission's cries for diversification of farm enterprises, SICA St-Pol-de-Léon accepted that cropping programmes had been too restricted on what were generally very small holdings. A programme was started to widen the scope of operations with crops of high output and value.

Visitors to the region in the late 1960s and throughout the 1970s were struck by the variety of crops being produced and the locations in which they were being grown: carrots in the sands just off the shorelines of Santec and Dossen; endives (chicory) further west along the coast, and shallots bursting through their plastic sheeting in odd strips of fields. But diversification into these crops—which also embraced nursery stock, bulbs and cut flowers—was not a panacea for everyone.

"We had to be careful in what we grew and we had to make certain that what we wanted would in fact grow productively and economically", says Kerdiles. "My land, for example, wasn't suitable for early potatoes nor for other of the specialities being produced within the region". But on the holding at Plouvorn, the cauliflowers and artichokes have gradually yielded space to calabrese, haricot vert, and maize for feeding to livestock.

The SICA exists not only to sell its members' produce, it is just as concerned with research and development. In the early 1980s, when iceberg lettuce was beginning to decorate plates in restaurants, a big Dutch buyer identified a two-week gap in the northern European market and asked a Breton exporter whether the region's growers could fill it.

A handful of growers accepted the challenge, but the first year's efforts were little short of disastrous. The Bretons responded by sending a small team of agronomists and

Preceding pages, a caravan holiday. Left, Alain Kerdiles on his farm.

The Farmer 77

growers on a crash course in California. Today, the lettuce, far from filling a two-week gap in the market, is recognised as an important regional crop.

Continuing research has improved the basic seeds and growing techniques and has made the region more competitive in traditional growing areas. Chicory and shallots are good examples: while other regions' productions and sales stagnate or decline, Brittany's has increased dramatically and new markets are being opened up.

Being a member of a growers' co-operative provides financial aid when markets are over-supplied, when prices are totally unrealistic and when bad weather wipes out

crops. But, of course, membership imposes constraints too.

"There is the discipline on the farmer to commit his produce to the co-op and there is the discipline of obeying the quality controls on the produce," says Kerdiles. In other words, great efforts are needed to ensure that the products are standardised. "It's like when the price of a car is announced. The type is also indicated so that the price means something."

The growing demand for beef and veal within France and elsewhere was met by the livestock farmers. And, with land prices still relatively high and in short supply, the only

way many could increase their farm size was through "buying extra acres" by erecting large buildings in which to keep pigs and poultry. Imports of young cows from Britain saw dairy herds become larger with a corresponding rise in the amount of milk each cow could produce daily.

Although surrounded by dairy farmers, Kerdiles took advantage of the favourable terms offered by Crédit Agricole, the farmers' bank, to expand his production through buildings. In those buildings he keeps 500 pigs, bought in when young and kept until mature.

"I needed a system which wouldn't involve too much labour nor time spent by that labour. This system of pig-keeping fits in very well with the growing of the vegetables outside."

A basic wrong: However, the implications of Europe's "green" currencies, which are used to determine farmers' prices, have seen the Bretons having to compete against what are essentially subsidised imports from other countries. This has sent shock waves through the industry. Frontier-post blockades and other actions by farmers in the streets have failed to right what Bretons see as a basic wrong.

"The result has been that farmers desperate to sell their pigs have been abandoning the co-operative system to see if they can do better as private individuals," says Kerdiles. "But this is not helping them, nor is it helping the industry and the only way we will succeed is if we stick together through this bad time."

Another cloud looms in the shape of the Single European Market in 1992. "A free market should be of benefit to us but how can it be free when we still have the unfairness of monetary policies which work against us? Will we see farmers and their workers all receiving identical pay throughout Europe? Will the same health and hygiene regulations apply to every country? Will we really be starting and competing from the same equal base?"

But, with the confidence and knowledge that they are masters of their craft in producing food and selling it, the Bretons are more likely than not to flourish in the 1990s.

Above, Alain Kerdiles at home. Right, in search of shade—or a scratch.

It wasn't altogether surprising that André Le Torrec, of Bourg de Nevez, Concarneau, in South Finistère, should become a fisherman. He's lost count of how many generations in his family have gone to sea in their trawlers from France's third largest and Finistère's second largest fishing port. Only Boulogne on the Channel coast and Lorient on the Atlantic coast are bigger ports.

"There was never any real question that, when I was 15, I would become a *matelot* on the trawlers," he says.

People apart: In those days, 27 years ago, commercial fishing—like agriculture—was a primary and traditional industry suffering from lack of investment and outdated marketing systems. The fishermen felt isolated because the Government, industry and commerce all tended to look eastwards and northwards from Paris to the heartland of the European Community, ignoring those living in France's northwest corner.

"The boats were old and traditional and, although pretty to look at by tourists and visitors, it meant that life at sea and catching fish was not easy," says André. "And when we returned to port with our catches there was never any guarantee that the fish would be sold or fetch what we felt to be a fair price. There was no real organisation among the fishermen."

The feeling of isolation was brought home to the crews of the trawlers as they battled against the elements, nets often damaged, and trying to catch what sleep they could in a corner on the deck with a coil of rope for a mattress and a piece of canvas for a blanket. But, in keeping with the old proverb that Bretons are "born with the waters from the sea flowing around their hearts", there was little option for people like André but to continue with the work they knew best.

During the early 1960s, though, a revolution was taking place in the fields, villages and towns in the northern part of the region as the farmers and growers began to loosen the shackles of an equally archaic marketing system for their crops and started to take

control of the selling of their produce. The fishermen in the south—André, now in his late teens, among them—watched with keen interest as the farmers gradually became masters of their own destiny.

Co-operatives and other groupings were formed among the fishermen and, as the region's economic expansion committee started drawing together all the strands of economic and social life to announce the renaissance of Brittany, the fishing industry was an enthusiastic partner.

The farmers had their Crédit Agricole bank to assist them in financing expansion and modernisation through longish-term cheap loans for the younger people, either in or setting up business on their own accounts. The fishermen looked to Crédit Maritime for similar arrangements and were not disappointed. The impetus generated by the regional plan not only allowed the fishermen to buy new boats and the latest equipment but also provided the equally vital infrastructure necessary for the ports.

New power: As the old-fashioned sailing ships with their colourful sails gave way to power, dramatic changes were taking place at the harboursides of the traditional ports. The *criées* (auctions) were established in new buildings which allowed the fish bought to be processed to a primary stage in the same premises.

The *criée* at Concarneau is the most impressive, running the length of the harbour, part of a 70 million franc investment by the authorities at Quimper which included the ports of Guilvenic, St Guénolé, Loctudy, Lesconil, Douranenez and Audierne.

Despite these improvements, there was still ever-present danger for the men who took to the sea. In the early 1970s, André was shipwrecked for the only time in his life.

"We were returning to Concarneau in a dense fog and the boat was not equipped with radar," he remembers. "There was a scrunching noise and we ran aground on rocks off the Iles de Glénan, a few miles from the mainland. The boat was wrecked but fortunately there were no injuries and no-one was the worse for the watery experience."

When, in the early 1980s, André achieved

Preceding pages, lobster-pots at St-Guénolé. Left, André Le Torrec.

his ambition of having his own boat, he made sure he had the right equipment to help him through the treacherous weather found in that part of the Atlantic. He bought the 49-tonne *Albator II*, more than 67 ft (21 metres) long with a 500-horsepower engine, for £300,000 on favourable finance terms. "I was eligible for the younger person's arrangements with Crédit Maritime: a loan spread over 12 years at 5 percent interest."

Centred on Concarneau are 31 boats of the *Pêche Artisanale* class; most are less than five years old and only one is more than 15 years old. The cost of such boats has risen in six years from the £300,000 which André paid to £800,000, although prospective

owners under 40 can still obtain favourable banking terms.

Brittany's fishing industry may have been dragged into the late 20th century, but the strong, traditional elements of the life have changed little. With his crew of seven, André takes to the sea for a 14 or 15-day tour off the West coast of Brittany, the Western Approaches off Cornwall and the southern part of the Irish Sea. He adheres to the traditional arrival home time of midnight and to the sale of the catch seven hours later.

Above, André Le Torrec on his boat. Right, fishing fleet in port.

The *Albator II* has capacity for 105 tonnes of fish and the catches invariably include brill, cod, whiting, sole, and skate. These days André can land his catch knowing that it will be sold and that if, for some reason, the bottom falls out of the market, his co-operative will step in to support the price.

The boat owner and fisherman of 100 or even 50 years ago would not recognise the way in which today's men go to sea and the conditions under which they operate. No longer is it a case of pulling up anchor, heading out of port to the fishing grounds and returning with a full hold to sell to an eager market.

Today's fishermen work in an environment of quotas, licences and restrictions imposed by the European Community and its various member states. Most of the fishermen agree that some controls are needed if there are to be fish left for them to catch but they can't agree on how those controls should be implemented. Competition becomes ever fiercer as more traditional waters become fished out and more boats try their luck. Bureaucracy looms, too, in the shape of voluminous forms. Operations at sea are monitored by the fisheries protection vessels to make certain that there are no infringements of the regulations that come cascading in from Europe's various capitals.

Modern image: To watch André Le Torrec put to sea with his crew is not to see the old archetypal trawler skipper wearing thick fisherman's knit covered in oilskins. Only in emergencies will he don this attire. Normally he enters the wheelhouse looking like a casually dressed captain of industry and commerce rather than the captain of a small trawler.

The wheelhouse, too, offers a dramatic change from 20 or 30 years ago. The interior wouldn't be out of place in an office block or the administration centre of a large factory. Apart from the usual cockpit and equipment necessary to drive the boat, the rest of the area bristles with electronic equipment. Pride of place is given to a new computer to assist him in finding the best grounds and likely catches.

"I was able to learn very quickly how to make the best use of the computer and the information it gives me," he says. "It is a pleasure to operate and it saves me and the boat a lot of time".

Brittany, though a compact and coherent region, can satisfy the most hackneyed demand of travel writers: it is indeed "a land of contrasts". Wild seas buffet its jagged coastline, reshaping the ancient granite. Inland, quiet villages and eerie forests seem not to obey the laws of time. Armor, the country near the sea, complements Argoat, the country of the wood.

On the north coast, St-Malo, an old corsairs' town, is a popular resort, exuberantly mixing centuries of architectural styles. Dinard, self-proclaimed Queen of the Emerald Coast, has been compared favourably with Mediterranean resorts. To the east, Mont-St-Michel, though technically it lies a few metres across the border in Normandy, is a magnet for visitors.

To the west, the Granit Rose coast derives its name from the attractively pink boulders and offers great seascapes, unspoilt sandy bays and quiet little resorts.

North Finistère is rich in *parish-clos* villages, with spectacularly carved calvaries and people who have, more than most Bretons, tried to preserve the old tongue and the old ways. Finistère (literally "World's End") exudes a sense of the past, yet encompasses the startlingly modern architecture and bustling commerce of Brest.

Morbihan's visual range is just as wide: the industrial port of Lorient, and island-sprinkled inland sea, medieval towns, the sophisticated resort of La Baule and the mysterious megaliths of Carnac.

Central Brittany, often ignored, is ideal for those who like walking and wandering. Much history was made here, in the castle of Josselin and the forest of Paimpont, and Merlin is said still to conjure up rain and thunder.

The sense of history deepens as one travels eastwards. Castles such as Fougères and towns such as Vitré testify to a once turbulent relationship with a hostile France.

As regional capitals go, Rennes is more a market town, mixing just the right touch of modernity with its medieval past. Nantes, Brittany's old capital, is a bustling city with wide boulevards and elegant shops.

Best of all, the people of Brittany have managed to stop the demands of modern tourism spoiling the very attractions which visitors come to see. But then, with all those saints to look after their interests, what else would one expect?

Preceding pages: boats at Lorient; the Ponte du Raz; sunset at Mont St-Michel; farmer in southern Brittany. Left, two-wheeled transport.

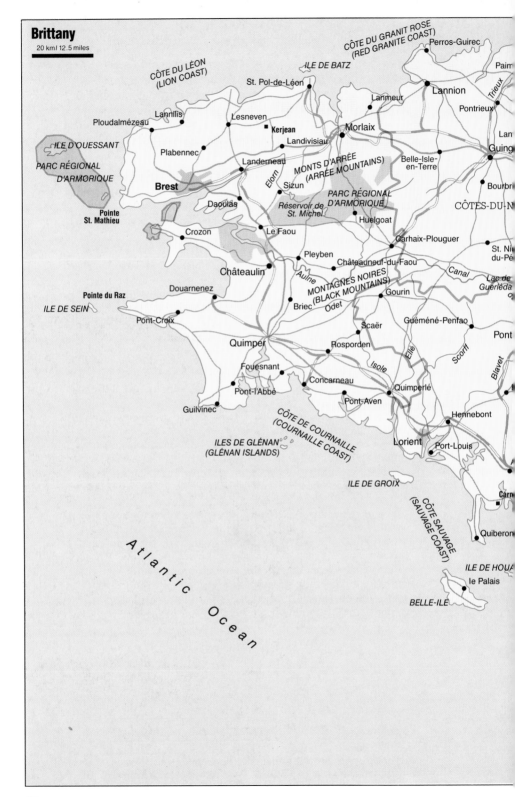

Brittany

20 km / 12.5 miles

CÔTE DU GRANIT ROSE
(RED GRANITE COAST)

Perros-Guirec

Paim

CÔTE DU LÉON
(LION COAST)

ILE DE BATZ

St. Pol-de-Léon

Lanmeur

Lannion

Trieux

Pontrieux

Lannilis

Lesneven

Kerjean

Guing

Ploudalmézeau

Landivisiau

Lan

ILE D'OUESSANT

Plabennec

Morlaix

PARC RÉGIONAL
D'ARMORIQUE

Landerneau

Belle-Isle-
en-Terre

MONTS D'ARRÉE
(ARRÉE MOUNTAINS)

Bourbri

Brest

Elorn

Sizun

Pointe
St. Mathieu

Daoulas

Réservoir de
St. Michel

PARC RÉGIONAL
D'ARMORIQUE

CÔTES-DU-N

Crozon

Le Faou

Huelgoat

Pointe
St. Mathieu

Carhaix-Plouguer

St. Ni
du-Pé

Châteaulin

Pleyben

Châteauneuf-du-Faou

Canal

Lac de
Guerléda

Douarnenez

Aulne

MONTAGNES NOIRES
(BLACK MOUNTAINS)

Gourin

Pointe du Raz

Briec

Odet

ILE DE SEIN

Scaër

Guémené-Penfao

Pont-Croix

Quimper

Rosporden

Elle

Pont

Fouesnant

Isole

Scorff

Blavet

Pont-l'Abbé

Concarneau

Quimperlé

Guilvinec

Pont-Aven

Hennebont

CÔTE DE COURNAILLE
(COURNAILLE COAST)

ILES DE GLÉNAN
(GLÉNAN ISLANDS)

Lorient

Port-Louis

Carn

ILE DE GROIX

CÔTE SAUVAGE
(SAUVAGE COAST)

Quiberon

ILE DE HOUA

ILE DE HOUA

le Palais

BELLE-ILE

Atlantic Ocean

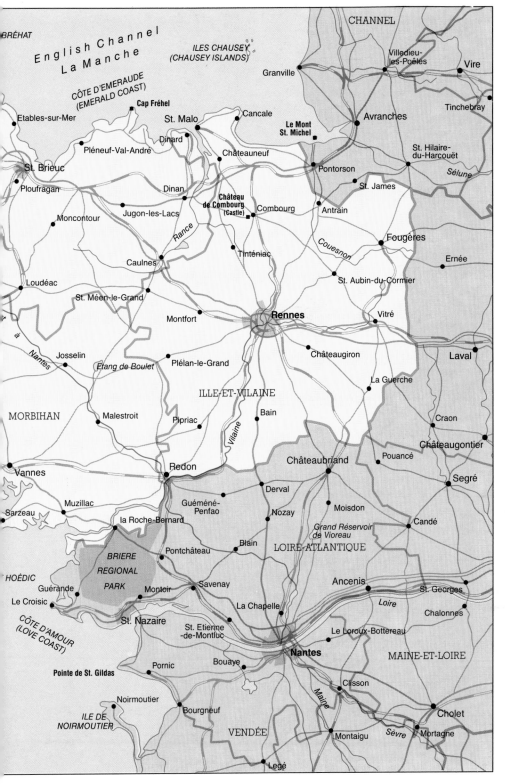

BRÉHAT

English Channel
La Manche

CÔTE D'EMERAUDE
(EMERALD COAST)

CHANNEL

ILES CHAUSEY
(CHAUSEY ISLANDS)

Granville

Villedieu-
les-Poêles

Vire

Tinchebray

Cap Fréhel

Etables-sur-Mer

St. Malo

Cancale

Le Mont
St. Michel

Avranches

Dinard

Pléneuf-Val-André

Châteauneuf

Pontorson

St. Hilaire-
du-Harcouët

St. Brieuc

Dinan

Château
de Combourg
(Castle)

Combourg

Antrain

St. James

Sélune

Ploufragan

Moncontour

Jugon-les-Lacs

Rance

Fougères

Caulnes

Tinténiac

St. Aubin-du-Cormier

Ernée

Couesnon

Loudéac

St. Méen-le-Grand

Montfort

Rennes

Vitré

Laval

Nantes

Josselin

Étang de Boulet

Plélan-le-Grand

Châteaugiron

La Guerche

MORBIHAN

Malestroit

Pipriac

Bain

ILLE-ET-VILAINE

Craon

Châteaugontier

Vannes

Vilaine

Redon

Châteaubriand

Pouancé

Segré

Muzillac

Guéméné-
Penfao

Derval

Moisdon

Candé

Sarzeau

la Roche-Bernard

Nozay

Grand Réservoir
de Vioreau

HOÉDIC

BRIERE
REGIONAL
PARK

Pontchâteau

Blain

LOIRE-ATLANTIQUE

Guérande

Montoir

Savenay

Ancenis

St. Georges

Le Croisic

La Chapelle

Loire

Chalonnes

CÔTE D'AMOUR
(LOVE COAST)

St. Nazaire

St. Etienne
-de-Montluc

Le Loroux-Bottereau

Pointe de St. Gildas

Pornic

Bouaye

Nantes

MAINE-ET-LOIRE

Noirmoutier

ILE DE
NOIRMOUTIER

Bourgneuf

Clisson

Maine

Cholet

VENDÉE

Montaigu

Sèvre

Mortagne

Legé

ST-MALO AND THE CÔTE D'EMERAUDE

Of all the approaches to Brittany, surely none can match that to **St-Malo** from the sea. The glass-blue clarity of the water, the coastline serried with rocky inlets, the backdrop of heather and bracken covered cliffs which, if you catch them before they have turned to the purples and russets of high summer, demonstrate in a blaze of green why the French call this the *Côte d'Emeraude*, the Emerald Coast. And then, as your boat rounds the **Mole des Noires**, you see the tall houses of the *cité intra-muros*, rising above the rampart-walls, their high steep-pitched slate roofs broken by rows of dormers.

Along the wharfs as your ship enters port, the sheer variety of craft—yachts, freighters, cross-Channel ferries, perhaps a Cancale *bisquine*, loveliest of all fishing vessels—are there to remind you that this is a place where sea and land commingle inextricably and that, for the Breton, the one has always shared equal place with the other as a source of livelihood.

Rich and poor: For most it was a meagre and dangerous living, as the coastal cemeteries affirm. The great houses of St-Malo, however, show that it was not so for all, for these were the homes of the ship-owners, the *armateurs* of the 17th and 18th centuries.

In some of the cellars are the remains of mooring posts where their vessels would tie up after a season's cod-fishing off the Newfoundland coast—St-Malo still has its cod-fishing fleet—or after voyages of discovery or slave-trading or preying as privateers on British and Dutch shipping, an activity which gave St-Malo its nickname of "City of the Corsairs". If you want a glimpse of the affluence these activities provided, try strolling along the ramparts at twilight, when window-shutters are yet unclosed but room-lights have been turned on.

Within the ramparts, especially in the French holiday season from the first week in July to the end of August, a very different scene is presented: the tourist St-Malo. Narrow streets thronged, its cafés and those souvenir arcades offering articles to be found in their counterparts up and down France, stiff with humanity.

Yet, for all this, it has a kind of fairground colour and vibrancy, an atmosphere occasionally reinforced by the sounds of a group playing the *vielle*, the Breton hurdy-gurdy, now rarely heard outside the city. Prices may be high at this season, but enjoying the passing-show need cost you no more than a cup of coffee or a *bière à pression* when you grow footsore.

For example, there is the stall in the shadow of **St-Vincent's Cathedral** where the burly proprietor, shouting to attract custom, slings a great transparent blob of molten sugar—red, yellow, orange or green—over a hook on his wall, pulls it out, loops it over the hook again, loops and pulls, loops and pulls, until it is a silken cord to be chopped into humbug shapes for sale.

Or there are the more run-of-the-mill

Preceding pages: St-Malo from the air. Left, St-Malo's Porte St-Vincent. Right, where town meets sea.

confectionery stalls piled with tins of silver-foil wrapped chocolate sardines—the sardine is traditionally fished in these waters—or with sweets which are perfect replicas of beach pebbles packed in scallop shells or in boxes like miniature matelot caps.

There is something reminiscent of the fair even in St-Malo's regular attractions: its aquarium and exortarium with crocodiles, iguanas, snakes and scorpions, the doll museum and the wax-work figures from local history in the **Quic en Groigne Tower**.

The Quic en Groigne, at the southeastern corner of the walled town, is part of a castle now used as the Hôtel de Ville. The castle was built by Duke Jean V of Brittany in 1415, more, it was said, to keep an eye on the turbulent *malouins* than to protect them from intruders—though there was no lack of those, either. The tower was added despite local opposition by one of Duke Jean's successors, the young Duchess Anne who, though devoted to her subjects, had a will of her own and defiantly called it "Quic en Groigne", complain who will.

Also within the walls is St-Vincent's Cathedral, a stylistic hodge-podge, but worth visiting on a sunny day for the light-show of its stained glass.

Outside the Walls: St-Malo is more than the walled city, of course. The ramparts themselves shelter fine sandy beaches and safe waters for swimming and water sports. Accessible from them at low tide are **Grande Bé Ile**, where the novelist René Châteaubriand is buried, and the **National Fort** designed to defend the *malouins* from the British and Dutch seeking reprisals for the harassment of their shipping.

The rest of St-Malo *extra-muros* is modern and characterless and includes the casino, *palais de congrès*, railway station and two yacht-marinas, though it has two-and-a-half-miles of firm sand stretching to **Rochebonne**.

St-Servan: Properly speaking, St-Malo is a complex of resorts running one into another and to the south is St-Servan, less elegant and more workaday and hence somewhat less crowded.

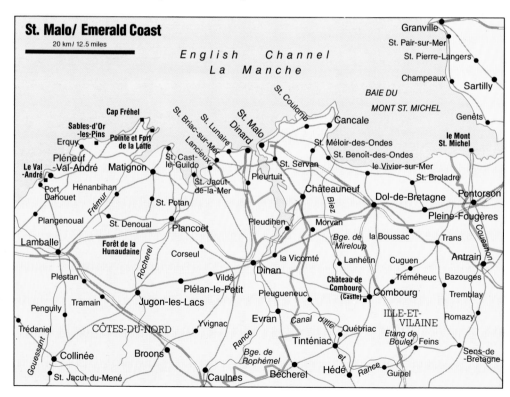

It is older than St-Malo for it was here that Saint Maclou, from whom it gets its name, landed in the sixth century to convert the natives. The splendid **Tour Solidor**, actually twin towers, stands foursquare to the elements, as it has stood since the 13th century, commanding the tip of a small promontory, and today houses a collection of memorabilia of the Cape Horn sailors, among them Sir Francis Drake and Captain Cook.

The **Fort de la Cité** on St-Servan's Aleth Corniche was the scene of heavy fighting during the battle to liberate Brittany in 1944 and though the pine-clad promontory footpath has long since recovered from the devastation of war, it still bears its marks. The steel gun-emplacements, two or three inches thick (50-80 mm), commanding the Rance estuary were ripped and lacerated by the shells of the American VIII Army Corps as if they had been modelled from plasticine.

Paramé and Rothéneuf: East of St-Malo is **Paramé** which, besides its streets of 19th and early 20th-century villas, is a spa with a large centre for the sea-water treatments so popular with the French. Further on, **Rothéneuf**'s principal claim to fame are its **Rochers sculptés**, the lifetime labour of a 19th-century priest, Abbé Foure who, between his pastoral duties, chiselled the foreshore rocks into a host of grotesque human, animal and vegetable forms.

Le Manoir de Limoelou, just outside, was the country home of Jacques Cartier, the 16th-century discoverer of Canada, and now houses a museum of memorabilia. Beyond Rothéneuf are a scatter of coves at the foot of pine-clad hillsides, **Le Lupin**, **La Guimorais** and **Le Verger**, **Port Mer**, **Basse-Cancale**, **Port Briac**, situated on either side of the headland of **Point Grouin**. The attractions of their setting, however, is marred by numerous camping and caravan sites.

Oysters galore: Eastwards round the Grouin Point is **Cancale**, a holiday resort and a busy fishing-port famous for its oysters. In pre-Revolutionary times,

The cannon is silent, the child is not.

bushels of them were rushed to the royal table twice a week.

The trade still flourishes and the beds, visible at low-water, cover 1,800 acres (730 hectares), producing around 25,000 tonnes per year. To harvest them, flat-bottomed *chalands*, powered by ancient engines, shuttle ceaselessly between beds and shore. Not surprisingly, seaweed draped harbourside stalls selling them, as well as other shellfish, and restaurants and cafés offering *dégustations* are even more common at Cancale than elsewhere along the coast.

It is an indirect compliment to the Cancale oyster that it has so frequently offered an irresistible temptation to the unscrupulous and the pillaging of the beds, particularly by the British, has repeatedly endangered the livelihood of the *Cancalais*. On other occasions it was life itself which was endangered by the invaders, whose reputation for wanton destruction was such that they came to be called "*les insensés*", the mindless ones.

As well as oysters, Cancale also produces mussels and the rows of posts on which they hang in clusters, like blue-black grapes in a marine vineyard, can also be seen from the shore. The fishing-fleet of about 30 vessels catches sole, plaice and turbot.

For the holidaymaker who does not intend to spend every minute on the beach, there are Cancale's footpaths to explore, among them the **Sentier des Douaniers** used by coastguards and customs men, which leads to Point Grouin and, if you are energetic enough, to Rothéneuf, Paramé and St-Malo.

Among the attractions of the town itself, reached by a fairly strenuous ascent from the port, are a collection of wood carvings by a Cancalais priest, Abbé Quemarais, and examples of costume and model boats in the museum.

The Polders: East of Cancale, the landscape becomes flatly monotonous. High tides relieve the appearance of the seaward side of the coast road (the D155), but when the tide is out a vista of

St-Malo's distinctive skyline.

mud and seagrass seems to reach the horizon, while the landward side of the sand-blown street is lined with squat granite cottages.

Behind stretches a bleak, featureless plain, which is in fact reclaimed land used for growing cereals, vegetables and fruit. This is also the habitat of the *pré salé* sheep which yield the succulent lamb used in many Breton dishes. The work of land reclamation goes on vigorously in the coastal area known as the *polders*, after the system of dykes used by the Dutch.

The road continues to **Le Vivier**, the largest mussel-farming centre in France producing between 10,000 and 12,000 tonnes a year, and port of embarkation for the *Sirène de la Baie*, a 90-ft long, 150-seater amphibious vehicle, which rolls across the mudflats on large wheels, then combines a trip round the bay with a full-course meal based on the *fruits de mer*, shellfish of the area.

France's marvel: A few kilometres beyond Vivier the road swings away from the coast toward St-Broladre and La Poultière before again swinging further inland toward the Normandy border at Pontorson. Neither **St-Broladre** or **La Poultière** are of great interest, but you have to go to Pontorson to reach **Mont-St-Michel**. This is one of France's greatest showplaces visited by more than half a million people each year which, undeterred by the fact that a change in the course of the Couesnon, their historical boundary, means it is now technically in Normandy, the Bretons continue to claim as their own.

Though most of its half million visitors will seem to have chosen to come on the same day as you and despite its officious car-park attendants, its kitsch souvenir shops and the breathless climb to the summit it should not be missed.

Poised on a sheer pinnacle of rock are buildings which, though constructed over more than five centuries, form a glorious and harmonious whole. Features such as the cloister, in which lacelike arcades of stone form the sides of a garden floating between sky and sea, or the magnificent, soaring Gothic

Oyster beds at Cancale.

THE MAKING OF MONT-ST-MICHEL

In the year 708, Aubert, Bishop of Avranches, dreamed a dream in which he was commanded by the archangel St Michael to build a church on top of the 258-ft (78-metre) cone of rock which thrust itself up out of the Forest of Scissy near the mouth of the River Couesnon.

As judge of the dead and commander of the angelic hosts who had defeated the mutinous Lucifer, St Michael was a member of the celestial hierarchy worth cultivating. By the 10th century Bishop Aubert's church, capable of containing some 100 souls, was too small for the masses of pilgrims who converged on it and was replaced by a bigger one.

Not long after its consecration, catastrophe struck: the sea engulfed the Forest of Scissy. Approach to the rock was restricted to a single causeway which could be crossed only at low tide, with treacherous pools or quicksands threatening the unwary.

Its days as a major Christian shrine might well have been over, but for the arrival of a new wave of invaders—the Northmen—to the area that came to be called Normandy after them. With none of their restless energy blunted by conversion to Christianity, they found in the archangel Michael a figure so congenial to their own warrior instincts that they decided to give him a fitting sanctuary.

Undismayed by the difficulties of building on this sea-girt pinnacle of rock, the Abbot Hildebert II and Richard II, fourth Duke of Normandy, gave the task to monks of the Order of St Benedict, patrons and practitioners of philosophy and the arts, and particularly the revolutionary Romanesque architecture which made possible buildings on a scale hitherto unimaginable.

It was an undertaking comparable with the building of the pyramids. From 1017 an army of labourers began denuding whole forests for wood, while another toiled in the Chaussey Isles quarrying and dressing chunks of granite into building blocks often higher than a man. These had then to be shipped over 20 miles (32 km) of water to specially built and equipped jetties, which the heavily laden vessels could approach only at high water. Once unloaded, they were man-handled up the long zigzag path to the summit, work both back-breaking and dangerous, since the blocks were liable to slide backward on their rollers especially in winter when the going was slippery. Finally each one had to be manoeuvred into its exact position.

Overseeing the actual building was the brilliant Benedictine architect Guilliaume de Volpiano, who recruited a corps of craftsmen, specialists in the Romanesque, from Italy. Besides using their own skills, they instructed local men in techniques from forging metal and mixing mortar of the right consistency to painting frescoes and working in stained glass. By 1080, after nearly 60 years, the abbey, with its dormitories, crypts and hostelry, was ready to receive pilgrims.

It stood for over 100 years. Then, early in the 13th century, Normandy was annexed to France and during the struggle part of the abbey was burnt down. The French king, to win over his new subjects, undertook to erect a new abbey which, thanks to the latest architectural discoveries—the Gothic—would be even higher, more spacious and lighter.

Work began in 1204 and continued for 17 years. What emerged was a cliff of stone and glass, its buttressed walls soaring three storeys high. Among exciting innovations was a cloistered garden at roof level where the monks could meditate amid lawns and flowers. The whole way christened *La Merveille*, the marvel.

Mont-St-Michel was again in the front line in the Hundred Years War, but the only result of repeated English sieges was another fire. After the expulsion of the invaders, in 1446, the abbey was reinstated in yet greater splendour.

Its importance declined with the waning of the post-war urge to thank St Michael for his part in liberation and it deteriorated gradually. By the 18th century lax abbots and venal monks gave it a notoriety exploited by the anti-clericalists of the French Revolution, who turned it into a prison. It was only in the last quarter of the 19th century that, taken over by the state, it was restored to become one of France's top tourist sites, attracting hundreds of thousands of visitors a year.

buildings on the north side, merit the French adjective *inoubliable*, unforgettable. One can understand why, on first seeing the latter the amazed 13th-century locals immediately christened it "la Merveille", the marvel.

Dinard to Le Val-André: St-Malo stands guard over the east side of the estuary of the **Rance**, the greatest of Brittany's many rivers. Watching over the west is Dinard and until 1967 getting from one side to the other by road entailed a long drive up river and an equally long one back down. The alternative was to make the crossing by one of the motor-launches, the *vedettes blanches* or *vertes* which still ply the river mouth.

Easier access came about with the opening of the **Rance Barrage**, the world's largest tidal barrage and one of the great achievements of French engineering. Even more impressive than the scale is an ingenuity of design which enables it to harness both rising and ebbing tides to produce something approaching 600 million kilowatts of electricity a year—far more than most

nuclear reactors—through 24 AC generators, housed in a tunnel running through the core of the dam. There are guided tours of the barrage in which its operation is explained through a variety of visual aids.

A disputed queen: The D169 traverses the 800-metre long dam and there are those *malouins* who complain that it has brought **Dinard** that much nearer. To be sure, nowhere could contrast more sharply with the old City of the Corsairs and, whether you love it or loathe it will depend on whether you are after the historical Côte d'Emeraude or the one of white beaches and safe waters. Of the latter Dinard is the queen—not quite an undisputed one, it is true, for La Baule, on the Atlantic coast, is a rival claimant—and, with its palms, camelias and tamarisks, it bears favourable comparison with many Mediterranean resorts.

The mid-Victorian mania for sea-bathing first attracted wealthy Britons to the fishing village near the market town of **St-Enogât**. Soon it was discovered by Americans, and in particular by

Emmanuel Lansyer's *Le Cloître du Mont-St-Michel* (1881).

a millionaire named Coppinger who built a mansion in the turreted-style one might call "stockbroker's château" which was to become Dinard's contribution to the repertoire of the French architect.

Within a few years a community of 800 villas, many of them more modest imitations of Coppinger's, had sprung up and the pace of development continued over the next half century. Most were occupied by Americans or Britons, the latter introducing the French to lawn-tennis, just becoming popular in their native land.

One of Dinard's attractions for these latterday Anglo-Saxon settlers must have been the climate, but another was certainly its beaches, and it is here that the extraordinary French skill in bringing civilised amenities into every milieu displays itself. Not for them the whelks, seaside rock and indifferent cafés of British resorts. On the promenade of **La Grande Plage**, a vast crescent between Étêtés and Moulinet Points, you can sip your pre-lunch apéritif followed by a three- or four-course meal, while admiring or envying the tanned bodies on the sand below.

The casino backs on to La Grande Plage, so that, on warm summer nights, gamblers were able to cool off from a session at the tables with a quick dip in the phosphorescent sea, though one hesitates to conjecture what uses those whom luck had not favoured made of it. But as well as the cafés and restaurants the promenade has shower rooms and changing rooms and shops selling the equipment of seaside life from water-wings to sun-tan lotion.

As at other Breton resorts, the tide goes out a long way at Dinard, but at the **Moulinet Point** end of La Grande Plage is a sea-water pool, in summer holidays shrill with children, so that it is possible to bathe even at low tide. Children are also catered for in a supervised beach play area with swings and slides, a resident swimming teacher and even facilities for activities such as windsurfing.

If the attractions of La Grande Plage pall there are at least two other beaches:

Delicate beach arrangements at Dinard.

St-Enogât, beyond Étêtés Point, and **Plage du Prieuré**, at the end of Clair de Lune Promenade. And, like any self-respecting resort, Dinard offers its visitors a variety of boat-trips, which include St-Malo, Cap Fréhel, Dinan (via the Rance), Cézembre and the Chaussey Isles.

Dinard tends to be a fair weather place, but you can always pass a wet morning or afternoon at its aquarium and marine museum or at the Musée Historique.

Saints and sailors: One way of describing the Côte d'Emeraude west of the Rance is as a series of resorts, some large, some small. Frequent visitors have their particular favourites, but all offer superb beaches and, in many cases, facilities for the yachtsman. It boils down to personal taste.

Taking the coast road (the D786), you next come to **St-Lunaire**, in some ways a lesser Dinard, with its two *plages*, **St-Lunaire** and **Longchamp**, separated by Décollé Point which can be reached on foot over a natural bridge known as

Le Saut de Chat, the cat's leap. On the far side of the bridge is the **Grotte des Sirènes**, the siren's grotto, a cave seen at its best as the rising tide begins to wash into it. In the town itself, near the *place du Pilori*, the site of the old pillory, is the 11th-century church containing the tomb of the Irish saint, Lunaire, from whom it takes its name.

A short distance further on, **St-Briac-sur-Mer**, at the mouth of the Frémur, has pretty coves and across the 1,000-ft (300-metre) Frémur Bridge is **Lancieux**, an unspoiled bay with rocks, fine sand and the added attraction of L'Islet, a little island accessible at low water. **St-Jacut-de-la-Mer**, across the Bay of Lancieux, is a small fishing port with a number of inlets, popular for sailing, but to some extent spoiled by camping and caravan sites.

Beyond is **Chevet Point** with its commanding views and, to the west, the estuary of the Arguenon, once dominated by the Château le Guildo, now a romantic ruin. It was here that the 15th-century poet-prince Gilles de Bretagne,

Fishing line-up at Erquy.

youngest son of Duke Jean V of Brittany, surrounded by young blades from the English court, embroiled himself in the political intrigues which led to his murder.

Across the Arguenon bridge is the village of **Notre-Dame du Guildo**. Following the lane out of it, which takes you along the riverbank, you come to *les pierres sonnants*, boulders which when pounded against one another by the sea set up an eerie ringing sound.

From Notre-Dame du Guildo the D786 turns inland towards the dull little town of Matignon. However, before reaching it you can turn off on to the D19 up to **St-Cast-le-Guildo** which has a good beach, la Grande Plage, between the two headlands, La Garde and St-Cast Points. At the **St-Cast Point** end of the bay is a small fishing and yachting port and, near the point's summit, a monument dedicated to the Frenchmen and women who escaped from Nazi captivity during World War II.

An earlier monument, portraying the greyhound of Brittany at grips with a lion, commemorates the 1758 victory over a British invasion force. A story, probably apocryphal, tells how the attackers, drawn from Welsh regiments, were marching to battle singing a national song. The Breton defenders, recognising the melody as that of one of their own songs, picked up the refrain. The marchers immediately halted with friend and foe falling on each others necks as brother Celts.

The western flank of St-Cast Point forms the tip of **La Frênaye Bay**, a deep, rectangular inlet at the end of whose other arm is the Medieval **Fort La Latte**. Perched dramatically on a spur of rock its natural defences include deep crevasses traversed by drawbridges.

It has links with British history for, in 1715, James Stuart, "the Old Pretender", used it as a base in his ill-starred bid for the throne. During World War II it was a German strongpoint and in more recent years was chosen as the location for the Hollywood epic *The Vikings*. Nearby is a *menhir* (standing

The River Rance at Dinan.

stone) known as "*le doigt du Gargan-tua*", Gargantua's Finger.

Majestic views: From the fort, the road turns northward to **Cap Fréhel**, one of the most majestic on the entire Breton coast. Rising nearly 250 ft (75 metres) from the granite rocks which whip the water into an angry, white froth to the lighthouse on its peak, on a clear day there are views from the Ile de Bréhat 30 miles (48 km) away to the left and to the Channel Islands on the right. Just beyond the cape are the **Fauconnière** rocks, nesting-place for hosts of sea-birds. As well as the landward approach, it is also possible to visit Cap Fréhel by taking an excursion trip from Dinard which gives a particularly striking impression of it.

From the cape, the road (the D34) follows the Lande de Fréhel gradually descending to **Sables-d'Or-les-Pins**, named after the immense beach of truly golden sand at the foot of pine woods. After Sables, the land rises to **Cape Erquy**, though the D786 turns inland to follow the bottom of the cape to **Erquy** itself. This is a fast growing scallop-fishing port which also offers the holidaymaker a selection of coves, beaches and resort facilities, besides pleasant footpaths for the walker.

From Erquy, the road again turns inland to emerge at Le Val-André, which prides itself on having one of the best beaches on the north coast of Brittany. From **Val-André** it is possible to take the Watchpath, once used by coastguards and excisemen in their war against smugglers, to **Port Dahouet**, a small yacht and fishing harbour set in a deep inlet of gorse-covered cliffs.

Turning inland: To regard the Côte d'Emeraude as no more than a coastal strip would be to miss some of its greatest delights: its patchwork hinterland of fields, of ancient castles, towns and villages. Indeed, one way of exploring the area is to use an inland town as a base for daily excursions, and ideally structured for this is the lovely medieval town of **Dinan** from which the road-system radiates like the spokes of a wheel.

Dinan: good example of a medieval town.

There is no doubt that the most delightful approach is up the Rance which spreads like a chain of lakes, passing gorges, water-meadows, inlets and riverside villages, to taper just before landing you among jostling stone houses and the little Gothic bridge under Dinan's ramparts. A winding, cobbled street which takes you through the **Porte Jerzual**, once the most important of the town's four gates, leads up to the town.

The climb, though steep, can be relieved by frequent halts to admire the ancient, corbelled buildings. Many are now restaurants and *crêperies*, potteries, the workshops of weavers, wood turners and the makers of antique reproductions of such painstaking craftmanship as to be indistinguishable from originals.

This impressive introduction to one of the best conserved towns in France might seem to be reserved for yachtsmen and women, and it is true that they are well catered for. The Rance below Dinan has been converted into a marina and there is also a newer and smaller one at **Port Lyvet**, a few miles downstream. However, it is available to anyone who takes one of the vedettes which sail upriver from Dinard and St-Malo, though as the Rance is tidal it is not possible to go in both directions on the same day.

Whatever means you use to reach it, Dinan transports you into the past. It was at its centre, the **Place du Guesclin**, which serves as marketplace on Wednesdays and car park for the rest of the week, that, in 1359, the truce-violator Thomas of Canterbury was vanquished in single combat by the great Breton soldier, Bertrand du Guesclin. His equestrian, sword-brandishing statue commands the *place*.

As not infrequently happened in the Middle Ages, when he died there were rival claimants for his remains. One was the basilica of St-Denis in Paris, burial place of kings and heroes; the other was the town with which he had always been so closely associated.

The dilemma was resolved by interring his body in St-Denis but removing his heart and sending it to Dinan in a silver-casket. It is preserved in **St-Sauveur's Basilica**, one of the town's two great churches, whose tower, topped with a particularly elaborate version of one of those peculiarly Breton slate pagoda-like spires, is a landmark for miles round. Behind St-Sauveur is the **Jardin Anglais** with marvellous views from the ramparts to the valley of the Rance.

Hotels occupy much of the Place du Guesclin's southern side, but at the southwest end are the Tour Duchesse Anne and Tour de Coëtquen, erected in 1382. They are less the towers their names imply and more like castles. The former is now a historical museum containing, among other things, a collection of Breton *coiffes*.

On long summer evenings the **Promenade des Petits Fossés** behind the castles is a rendezvous for boule players, but the best time to visit it is during an after-dinner constitutional when rampart walls and the castles are magnificently floodlit.

Small cars suit Dinan best.

112

The northern and western sides of the Place du Guesclin give on to narrow streets and alleys with names—**Place des Merciers**, **Rue de la Ferronerie**, **Rue de la Lainerie**, **Rue de la Poissonerie**—recalling the medieval guilds who once practised their crafts there.

Among buildings worth noting are the **Hôtel Kératry** with its leaning upper storey supported on granite pillars and now the home of the Tourist Information Centre; the **Governor's House** in the Rue du Petit Fort; the former **Beaumanoir château**; and the **Franciscan monastery**; as well as the **clock tower** in the Rue de l'Horloge, the clock from which it takes its name being the gift of Duchess Anne. Within the purlieus of the old town is the **Church of St-Malo**, started in the 15th century in the Flamboyant Gothic style but not completed until the 19th.

Upstream of Dinan is the village of **Léhon** with the remains of its castle and a priory, St-Magloire, with splendid 17th-century cloisters. Léhon can be reached by the D12, but is a pleasant

Brittany's roofs are distinctively steep.

hour's walk along the riverside, while within walking distance in the opposite direction is **Taden** whose ruined Château de la Garaye was the seat of a family of aristocratic benefactors still revered in Dinan. Also at Taden are two earlier relics: the remains of a Gallo-Roman villa and a Neolithic standing-stone, the **Menhir de la Tiemblaye**, covered in hieroglyphs.

West from Dinan: Leaving by the St-Brieuc road (the D794) you come to **Corseul**, a name derived from the Celtic Curiosolites tribe for whom it was once the capital. It has a small archaeological museum and the remains of a Roman Temple of Mars.

Further along the D794 is **Plancoët**, a town remarkable only for its incongruous Japanese style bridge spanning the Arguenon. Here you can either continue in the same direction or turn inland on to the D792 which will take you to the Forest of **Hunaudaie** where among the trees rise the five towers of a 13th-century castle.

The castle's present ruinous state is

less the result of enemy action or the erosion of time, than pillage.

It lost its last occupants during the Revolution; after that, the custom of helping oneself to its stones or whatever else one fancied quickly spread and continued into the present century, until the castle became national property in 1930. This was too late to prevent the removal of its grand staircase which now adorns a Loire château. Hunaudaie can be visited between 1 July and 31 August.

Whether you make the detour to see Hunaudaie or not the next town of any size is **Lamballe**, today known mainly for the huge stud farm on its outskirts. This is closed from mid-February until mid-July, when the stallions are sent out for mating, but is open daily the rest of the year.

Though Lamballe has fewer interesting buildings than Dinan, one fine example is the 15th-century **Maison du Bourreau** (the Executioner's House) now shared by the Syndicat d'Initiative and a museum dedicated to the illustra-

tor Mathurin Meheut. The long *place*, lined with shops and ending in a flight of stone steps up to the late Gothic church of St-Jean, presents a pleasant prospect. The octagonal tower overlooking the *place* is capped by another of those Breton-style slate roofs. A second Gothic edifice, the **Collegiate Church of Notre-Dame**, stands on a terrace overlooking the Gouessant Valley.

After Lamballe the D768 goes to **Moncontour**. However, before reaching the town, you can turn on to the D6 and visit the Church of Notre-Dame du Haut at **Trédaniel** whose seven saints, Mamertus, Livertin, Eugenia, Leobinus, Méen, Hubert and Houarniaule, portrayed in carved wood, can cure everything from night-sweats to dogbites, not forgetting colic, migraine, rheumatism and madness. Nearby is **Touche-Trébry Castle**, a 16th-century medieval imitation, open to visitors during July and August.

To get to Moncontour itself, you must back-track down the D6 to the D768. The town is terraced up the hillside with

Mighty Combourg.

stone steps or steep lanes connecting the various levels and giving vistas of stone and half-timbered buildings. Out of Moncontour, you can either head straight back to Lamballe and take the N176 to Dinan or follow the more circuitous D-roads through the Breton countryside, a route full of minor delights.

Notice one very local characteristic: the bushes of mistletoe sprouting, especially in the poplar trees. Mistletoe is deeply embedded in Celtic folklore and, according to the Elder Pliny, was esteemed by the Druids as a cure-all.

East from Dinan: The east route also has a great deal to offer. About seven miles (11 km) along the D794 is a turning to the right on to the D137 which takes you to the **Château de la Bourbansais**, built in the 16th century and considerably enlarged in the 18th.

The château, with its conical-roofed turrets and pavilions, reveals itself as you drive up an avenue of fine beech trees. Once the home of the Huarts, members of the States of Brittany, it is set amid typically French formal gardens and, as an added attraction, has a zoo.

More impressive still is the château at **Combourg** with its towers, rearing out of the huddled roofs of the little town and the foliage of its trees mirrored in a natural, reed-margined lake. Once the home of the du Guesclins, it was acquired in the 18th century by the Comte de Châteaubriand, father of the novelist René de Châteaubriand who describes life there in his *Memoirs*. It is open from Easter until the end of September and visitors can see the author's room and a small museum dedicated to him.

The only large inland town, **Dol-de-Bretagne** on the western side of Dinan, is reached from Combourg along the D795. However, instead of making straight for it, it's worth a diversion via **Croix-de-Bois** and **Epiniac** to the 15th-century **Landal Castle** set amid lawns and a lake.

Just before Dol itself is the **Menhir de Champ Dolent**, a 30-ft (nine-metre) horn of stone which is the subject of two

Farming near Dol-de-Bretagne.

local legends. One claims that it was hurled from heaven to separate two brothers who, with their armies, were locked in the appallingly bloody combat from which it gained its name, "the field of grief". According to the other, the menhir sinks an inch every century and the world will end when it disappears altogether.

In fact, this entire area is studded with Neolithic remains, including the passage-grave at **Tressé**.

Dol is a former bishopric. Its first incumbent, the greatest of the missionary saints, Samson, is commemorated in its vast and oppressive granite cathedral, the successor of one destroyed by English troops in 1203. Among its most interesting features is the great 14th-century porch, though the beggars who often linger there can be rather depressing to the spirits.

The small **Trésorerie Museum** nearby is devoted to the town's long history and includes a collection of carved wood and faïence statuary. The town is second only to Dinan in the number of its ancient houses, the **Maison des Plaids**, going back to the 11th century and offering one of the best examples of Romanesque arcading in Brittany. Like most of Dol's old houses, the Maison des Plaids stands, not inappropriately, in the Grand Rue-des-Stuarts which takes its name from the fact that James II, the last of his line, spent some years in exile there.

North of Dol on the D155 is **Mont Dol**, a 2,208-ft (673-metre) escarpment of rock bursting from Dol Marsh which can be ascended by car up a precariously narrow road. Today it is surmounted by the remains of a semaphore station, a huge chestnut planted in the 17th century and the chapel of Notre-Dame de l'Esperance, still a place of pilgrimage.. However, its habitation since prehistoric times is shown by the discovery of numerous flint tools.

Before the semaphore station could be built in the late 19th century, two chapels had to be pulled down. Their altar stones were found to be pierced by rows of regular funnel-like holes and archaeologists realised they had stumbled upon relics of a temple of Mithraism, the Persian cult which swept through the Roman army just before the conversion to Christianity.

Initiates were required to undergo a baptism of blood which involved crouching under an altar on which a bull, the animal sacred to Mithras, was slaughtered. The blood poured down on his naked body through the holes in the stone.

Good triumphs again: Since then the mount has been subsumed into Christian legend as the site of a frightful struggle between St Michael and Satan. The archangel hurled the Tempter down from the rock, creating at the same time a hole through which he intended to drive his enemy back to the lower regions. But Satan reappeared on Mont-St-Michel—at that time, like Mont-Dol itself, an outcrop in the Forest of Scissy.

Naturally, St Michael finally won, but, as in all such encounters, it was to prove a transient victory and the wily devil was to continue to tempt and deceive humanity.

Left, Mont Dol. Right, St Sampson's Cathedral, Dol-de-Bretagne.

FROM ST BRIEUC TO LOCQUIREC

St-Brieuc starts with two great advantages. First, it lies just to the west of the vast Anse d'Yffiniac, which pours out into the even wider Baie de St-Brieuc, and thus has access to some splendid beaches and a dramatic section of the coast; second, it is the capital of the *Goëlo* country, a region of rambling hills and dunes, cloaked in flowers and flaming gorse, set just behind the coast.

As for St Brieuc, who is just one of the seven thousand, seven hundred and seven score saints who are said to have lived in Brittany, he was a Celt who arrived in Brittany some time in the fifth century, in the days when it was still Armorica, fleeing from the Northmen.

The town of St-Brieuc is now a rather modern place, much rebuilt after being severely damaged in the heavy fighting of 1944, but still dominated by the **Cathedral of St-Etienne**, or St-Stephen. The cathedral, like the rest of St-Brieuc, has been pillaged and buried and generally battered about since it was first built in the 12th century, notably in 1944, but long before that, during the War of the Breton Succession and the Wars of Religion. As Breton cathedrals go, St-Etienne's is rather on the small side, but it was once fortified and is still a splendid building, with a sanctuary to another Breton saint, St William, in the chancel.

St-Brieuc has little to detain the traveller, but the surrounding countryside is very fine, especially at evening time, when the westering sun does wonders for the colours of the gorse and the great sweep of sea before the Baie de St-Brieuc.

From St-Brieuc there are two ways west: one round the Granit Rose coast; the other, the main route west, through Guingamp. They offer different aspects of the region and the coast route may be considered first.

Etables-sur-Mer, as the name implies, is a beach resort, although the beaches here are rather on the small side and set in between the cliffs of what is now called the "Granit Rose" coast. This runs from here all the way north and west as far as Lannion. This is a beautiful region of Brittany, where fine beaches are guarded by great tumbled rocks, many of which are indeed distinctly pink in colour.

The main sight to see at Etables, apart from general views along the coast, is the Chapel of Notre Dame d'Espérance, near the resort of **St-Quay-Portrieux**, which was once a fishing port, sending trawlers to fish for cod on the Grand Banks off Newfoundland. St-Quay still has some boats engaged in inshore fishing, but is now mainly a seaside resort for summer visitors. There are good seafood restaurants along the *quai*, where local lobsters are available, though at a price; four excellent sandy beaches, a swimming pool if the sea is too chilly, even a casino, and for just one good excursion, boat trips north to the **Ile de Bréhat**.

A little further north lies **Plouha** and a little inland from there, the Church at **Kermaria-Nisquit**. Plouha is generally regarded as the point where the French language gives way to the native Breton tongue, and anywhere to the west of this point, Breton is—or certainly was—the common tongue of the country people. Plouha itself is now a tourist town, as are most of these seaside places on the Granit Rose coast, but it is also a favourite retreat for naval pensioners, so the back streets of the village are full of neatly kept cottages, each with a delightful garden.

The little chapel of Kermaria is built in yellow stone and contains a fine collection of statues of Breton saints and, rather more rare, a Doom. Dooms, which are visions of the Last Judgement and show the judged souls departing for Heaven or Hell, were once very common in churches, but are now becoming hard to find. The one here is in the form of the Dance of Death, a popular piece of medieval imagery, and dates from the mid-15th century.

Steep cliffs mark the coast from Plouha north, past Bréhec up to the bay of **Paimpol** and the first of those jagged northern peninsulas which add ears to the snarling wolf's head outline of the Brittany coast. First stop here, at the foot of the Paimpol peninsula, is the **Abbey of Beauport**, which is now in ruins, having been sacked and burned two centuries ago, at the time of the Revolution. Even so, like so many ruined abbeys, it remains an evocative, beautiful place, and parts of it, like the Norman chapterhouse, have recently been repaired, while parts of the church and many of the cellars survived destruction.

Paimpol is a fairly large town for rural Brittany, with 10,000 inhabitants, many of whom were once fishermen but now devote themselves to the summer tourist trade or the cultivation of oysters. That apart, Paimpol is best known in France as the home of the 19th-century novelist, Pierre Loti, who wrote several of his books in the town and set his most famous, *Pêcheur d'Islande*, (Fisherman of Iceland) in a Paimpol setting.

From Paimpol there are a number of excellent short excursions out to the nearby coast, to the tiny fishing village

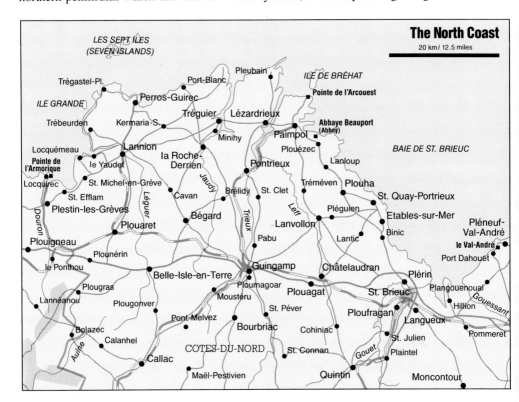

The North Coast

20 km / 12.5 miles

at **Pors-Even**, or to the **Pointe de l'Ar-couest**, which is a fine viewpoint overlooking the scattered offshore islands, especially the island of Bréhat, which is one place no visitor to this part of Brittany should miss.

Bréhat is a flat, red-rock island, some two miles long by a mile wide, and a paradise for birdlife. The centre of the island is seamed with tiny footpaths and there is a rich variety of trees, including mimosa and figs. The people of Bréhat are great seafarers and believe that one of their ancestors told Christopher Columbus about the Americas long before the Genoese explorer set sail for the New World, the local man having seen it himself during a fishing trip to Newfoundland. Well, who knows?

Tréguier is the largest town on the Granit Rose coast and a very splendid one. To get there it is necessary to take the bridge over a wide, deep estuary, or *ria*, as they are called in North Brittany, a feature which, to the east of Brittany, in Finistère, is better known as an *aber*. Whatever they are called, they are very striking inlets, and make perfect harbours.

The heart of Tréguier is in the **Cathedral Church of St-Tudwal**, who came to Brittany from Cornwall and is said to be a relative of King Arthur. His fame is rather overlooked by that of the Cathedral's principal relic, the heart of St Yves, patron saint of lawyers. Most Breton saints are semi-mythical figures, but St Yves certainly existed and was a well-known—and notably honest—advocate during the 13th century, when he was chaplain to the Bishop of Rennes. His saintliness was attributed to the fact that he refused bribes and became very testy indeed with litigants who wouldn't tell the truth under oath. He died full of years and honours in about 1303, but his shrine still thrives and is visited to this day by lawyers on pilgrimage.

Other interesting sights in this fine cathedral include the tomb of Duke John V, who was briefly allied with the English King, Henry V, during the Hundred Years War, and died in 1442.

Solitude near Tréguier.

Tréguier is a breezy, brisk, little town, with the remains of medieval fortifications here and there, including two fine towers by the port, and more up-to-date, the house of Renan, the agnostic philosopher who was born in Tréguier in 1823 and lived here for most of his life.

From Tréguier, which lies on the River Jaudy, there are excursions north up two peninsulas to the east and west, but the most enjoyable are those to St-Gonéry and the Pointe du Château to the west and on the north coast, the one to the little resort of Port Blanc.

St-Gonéry has a beautiful chapel, parts of it 10th century, and the **Pointe du Château** offers the usual marvellous seaviews, especially at sunset. **Port Blanc** has the minute Chapel of Our Lady, perched on a rock above the beach and completely cut off from the shore at high tide. Port Blanc is a beautiful little resort, set a little off the well-trodden track and definitely not to be missed. It also has a very fine hotel, Le Grand, which serves Breton specialities

and excellent seafood. Other local places worth visiting include Minihy-Tréguier, where St Yves was born, and the fine castle at **La Roche Jagu**.

La Roche-Jagu can be reached by the inland route from St-Brieuc, via Guingamp. **Guingamp** is one of those towns which time has overlooked and is said to be the place where gingham cloth was first woven. Guingamp was certainly a weaving centre. It is now best noted for its food, having many fine restaurants, notably the Relais du Roy.

The old town of Guingamp is medieval and retains sections of the old ramparts, while the town church, **Notre Dame de Bon Secours**, contains one of those rare Black Virgins which are said to originate in the East and were brought to France by returning Crusaders. This Virgin is the object of a great *pardon* on the first weekend in June.

West of Guingamp lies the **Chapel of St Hervé** on the hill of the Menez-Bré, whilst to the north is a famous Breton chapel to **Les Sept Dormeurs**, the Seven Sleepers. Other places worth

Port Blanc.

seeing in this otherwise quiet country-side, are the ruined castle at **Tonquédec** and yet another chapel at **Kerfons**, south of Lannion. Brittany is full of chapels and the wise traveller can afford to be selective. **Minihy-Tréguier**, a mile south of Tréguier, is full of reminders of St Yves, and hosts a great *pardon* on 19 May.

Lannion, 10 miles (17 km) to the west of Tréguier, lies inland from the sea at the end of the long estuary of the River Léguer. It is a large town by local standards, with a population of about 15,000, and is worth visiting for the many fine old houses in the centre, and as a base for exploring the surrounding countryside. These late medieval houses are found in quantity around the Place Général Leclerc, and date from the 15th and 16th centuries.

The **Eglise de Brélévenez** was built by the Knights Templar in the 12th century, although much of the present building dates from the 15th century, when the church was enlarged. It is reached up a leg-testing flight of steps,

from the town centre, but the climb is worth it for the views from the church tower over the rooftops of the town.

South of Lannion lie a number of attractive places, notably the great castle at **Kergrist**, which is set in attractive gardens and embellished with pepper-pot towers. Only the gardens are open to visitors, but at least this castle, which dates from the early 16th century, is still intact, while that of Tonquédec is now in ruins, having been "slighted" on the orders of Cardinal Richelieu, who was determined to destroy or reduce all those strongholds of the provincial nobility which might serve as centres for rebellion. The ruins are still very impressive and, in spite of Richelieu's command, two towers and part of the walls are still intact and give a good indication of what the castle must have looked like during the 15th century.

The peninsula northwest of Lannion is very attractive and full of good things to see. The best way to see them is on a circular tour heading first directly north to the resort of **Perros-Guirec**.

Left, Guingamp. Right, give us this day our daily bread...

This is another seaside resort formed around what was once a fishing harbour. The town, though much larger than the old port, still surrounds the harbour which is still full of boats and very picturesque. There are good, safe, sandy beaches on either side of the harbour, plus the usual viewing platform on the Boulevard Clemenceau.

From Perros-Guirec there are two excellent ways to get about; firstly, by following the old Customs path, the **Sentier des Douaniers**, along the cliff edge to the nearby resort of Ploumanach. These *sentiers des douaniers*, very common in Brittany, were once used to patrol the coast and keep an eye on the activities of local smugglers.

The other excursion is by boat, out to **Les Sept Iles**, the Seven Islands, which lie just offshore; they are a famous sanctuary for seabirds and therefore visited by ornithologists from all over the world. Some of the islands are fully protected and people are not allowed to land, but the largest, **Ile aux Moines**, can be visited. Apart from tens of thousands of auks, gannets and guillimots the island also contains a lighthouse and a 17th-century fort built by Vauban.

Trégastel-Plage has a very fine beach with huge, piled rocks, and some good walks along the cliff-top paths to the White Beach, but the great sight hereabouts is the Chapel of Notre Dame at **La Clarté**, which was built by the Lord of Barach in the 16th century as a place of worship and as a a leading mark for ships coasting off this rocky shore in fog or bad weather. The local fishermen hold a *pardon* here on 15 August.

Another even older sight near La Clarté is the great *menhir* of **St Uzec**, which stands in a field near the modern communications centre. This *menhir* was once the object of a pagan veneration, but has long since been Christianised and is now endowed with a cross, carved on the top of the stone to keep the old gods away.

Trébeurden, on the eastern tip of the Lannion peninsula, is a very popular resort, with fine beaches which lie on either side of the little promontory of the

Plage de Trestraou, Perros-Guirec.

128

Castel below the town centre. There are more magnificent views from the **Pointe de Bihit**, two and a half miles (four km) to the south of the town. This part of the Granit Rose coast is often called the Brittany Corniche. It's a fairly apt title for the road does skirt the cliffs and the cliffs look out over the sea to the offshore islands and those curious jumbles of pink rocks which make this coast so attractive and distinctive.

Some of these islands and the larger rocky outcrops can be visited from the shore, notably the ones around the **Ile Renete** near Trégastel-Plage, which is surrounded by huge wind- and wave-eroded rocks. Some rocks have names like the **Tête du Mort** (Death's Head), or one particular favourite, the **Tas des Crêpes** (the Pile of Pancakes), a very apt description for this flat jumble of rocks.

South of Trébeurden, across the mouth of the Léguer river, lies the tiny village of **Le Yaudet**. This was once more important than its present size might suggest, for it was the seat of a bishopric. All that remains now of the bishop's palace is the small Chapel of Our Lady, which contains a fine sculpture of the Holy Family and is the object of a popular local *pardon* held on the third Sunday in May.

West of here the Léguer widens out into the Baie de Lannion, and the road along the southern shore runs out to the Pointe de Séhar, for more fine views, past the village of **Locquémeau**. This is another of those attractive little places the tourist tide has not yet swamped, a small resort set round a fishing harbour, with a pretty little 15th-century chapel to round it off.

To the south lies **St-Michel-en-Grève**, and what is probably—no, certainly—the finest beach on this entire coast, the Lieue de Grève, which runs west from St-Michel for three miles (five km) to the village of St-Efflam at the foot of what is now called the Armorican Corniche.

St-Michel is just a beach resort, but the beach has made its fortune. The Lieue sweeps out to create a beach over

Below, Plage de Tresmeur, Trébeurden. Overpage, village bakery.

a mile wide at low tide, a paradise for sand yachts, and small freshwater streams, full of trout, run out of the low hills behind this vast expanse of sand, right across it, out into the sea.

The best view of this great bay is from the 250-ft (76-metre) vantage point of the **Grand Rocher**, which rears up on the shoreline in the middle of the bay. Seen from up here, the incoming tide is an awesome sight, especially if it is propelled before a westerly gale: great waves sweep in unhindered across the sound to dash themselves in spray against the seawall beyond the road.

St-Efflam is a tiny place with a small chapel hidden in the dunes, dedicated to the Irish hermit, St Efflam, who landed hereabouts in the fifth century and lived near the Grand Rocher until his death in A.D.502.

Past here and still heading west, the road turns up towards the **Pointe de l'Armorique**, which can be reached on foot, and then turns down towards **Plestin-les-Grèves**, which was sacked and burned by the retreating German Army in 1944. The church here, and not the one in his village, contains the tomb of St Efflam.

The coast road crosses another river estuary, that of the Douron, by another long bridge and arrives in **Locquirec**, which contains a fine church built as an almonry by the Knights of St John of Jerusalem in the late 15th to early 16th century. This church contains various statues of Our Lady and the Saints, and a very fine Pieta carved in alabaster. Locquirec marks the frontier of the Côtes du Nord; to the west lies Finistère, the true heartland of Brittany.

Recommendations: This section of the North Coast contains three areas that any visitor to Brittany should not miss. One of these, the Granit Rose coast, is quite distinctive, a part of France that you could only find in Brittany, while the Armorique and Brittany Corniches are also very beautiful, with great seascapes and quiet sandy bays. For towns, Tréguier and Paimpol are the essential places, and for that little place where the other visitors don't go, **Port Blanc** has to be the favourite.

NORTH FINISTÈRE

The western department of Finistère is divided into two, and the northern peninsula of Finistère, above the **presqu'île de Crozon**, is known as the Léonais. If the popular description of the Brittany peninsula is accepted—visualising Brittany as a wolf's head snapping at the Atlantic—then the upper jaw of the wolf is the peninsula of Léonais, the southern peninsula of Cournouaille forms the lower jaw, and the long Crozon peninsula in the centre could be taken for the tongue.

This region of Finistère is the Brittany of popular imagination, the place for calvaries and *parish-clos*, where ladies in black are seen occasionally in tall lace, Breton *coiffes*. Popular though this image may be, and one much used for promotion by the tourist authorities, *coiffes* and calvaries are actually quite rare in Brittany, but the best of these can be found here, in the north of Finistère, in the beautiful country of the Léonais.

Visitors coming in from the east, along the Côtes-du-Nord, as most do, should begin this visit at the pilgrim Church of **St-Jean-du-Doigt** (St John of the Finger) 10 miles (16 km) north of Morlaix. This is a great place of pilgrimage, for it contains the finger of St John the Baptist which the village obtained in 1437 and has guarded carefully.

The church is much too large for the village and owes its dimensions to La Duchesse Anne, who came on pilgrimage here in 1505 and left a donation large enough to complete this present building. Those who wish to see the reliquary of the Finger must apply to the village priest, but the church itself is very attractive and provides the perfect place to start a tour of north Finistère.

If St-Jean-du-Doigt must not be missed on the road to the Leonais, the countryside which surrounds it is also attractive. A good road runs from the pink rocks of the **Pointe de Primel** south through another seaside resort, **Primel-Trégastel**, to little **Diben**, a centre for local oyster beds, and then

beside the vast estuary of the River Dossen, which yawns across the bay to Roscoff, into the town of Morlaix, which actually straddles the frontier between the departments of Côtes-du-Nord and Finistère.

This part of the country, north of Morlaix, is a little-visited region of small valleys, high cliffs and rocky coves containing perfect sandy beaches. Morlaix Bay was created by the two rivers which flow into it, the **Dossen** and the **Dourduff**. Their courses have kept the bay from silting up so that it still contains several ports, notably Roscoff.

Morlaix itself is actually several miles inland, but can still be reached by cruising yachts and small coastal craft which tie up at *quais* in the town centre. It is a market town for the region and visually memorable for the vast expanse of the 19th-century railway viaduct, the supporting pillars of which march across the town like the legs of so many giants, reaching up 200 ft (60 metres) above the rooftops.

The town has kept some old areas which are very attractive and have seen much history through the years. The English and French fought a battle here at the start of the Hundred Years War in 1340—the English won—and later visitors have included Mary Queen of Scots and La Duchesse Anne. The latter seems to have visited every part of her native province and came here in 1505.

Morlaix is a rather quiet town today, more a centre for local farmers than a stopping place for tourists. It had a lively history, however, and the town crest, or arms, of a lion facing a leopard. recalls the day in 1522 when an English force sailed into the bay and marched on the town, and the townspeople rushed in from their fields to drive them away. The town today lies outside the tourist circuit and will not detain any traveller for long, although the houses on the Grande Rue and the 16th-century house attributed as a residence of La Duchesse Anne are worth inspecting.

Heading north out of Morlaix, along the left bank of the river estuary, a scenic route leads to **Pen-al-Lann** and the little port of **Carantec**. This stands on a small peninsula and has two of the best beaches close to Morlaix, the **Grève-Blanche** near the point, and the **Grève du Kehenn**, which is near the harbour. There is a good view of both beaches from the viewpoint north of the town called **La Chaise du Curé** (the Priest's Chair) plus two short but excellent excursions, each a half-hour walk to either the **Pen-al-Lann point** or the offshore island of **Callot**, which can be reached at most states of the tide.

A full visit here will take at least two hours, because there is quite a lot to see in the island's chapel, which is dedicated to Our Lady and contains a 16th-century statue of the Virgin, the objective of an annual *pardon* on 15 August. The Château du Taureau was built in 1512 to prevent more English raids on Morlaix, and became a State Prison in 1660.

Northwest of here, a tall spire rising out of the onion and artichoke fields marks the site of **St-Pol-de-Léon**. St-

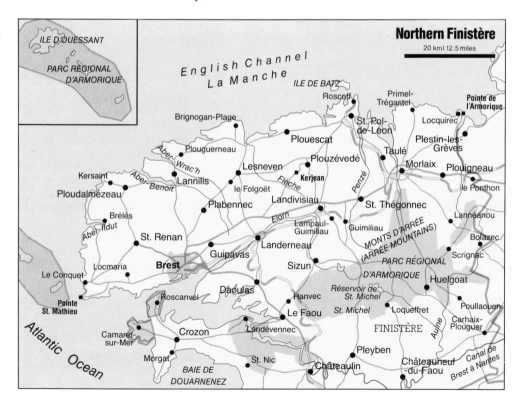

Pol is not a large town, with a population of less than 10,000, but it contains two worthwhile sights, the former Cathedral of St-Pol—or St Paul—and the famous Kreisker Chapel, famous for its magnificent belfry.

The **Cathedral of St Pol**, dating from the 13th century is a fine clean building with splendid lines, built not in local stone but in granite imported from Normandy. The interior is less stark than in many French churches, with 16th-century pews in highly-carved wood and the shrine of St Pol near the chancel. The exterior is set off by two twin towers, one of which contains a leper's door, through which lepers were admitted into a small area so they could view the services.

The 14th to 15th-century **Kreisker Chapel** lies a short distance away, at the far end of the Rue Général Leclerc. During the Middle Ages the Town Council used to meet in this magnificent church, and today it is the chapel of the nearby college.

The Kreisker is a marvellous medieval chapel, its belfry modelled on that of the Church of St Pierre in Caen, which is a splendid fluted affair, and the prototype for many other church towers in Brittany, though few can match the beauty of the original. The belfry may be climbed and gives great views over the coast and countryside. The interior of the chapel, if rather bare, is a fine example of medieval architecture.

Heading north, a short drive to the head of the peninsula brings the traveller to **Roscoff**, northern Finistère's major port, from whence the Brittany Ferries take passengers, trucks and Breton produce across the sea to England and Ireland. Roscoff is also a popular seaside resort in summer and a centre for thalassotherapy, or seawater treatments, as well as being a market centre for the local farmers.

There are three sights to see in Roscoff. First is the great **fig tree** in the Maison des Vacances in the Rue de Capuchins, which was planted by Capuchin monks in 1625 and has now grown and spread until it covers an area

Calm sea at Roscoff.

of about 750 sq yards (630 sq metres), surely making it the great-grandfather of all fig trees. It is still fruiting and can produce over 1,000 lbs (450 kg) of figs in a good year.

The second, rather more traditional attraction, is the **Church of Our Lady of Kroaz-Bas** near the harbour, a late-Renaissance building with one of the finest belfries in Finistère, and some fine alabaster carvings in the altarpiece. These are earlier than the building and must have been brought in from another church. Apart from the belfry, the most notable feature is the carvings of ships and cannon on the walls and towers, paid for by the local privateers whose raids on Channel shipping rivalled those of the St-Malo corsairs.

Roscoff's final main attraction is the **Charles Perez Aquarium**, which is open to visitors throughout the summer and contains species of most of the Channel fish—and very weird some of them are.

Roscoff is well worth exploring, as old seaports often are. It's an attractive little town of whitewashed houses and narrow streets and alleyways, with several good restaurants.

Just offshore lies the **Ile de Batz**, flat and treeless but edged by sandy beaches. The population of Batz is declining but those who remain keep to their traditional ways. The men are fishermen or farmers, the women grow vegetables or collect seaweed for fertilizer, and no man would dream of offering his wife assistance in her work, or she of helping him with the fish or the farm.

South of Roscoff: Minor roads lead down to the southern frontier of the Leonais with Cornouaille, and to those villages which bring visitors from all over the world; the *parish-clos* villages of St-Thégonnec, Guimiliau and Lampaul-Guimiliau, which although not the only ones, are certainly the finest such villages in Finistère.

A considerable number of Breton churches, but mainly those in Finistère, have these curious *parish-clos*. The full *parish-clos* consists of three elements:

Roscoff from the air.

140

the cemetery, an ossuary where bones were placed when old graves were cleared, and the centrepiece of it all, an elaborately carved calvary. These calvaries usually have the Crucifixion as the central element, and are always elaborately carved and embellished with the inclusion of scores (sometimes hundreds) of figures of saints and soldiers, or scenes from the life of Christ or the Passion.

Calvaries south of Morlaix date from the late 16th century, when France and much of Western Europe was in the throes of the Counter-Reformation. Records seem to indicate, however, that civic pride and jealousy of the calvaries erected by neighbouring communities had as much to do with the construction as religious fervour.

Of these three *parish-clos*, the one at **St-Thégonnec** is the most famous and has all the essential elements. There is a large church which, like most Breton churches, seems far too large for any conceivable congregation, an ossuary dating from the 17th century, and a tall calvary with three crosses surrounded by supporting figures, among which a keen eye will detect St Thégonnec and the wolves he harnessed to his plough after they had eaten his horses.

This church and calvary at St-Thégonnec cost a fortune and was built over the years as parish funds became available. The nave was rebuilt several times, the present one dating from about 1563. It contains a fine pulpit carved with the Cardinal Virtues and overlooked by a statue of St Thégonnec, while the apse and trancept are lined with 17th and 18th-century woodcarvings showing details from the lives of the saints.

The calvary was erected 50 years after the church was completed, in 1610, and shows scenes from the Passion. The ossuary, now also a Chapel of Rest, was not built until 1676.

This *parish-clos* at St-Thégonnec is the perfect place to start a tour of the others in the vicinity, and the Auberge-St-Thégonnec, just across the road, is noted for excellent local dishes.

St-Thégonnec's elaborate calvary.

CONNOISSEUR'S GUIDE TO CALVARIES

Why build elaborate works of sculpture in the open—especially when they are bound to be bruised by Atlantic gales and eroded by the sea air? The Breton calvaries are original in their very independence, standing away from chapel or church in symbolic, almost foolhardy, defiance of the elements. While so much Christian religious art hides within the darkened confines of churches or is incorporated into their architecture, Brittany's unique calvaries stand proud, their silhouettes beautiful against the sky.

To appreciate their full originality, one has to see them in the context of the particular development of the accompanying churchyard, known as the *enclos paroissial*. The distinguishing features of this "parish enclosure" lasted through the 16th and 17th centuries—although the oldest calvaries of Rumengol and Tronoën date from the mid-14th—the time when the bulk of Brittany's chapels and churches were built.

Brittany was prosperous then, but had few large urban centres or dominant landlords to encourage patronage. Religion being the most powerful social force, money and craftsmanship went into the Church monuments on a communal scale, parishes vying to outdo one another. A whole series of original architectural elements arose within the boundaries of the low stone wall separating hallowed ground from lay territory: the gate of the dead, the highly-decorated ossuaries, and the calvaries.

Stone crosses are commonplace in the Christian world. But Brittany's calvaries developed the symbol and message of the cross as nowhere else. With their didactic narrative, often used in sermons, and their symbolic purpose in the churchyard, they demanded their own new architectural structure.

Even if the stories and iconography of the Passion and Crucifixion are familiar, the calvaries are complex forms of Christian art, not in the least like the simple Celtic crosses. They concentrate the eye both on the story being unfolded, leading the observer round the sculptures, and on

the outline of the crosses, stretching up to the sky.

The grandest calvaries consist of a raised base, from a simple rectangle, triangle or octagon, to more elaborate forms such as the famed calvaries of Pleyben, with its pierced archway, or Guimiliau, with its stairway to the platform for delivering sermons. Two tiers of sculpted figures—one a frieze, the other usually on the platform—depict the Gospel scenes. Rising from the platform is a cross—more often three crosses. The central crosses, with their many branches, look like a complex candelabra, a figure on each branch.

Occasionally the calvaries portray a local figure. On the cross at Lannédern, for instance, a curious asymmetrical branch has been added where the local St Edern rides, as in the legend, on his deer. At Plougastel, Catell Gollet, a local servant of ill repute, is shown being tormented in the mouth of hell.

The calvaries fit in with the Breton chapels and churches in two evident ways. First, they are in unyielding granite, which scarcely allows for the fineness of carving in soft stone and which gives the characters a certain coarseness. Second, they are built to be accessible, like the squat chapels whose roofs you can sometimes touch. The sculpted tiers rest at eye level or slighly raised, easy to read and not over-imposing. They are on a human scale, their clarity striking.

However, the craftsmanship on most has suffered from wind and weather—or at least been transformed. (But just as an unfinished sculpture emerging from a solid mass has great mystery, so does a partially disintegrating work.) Many of Brittany's calvaries are battered, the granite features partly effaced; others are crumbling or even have figures missing. White, black, green and yellow lichen colour and disfigure some of the characters. Yet they remain captivating.

A great deal of pleasure is to be found coming across the calvaries dotted around Brittany. Like stark open-air museums, they attract you to walk around and decipher them. The postures, costumes and expressions of the figures as well as the calvaries's sites and silhouettes are easily enjoyed. But they retain a potent religious symbolism and have not degenerated into mere cultural exhibits of a remarkably rich culture.

South-west of St-Thégonnec lies the next *parish-clos*, that of **Guimiliau**, which is, if anything, even finer. The calvary here shows the usual scenes of Crucifixion and entombment, but also shows the fate of a local girl, Kate Gollet, who took the Devil as her lover. In one corner of the carvings there are scenes of Kate being torn to pieces by demons for this crime and for the sin of stealing holy wafers from the church.

The calvary at Guimiliau is one of the largest in Finistère, containing more than 200 figures and was carved between 1581 and 1588. The carvings also show scenes from the life of Christ and feature the Virgin and St John, as well as a local saint, St Yves, patron saint of lawyers.

Apart from this fine calvary, the church at Guimiliau is very fine, while the south porch is quite remarkable, heavily adorned with statues and carvings, including one depicting St Miliau, another local saint who was also the King of Cornouaille. These elaborate carvings continue outside the porch and around the door. More scenes from the lives of St Miliau, St Yves and St Hervé are shown inside the church, which is a fine example of a Breton church of the late Renaissance period.

The last of the three principal local calvaries and *parish-clos* south of Morlaix is at **Lampaul-Guimiliau**, and is much less elaborate than the other two. But any lack of detail on the calvary is compensated for by the magnificent church, built in stages during the 16th and 17th centuries, with much of the furnishings, like the 18th-century pulpit, coming from later periods still. Here, as elsewhere, it is the detail that catches the eye: the woodwork of the interior is elaborately carved and depicts the usual stories from the lives of the saints.

To enjoy these Breton calvaries and *parish-clos* takes a little time, for such is the detail and elaboration of the carving that it cannot all be absorbed in one swift visit. It pays to visit them on successive days, allowing plenty of time to explore each place slowly and at leisure,

Left, calvary at St-Thégonnec. Below, oyster hunters.

rather than attempting to take in all three or more during the course of one crowded day.

Brittany's Versailles: Moving back towards the north shore from Lampaul-Guimiliau, the first place reached is the little town of **Landivisiau** which, apart from several good restaurants, has no great attractions for visitors and is chiefly noted for its cattle fairs and markets, the biggest in France.

North of here again lies the castle at **Kerjean**, which is very splendid and has indeed been referred to as "the Versailles of Brittany", a considerable exaggeration. Kerjean stands at the end of a long tree-lined avenue, and although it dates from the late 16th century, the architect has provided the building with such medieval trimmings as a moat and a drawbridge leading through into a centre square.

The castle is built on an open plan with, on one side of the gateway, a gallows tree, from which the Lord of Kerjean would suspend such unlucky thieves and villains as fell into his

hands. The last Lord of Kerjean was guillotined in 1794 and this fine Renaissance building now belongs to the State, which took it over in 1911. It is in an excellent state of repair and so it should be, with walls 11 ft (3.3 metres) thick.

Today, the castle contains a small museum of Breton folk art. The usual tour includes a visit to the room where a Lady of Kerjean imprisoned four gallants from the Court of Louis XIII who had made a bet with her husband that one of them would seduce her.

Back again on the northern coast of Finistère, **Brignogan Plage**, west of the bay at Goulven, is a seaside resort with another of those magnificent Breton beaches and a magnificent *menhir*, the **Menhir Marz**. It stands 25 ft (7.6 metres) high, and like several other Breton *menhirs* is now topped off with a Christian cross, carved by some local missionary many centuries ago.

Once a home of wreckers, Brignogan Plage today is a small seaside resort, but it lies close to some splendid country, for to the west of here lie the *abers*, those deep, fiord-like fissures in the western coast of the Léonais. This region is therefore known as the **Côte des Abers**, or more colloquially, the **Land of Ac'h**, or even the Coast of Legends.

It is very striking and somewhat resembles the north coast of Cornwall, with which the people of Finistère have many links, both coming from Celtic stock. The local people, known as the *goemonniers*, have made a precarious living down the centuries by gathering in seaweed from the *abers* which, when burned, makes a form of potash and is a good fertilizer. This trade, which involves a great deal of hard, wet work, has declined considerably.

The main *abers*, **Aber-Wrac'h**, **Aber-Benoît**, and **Aber-Ildut**, are the unique feature of this part of the coast, and a tour up and down this indented shoreline would make an enjoyable couple of days. The little village of **Plouguerneau** is a good place to start. From here, the traveller can run up and down the two northern *abers*, into Aber-Wrac'h, which contains a small yachting port, and stroll to the tip of the Ste-

St–
Thégonnec's
carvings.

144

Marguerite peninsula. This is no great distance to walk but provides splendid views along the rock-littered coast.

The castle at **Trémazan** does have a legend: it was said to have sheltered those tragic lovers of the Arthurian legends, Tristan and Isolde. It was also the home and birthplace of a 15th-century knight, Tanguay du Châtel. He made his mark in history in 1419 when he killed John the Fearless, the Duke of Burgundy, on the bridge at Montereau, while the Duke was discussing a truce with the Dauphin Charles, later Charles VII of France. This blow ushered in the second stage of the Hundred Years War.

South of the ruins of Trémazan, the road stays close to the shore to Aber Ildut and minor roads from there, some little more than tracks, lead up to the high point of the coast at **Trézien**. Here there is a lighthouse out across the rock- and island-littered sea, a fearsome spot during a westerly gale.

Further on is the long low bulk of the **Ile d'Ouessant** or, as most mariners call it, **Ushant**. Ushant can be visited from the little port of Brélès in the Aber-Ildut, and if the sea is fairly calm the trip is well worth making, for Ushant is an interesting island.

The island is quite small, just four miles long by two and a half miles wide (seven by four km) but it packs a great variety of scenery and interest into that small space. As elsewhere, the men and women share out the work, the men working at sea while the women till the land. Even today, though, farming is at subsistence level, with just a few cows and some fields of potatoes, and small flocks of sheep grazing here and there on the wind-tugged grass.

It is also an island tradition that the women are the ones who propose marriage and Ushant is one of the few places in Brittany where traditional dress, including a small lace *coiffe*, is worn habitually and not just for church-going, weddings and *pardons*. Even so, the old customs are dying out.

The island's capital is **Lampaul**, a small port at the tail-end of a wide bay looking southwest and barely sheltered

Old and new on Ouessant.

by the offshore reefs, but covered by one long westerly headland which supports the **Chapel of Notre Dame de Bon Voyage** (Our Lady of the Safe Return). When a Ushant man dies at sea, his friends and relations make small wax crosses, called Proella crosses, which are kept in the church here or in the main church in Lampaul.

Even here however, tourism is becoming increasingly important, and more and more visitors, especially bird-watchers, are now crossing over from the mainland and staying with the island people. The climate of Ushant is very mild—even in winter, if no great gales are blowing—but the island becomes a very wild and lonely place when a sea mist settles on the rocks and cuts it off completely, sometimes for days.

Back on the mainland and moving south from Brélès, which is a small port at the far end of Aber-Ildut, the next significant stop is at **Le Conquet**, a fishing port famous locally for crabs and lobsters, close to **St-Mathieu's Point**. This tip of land, overlooking the Goulet Channel that leads up to Brest, once supported a fair-sized town, also called St-Mathieu, but this has now disappeared.

All that remains of it are a few abandoned cottages and the ruins of an ancient abbey, which may have been founded in the sixth century and is said to have once contained the head of St Matthew as its principal relic. Only parts of the abbey, such as the chancel, still stand, so the main reason for a visit here is to see the lighthouse and enjoy the marvellous views over the reefs and rocks and offshore islands, out to Ushant and south to the Raz deSein and the wild Crozon Peninsula, once a graveyard for ships.

Inland from here, but skirting the great town and naval base of Brest, the road runs through **St-Renan** and past the small calvary at **Locmaria**, to Le Folgoët in the centre of the Leonais. The chapel and calvary at Locmaria need not detain us, but **Le Folgoët** is a marvellous spot, and home of a *pardon* so popular in Brittany that it is known as

Two generations on Ouessant.

"The Great *Pardon*". It takes place either on 8 September or the Sunday before it, when thousands of people from all over the province flock to attend.

The reason for all this goes back to the 14th century, when a boy called Solomon lived hereabouts. Solomon was probably half-witted, for he lived in a tree, speaking only one phrase endlessly, "Oh Lady Virgin Mary". When he died and was buried in Le Folgoët, a lily sprung from his grave bearing those very words, and on excavation it was discovered that the lily grew from his mouth.

The first stones of the great church which now stands on the green at Le Folgoët were laid by Duke John de Montfort to celebrate his victory over Charles of Blois at Auray in 1364, and the church, which soon became a famous pilgrimage centre, was finally completed in 1423. Le Folgoët attracted thousands of pilgrims every year, one of them inevitably La Duchesse Anne, who came with her entire court in 1505.

The church is quite magnificent, built in the local blue granite from Kersanton and in the late Gothic style. Thanks to its popularity with the local people, it has somehow survived the Wars of Religion and the French Revolution intact.

The church is square in shape, topped off with a fine belfry, and among other treasures it contains the original 15th-century granite rood-screen and contemporary statues of Notre Dame de Folgoët and five fine granite altars.

Finistère is the one *département* of Brittany which has retained its Breton culture and heritage better than any other and is, indeed, reviving them. Breton is again being taught in the schools and is probably still the first language spoken in the home, in spite of the erosion of Breton culture and traditions over the centuries.

Recommendations: Essential sights to see here include the *parish-clos* villages of St-Thégonnec, Guimiliau and Lampaul-Guimiliau, the *aber* coast and Le Folgoët, while those who have the time and no fear of *mal-de-mer* should cross the stormy sea to Ushant.

A local pardon.

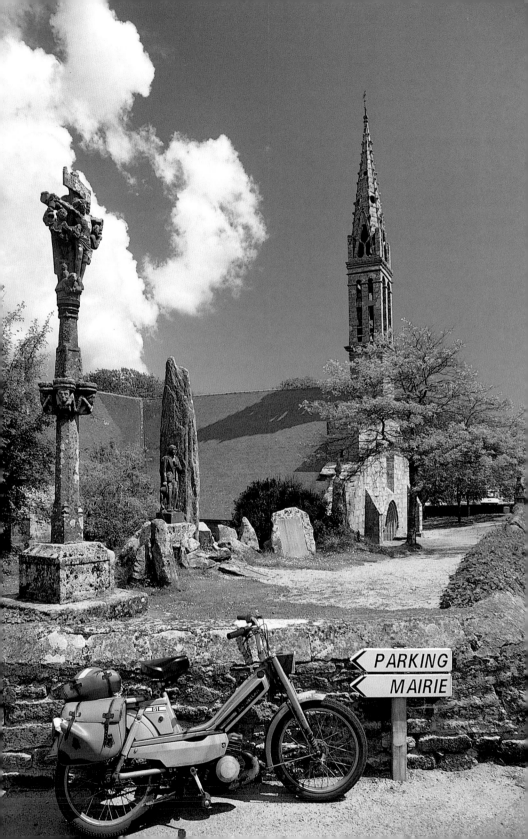

WORLD'S END

Brittany is formed of rocks that are amongst the oldest in the world, and romantics insist that this ancient geological foundation somehow determines the character of the place. Certainly, the sense of the past is powerful in the far west—although for the prosaic reason that traditions often linger in far-flung places insulated from the creeping tide of cosmopolitanism.

Finistère, south as well as north, contains savage, refreshingly uncivilised stretches of coastline not to be found in the more settled areas of Brittany. Parts of this seaboard are bleak and chilling. Other parts are spectacular (especially the numerous rocky headlands along this shore), sheltered and sandy. The further west you travel, the more untouched the seascapes become—although this rule is broken by Brest, the largest port in northwestern France.

There's a view of **Brest** from the Pointe des Espagnols on the Crozon Peninsula across the bay—referred to as the *rade* or roadstead—which is quite flattering. The port's dazzling white post-war architecture, resembling a low-rise New York, looks most impressive when highlighted by a sudden burst of sunlight against a backcloth of grey, scudding skies. But it flatters only to deceive: close up, the place loses that distant appeal.

The naval port and dockyard of Brest occupies one of Europe's finest natural harbours, the sheltered, deep waters of the Rade de Brest, fed by the rivers **Élorn** and **Aulne**. It paid dearly for its favoured location, for while in German hands between 1940 and 1944, Brest was bombed almost incessantly. Almost half the town, including the old centre, was destroyed.

Unfortunately, the new town that rose amongst the ashes of the old—a mishmash of utilitarian tower blocks, apartments, busy road systems and industrial suburbs built on a geometric plan—is remorselessly modern. Apart from a scattering of historic sites (the castle and maritime museum, for example) only the naval traditions remain. The dockyards, founded by Richelieu in 1631 and developed by Napoleon, today serve as the base for the French Atlantic fleet.

Take a walk along the **Cours Dajot**, a promenade alongside the commercial port, for fine views across the vast anchorage of the roadstead. If your tastes extend to modern municipal architecture, also take a look at the **Place de la Liberté** with its cenotaph and gardens, surrounded by rigid, grid-iron streets.

Outside Brest, these wild, western shores almost immediately recover their composure and revert to type. A spectacular bridge more than half a mile long, the **Pont Albert-Louppe**, crosses the mouth of the Élorn, the road then cutting across the stubby little Plougastel Peninsula which, although only a short drive from Brest, has kept its distance from the modern world.

At **Plougastel-Daoulas** there's a famous calvary of 1602-04, built to give

Preceding pages, Pointe du Raz. Left, Plozévet. Right, tall tales at Concarneau.

thanks for the end of a plague. This intricate monument depicts 180 figures gathered around the cross, together with the gruesome tale—unique to Brittany and an insight into the darker side of rural communities—of Catell Gollet, a servant girl who was torn to shreds by demons in punishment for stealing consecrated wafers for her lover, the Devil. Nearby Daoulas contains an abbey, founded in the 12th century by Augustinian monks, in which is preserved Brittany's only Romanesque cloister, an elegant structure adorned with foliated and geometric decoration.

Le Faou, a pretty little place with a small harbour and old houses faced with slate, stands on the approach to the **Crozon Peninsula**. This is one of Brittany's loveliest peninsulas, a narrow neck of land which opens up like an umbrella to form a wild, cliff-bound coastline, part of which faces west into the stormy Atlantic, while other stretches of sandy cove face eastwards into calmer waters.

This beautiful peninsula, part of the Parc Regional D'Armorique, is sufficiently far-flung to avoid the excesses of tourism. For an introductory overview of this peninsula, go first to **Ménez-Holm**, a 1,082-ft (330-metre) summit which commands vast panoramas across to Brest, the Pointe de Penhir and Douarnenez Bay.

The road westwards from Le Faou is most scenic as it loops along the coast then across the mouth of the Aulne by the Pont de Térénez. It's worth taking a short detour just after the bridge for **Landévennec**, a pleasant village which occupies a peaceful promontory on the Aulne Estuary. The ruins of a fifth-century abbey stand in a wooded setting at the tip of the promontory.

The scant remains fail to convey the influence which this site once had in both religious and political circles during pre-medieval times. The early Breton monarch King Gradlon is said to have been buried here. By the 18th century, the abbey had finally been abandoned. A modern replacement stands nearby.

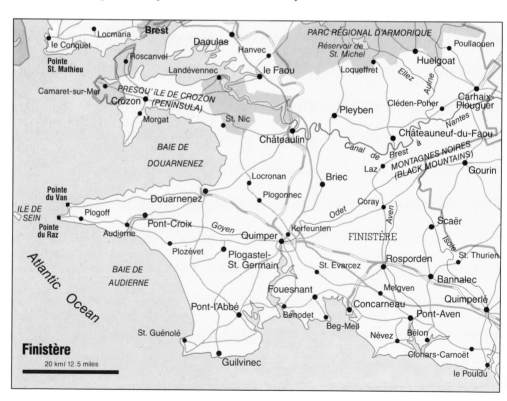

The largest town on the peninsula is **Crozon**, an uninteresting place that you'll need to pass through to reach the little resorts and fishing villages further west. Nearby **Morgat** is an attractive seaside resort and sailing centre with a sheltered, east-facing crescent of sand backed by pine woods.

A group of small caves on the rocky spur dividing the beaches at Morgat and Le Portzic is accessible on foot at low tide. The great attraction here, though, are the large, multi-coloured *grottes* (caves) a little way south along the coast, which can be viewed on boat trips from the harbour.

Those who like their seasides unadultereted by any overt commercialism are bound to fall in love with **Camaret**, an unpretentious old lobster port with a shabby quayside lined with excellent seafood restaurants. It is protected by the sillion, a strange natural breakwater at the end of which are the Gothic chapel of Notre-Dame-de-Rocamadour and Vauban Castle, both of the 17th century, the latter named after the military

Cruising at Châteaulin-sur-l'Aulne.

architect who had much influence in this part of the world.

Aficionados of historical oddities will be interested to know that the first submarine—a rudimentary, leaky wooden craft—was tested in the bay in 1801 by an American, Robert Fulton.

From the Pointe des Espagnols north of Camaret, you can enjoy that flattering view across to Brest. Better still are the vistas from the **Pointe de Penhir**, the finest headland on the peninsula. A towering curtain of cliffs, over 200 ft (60 metres) high, topped by a memorial to the Breton resistance. Below are the **Tas de Pois**, a spectacular jumble of sea-washed granite. On a clear day, the views extend across the Bay of Douarnanez to the Pointe du Raz, the westernmost point in mainland Europe.

On the way down to Douarnanez, it's worth detouring inland a little way. First, there's **Châteaulin** in the green, shady valley of the Aulne (pleasant riverside walking and excellent salmon and trout fishing here). And to the southwest, on the road back to the coast,

there's **Locronan** (though it can be a bit of a tourist crush in high summer). Locronan was the "typical English village" in Roman Polanski's film *Tess*, based on Thomas Hardy's novels.

This is a place where a medieval atmosphere, albeit French more than English, is particularly well preserved. Named after an Irish saint, Ronan, who arived here in the fifth century, Locronan is probably the most picturesque village in Brittany. It sits in an attractive setting beneath the 948-ft (289-metre) Locronan Mountain, and wraps about it a most convincing air of authenticity.

The town's 18th- and 19th-century decline from being a prosperous sail-cloth centre had the one benign effect of preserving the medieval town centre from modern development. Today, it is again prosperous as a thriving arts and crafts centre. Perhaps it's a trifle twee; but, if your sensibilities are offended by up-market tourist artefacts, you can at least turn to the magnificent late 15th-century Church of St Ronan with its massive tower and pulpit painted with scenes from the saint's life.

Also, you can soak up the architectural sights amongst the village's narrow streets (where the leaning houses on opposite sides almost touch each other) and along the square, still lined with the granite houses built during the Renaissance.

There's nothing precious or pretentious about Douarnenez. This is a working, workmanlike Breton port and canning centre. For a whiff of the sea, go down to the harbour when the sardine, lobster and deep-sea fishing boats are unloading their catches.

The market here is well-patronised by visitors on self-catering holidays. For those who prefer not to cook, the quayside at the **Port de Rosmeur** is lined with restaurants.

Douarnenez is an out-and-out commercial port. For the sand and the sea, resort-style, you have to cross the Port-Rhu River to neighbouring **Tréboul** and the popular **Sables Blancs** beach.

On the main road west from Douarnenez, the next major stop is at **Audierne**. Unlike Douarnenez, this port, on the mouth of the River Goyen overlooking Audierne Bay, manages to be both busy and handsome. The quaint old harbourside, spread out below a wooded hill, is again renowned for its bountiful supplies of seafood, especially langoustines.

This far southwestern part of Finistère is not famous for its beaches. The coastline here is bleak and inhospitable, with mile after mile of rocky or marshy foreshore. Audierne is fortunate in having a beach near **Ste-Evette**, a mile from the town.

The long promontory north of Audierne and to the west of Douarnenez is known as the **Sizun Peninsula**, which ends at the famous Pointe du Raz. The main route to this much-visited spot is via Audierne. Quieter back-roads run along the northern shore of the peninsula, taking in a string of lesser known but spectacular headlands (the **Pointe du Millier**, **Pointe de Beuzec**, and **Pointe de Brézellec**, where you'll be able to view Brittany's longest stretch of sheer cliffs and jagged rocks). This

Left, Douarnenez. Right, traditional busking on market day.

undisturbed north-facing coast also contains a bird sanctuary at Cap Sizun.

Whichever way you go, all roads west eventually lead to the incomparable **Pointe du Raz**. Forget the fact that you'll be joining a lemming-like stream of visitors in the summer months: this is Finistère's most breathtaking sight, a coastal spectacle that eclipses all others. The savage, serrated Pointe du Raz is a magnet for tourists, despite its inaccessible location at the northern end of a bay largely devoid of interest.

Come early or late in the day, or out of the main holiday season, to enjoy the Pointe du Raz at its best. The approach is somewhat spoilt by the usual tourist blight—poorly landscaped car parks and souvenir shops—but, once past the man-made detritus, natural spectacle takes over. A pathway, precipitous in places, across worn, polished stones leads out to the razor-sharp sea-pinnacles at the point itself. (The French tend to adopt a rather cavalier attitude to visitor safety, so do yourself a favour and wear sensible shoes.)

Just off the point is the **Ile de Sein**. Looking out to this tiny island, it's not difficult to believe the legend which states that this was the last refuge for the druids in Brittany. The ferocious currents offshore can sometimes be seen when a small fishing boat makes painfully slow progress, inching its way northwards against the tides in the channel between the Pointe du Raz and the island.

These are treacherous seas. Between the Pointe du Raz and the Pointe du Van further north, there's the **Baie des Trépassés** ("The Bay of the Dead"), another darkly beautiful stretch of coast where the bodies of drowned sailors, their ships wrecked on the Pointe du Raz, were washed ashore. The bay is also one of the many possible sites for the fabled, drowned city of **Is**, the legendary capital of the kingdom of Cornouaille (echoes of Cornwall here) and the home of King Gradlon, whose daughter, under the influence of the Devil, opened the sluices which flooded the city.

Pointe du Raz.

If the crowds are too great on the Pointe du Raz, make for the **Pointe du Van** instead—although this promontory, with its tiny 15th-century chapel, is not as spectacular as its famous neighbour across the bay.

Whereas the Baie des Trépassés is small and enclosed, **Audierne Bay** is an immense, open stretch of coast running all the way down to the Pointe de Penmarch. The shoreline here, unprotected from weather sweeping in from the west, is rather featureless and desolate, with exposed shingle beaches backed by a hinterland of scattered farms.

The old church at **Plozévet** has a 15th-century porch and sacred fountain. Within about half a mile there's another religious site, the Chapel of the Holy Trinity, a T-shaped building dating from the 14th and 16th centuries.

The ruined Languidou Chapel at **Plovan**, with its delicately carved rose window, is better still. Best of all is Languivoa Chapel near **Plonéour-Lanvern**, with its rose windows, classical features and Gothic arcading. The most famous religious site of all in this area is tucked away in the obscure southern corner of the bay at **Tronoën**, home of the Notre-Dame-de-Tronoën calvary, the oldest in Brittany, which has 100 figures around the cross.

The principal town in this corner of Finistère is **Pont l'Abbé**, named after a bridge built by the monks of Loctudy. It stands at the base of the Penmarch Peninsula and is also the capital of the district known as the **Pays de Bigouden**, a regional name derived from the elaborate lace *coiffes* you sometimes see in this part of Brittany.

This traditional, decorative headdress is quite unmistakable, for it takes the form of a tall cylindrical white pillar, often invisibly propped up by cardboard, which somehow stays erect on top of the head. There's more information on traditional dress and local regional life at Pont l'Abbé's **Bigouden Museum**. This is located within the town's castle, a 14th-century fortress with a large round tower.

Loctudy, on the coast to the south, is

They'll grow bigger with the telling.

a more attractive place. This small port-*cum*-seaside town has a good beach and fulfils the role of a well-located, uncommercialised little resort. Its church, founded in the early 12th century, is the best preserved Romanesque building in Brittany, with a richly decorated, elegant interior. The boat trips from Loctudy up the wide and wooded River Odet to Quimper are highly recommended.

West of Loctudy, Brittany's wild Atlantic personality once more asserts itself. **Guilvinec**'s sheltered harbour is a base for sardine and tunny boats, but after the smaller port of Kérity, on the approach to the Pointe de Penmarch, fishermen wave goodbye to safe anchorages.

The huge **Eckmühl Lighthouse** on the Pointe de Penmarch is a testament to the ferocious power of these seas. Standing 213 ft (65 metres) tall, with a range of over 30 miles (48 km), it is also a conspicuous landmark visible from great distances across the flat terrain of south-western Finistère. In complete

contrast to the towering bulk of the lighthouse, visit the fortified little 15th-century chapel on the reefs alongside.

A short distance to the north, at **St-Guénolé**, is the **Finistère Prehistoric Museum**, with exhibits from Stone Age to Gallo-Roman times, including a reconstruction of an Iron Age cemetery, polished axes, flint arrowheads and bronze weapons. The otherwise inhospitable coast around the point does have one sandy beach: the **plage de Pors-Carn** along La Torche Bay east of St-Guénolé.

Brittany's coastline inevitably captures the lion's share of attention. This sometimes does a disservice to the province's fine historic towns, which don't always therefore receive the attention they deserve. **Quimper**, for example, is as laden with historic buildings as one would expect of the oldest Breton city, once the capital of Cornouaille, a duchy of medieval Brittany that extended as far north as the neighbourhood of Morlaix and east to Quimperlé.

Legend has it that Quimper's first bishop—St Corentin—came from Cornwall, establishing a "Little Britain" here sometime between the fourth and seventh centuries. When King Gradlon's legendary city of Is was inundated by the sea, he travelled inland and founded his new capital at Quimper, making St Corentin his first bishop.

Gradlon makes an appearance at Quimper's **cathedral**, a soaring building dedicated to St Corentin. Constructed between 1239 and 1515, it is the most complete Gothic cathedral in Brittany. King Gradlon is represented as a mounted figure between the cathedral's two graceful towers (their modern spires were part of a sympathetic 19th-century restoration which thankfully did not compromise the cathedral's ancient character).

Built from the local hard granite, this impressive cathedral is embellished with decorative features which speak volumes of the skills of the medieval stonemasons. There is, however, one blemish, imposed apparently by the lie of the land: the 13th-century chancel is

Left and right, Quimper.

out of alignment with the 15th-century nave, giving the interior a slightly crooked look.

Alongside the cathedral stands the **Bishop's Palace**, mostly an early 16th-century building with a noteworthy spiral staircase beneath a splendidly carved oak canopy. The palace now houses a local musuem devoted to the history, archaeology and folklore of Finistère. The **Museum of Fine Arts**, located in the Hotel de Ville, is also worth a visit. On display are works by French and other painters from the 16th to the early 20th centuries, including those of the local Pont-Aven school, a unique style of painting associated with the likes of Paul Gauguin and Emile Bernard (Bernard's *Breton Women*, which is said to have had an influence on Gauguin, is one of the exhibits).

Quimper is named after its location at the confluence of two rivers, the **Odet** and the **Steir**, *kemper* denoting a meeting place. The old quarter of the city, bounded by the two rivers and the cathedral, is ranged around the Rue Kéréon.

The streets of the old town, which contain plenty of examples of well-preserved half-timbered houses and an enticing selection of shops, are delightful. And don't miss the covered market; nor the pottery workshops (the **Faïenceries de Quimper**), which are part of a tradition of pottery making in Quimper going back to the late 17th century.

You can catch a boat downriver to **Bénodet**. This is one of Brittany's most picturesque resorts, with a small harbour, splendid sheltered beach and a good complement of facilities for seaside family holidays. Small and popular but not too commercialised, Bénodet stands at the mouth of the Odet in a pretty setting backed by a most attractive, wooded hinterland.

Across the Odet is **Ste-Marine**, an equally pretty little resort with a good sandy beach (it's easy to commute between the two on a passenger ferry which operates across the narrow neck of water). Offshore are the **Les Glénan** (accessible by boat from Bénodet), an

Bénodet market.

archipelago of nine islets, some of which are bird sanctuaries.

In character, this south-facing coastline is more placid and gentle, unlike the stark, uncompromising stretches further west with their rocks, cliffs and dramatic seas. **Beg-Meil** is another of its little resorts, standing on a headland east of Bénodet overlooking La Forêt Bay (take in the **Pointe de Mousterlin** on the way for more extensive sea views across to the Glénan Islands). This resort, scattered amongst the pines, has excellent sandy beaches, rocky coves and dunes.

At the head of the bay, on the way to Concarneau, is **La Forêt-Fouesnant**, a peaceful village whose church contains a 16th-century calvary. Unless in a rush, take the minor road from here which runs down to the coast via Kerleven beach to the large (by Brittany standards), well-known resort of **Concarneau**. The beaches here, although extensive, are something of a disappointment: they are not very appealing at low tide, when you have to slip and slide

your way across a slimy carpet of seaweed to reach the sea.

The resort is not too heavily built up behind the beaches: most of the development is confined to the busy town and the huge fish market. In fact, it's more accurate to say that Concarneau is first and foremost a commercial fishing port (the third largest in France), and only secondly a holiday resort. The tourists all flock to the old walled town—the *Ville Clos*—located in the middle of the harbour on what was once an island but is now accessible by a slender causeway.

This irregularly shaped island, the nucleus around which Concarneau later developed, has been fortified for 1,000 years. By the 14th century, this bastion was regarded as being virtually impregnable, a reputation that presumably became even more formidable when the walls were extensively strengthened in the 17th century by the great military architect Vauban.

Enclosed within the sturdy granite ramparts is a charming area of narrow

Wineseller at Forêt-Fouesnant.

streets with, predictably, lots of tourist shops. The atmosphere, though, is pleasant and colourful, enhanced by the flowers that seem to grow everywhere within the walls.

Fishing remains the lifeblood of Concarneau. The wide harbour provides shelter for a huge fleet of trawlers whenever winter storms are blowing. When the boats are working and the catch has been landed, bartering takes place at the lively fish auction market and stalls on the quayside are amongst the first recipients of a huge variety of freshly caught fish.

Concarneau's historic dependence on the sea is the theme of the **Fishing Museum** in the old town. The building contains rooms on whaling, tuna and herring fishing, and sardine canning, while other exhibits reflect the evolution of the port. Among the oddities here are fishing-related items from all over the world, including a whaleboat from the Azores, the swords of swordfish, and a Japanese giant crab.

Each year the port holds its Festival of the Blue Fishing Nets, a folk event which takes place on the penultimate Sunday in August and in the evenings of the preceding week. It's very crowded, though.

Pont-Aven attracts admirers of Paul Gauguin. The painter came here to paint in the 1880s, before he took himself off to Tahiti in the South Seas. Many Pont-Aven scenes ended up on his canvases, including the 16th-century wooden figure of Christ in the Trémalo Chapel which was the model for his *Yellow Christ*, and the Romanesque calvary in the little church at nearby Nizon, which inspired his *Green Christ*.

Gauguin inaugurated the so-called "Pont-Aven school" of painting, which took Impressionism a stage further by giving free rein to the intuitive feelings of the artist. Unfortunately, Gauguin's works are usually conclusively outnumbered—or conspicuous by their absence—in the galleries within the town's museum, where changing exhibitions feature paintings by the school's numerous followers.

American painters gather outside the Pension Gloanec in Pont-Aven in the 1880s.

The inspiration which the town gave to these painters is easy to appreciate. Pont-Aven occupies a most agreeable setting between the rocky upstream course of the River Aven and the point where it opens out into a tidal estuary. Although the water mills may have been superseded by art galleries, Pont-Aven cannot have changed all that much since Gauguin's time. Take the lovely wooded walk to the **Trémalo Chapel** through the **Bois d'Amour**, along which there are signposts pointing out locations which inspired the artists.

There must be something inspiring about Pont-Aven, for the town was also the home of the poet Théodore Botrel, who founded the Gorse Flower Festival which is held here on the first Sunday in August.

East of Pont-Aven, the coast is broken by estuaries as far down as Le Pouldu. One of the rivers, the **Bélon**, is famous for its oyster beds. The commercial maturing beds in this river estuary, among the largest on the Atlantic coast, can be seen at low tide. Another Breton favourite, cider, comes from the countryside around the small fishing port of **Doëlan**, a little further east.

Le Pouldu is a small port on the mouth of the River Laïta. Upstream is the oak and beech forest of **Carnoët** and the town of **Quimperlé**, which stands on the border between Finistère and Morbihan. The rivers **Ellé** and **Isole** meet here to become the **Laïta** (hence the "*kemper*" as in Quimper).

Quimperlé is an old place which shows its age well, particularly in the medieval streets grouped around the church of Ste Croix beside the two rivers in the lower town. Dating from the 12th century (but largely rebuilt in the 19th, though in a style faithful to the original), the church was modelled on the Holy Sepulchre in Jerusalem, probably thanks to drawings brought back by the crusaders. The upper town is also dominated by a substantial place of worship, the square-towered Church of St Michael, which dates from the 13th century.

Paul
Gaugin's
*Les Quatre
Bretonnes*
(1886).

MORBIHAN

In no other region of Brittany, itself a land of contrasts, can there be found such variety within such a small area. Confined within its limits are a large industrial port, a unique inland sea sprinkled with islands, time-warped marshlands and saltpans, and Brittany's most sophisticated beach resort. In addition, there are enchanting medieval towns, fishing villages, peninsulas, marinas and deep-probing rivers.

The climate is unusually mild, and the south-facing aspect ensures that the vegetation is more Mediterranean than Atlantic. The attractions to the tourist are obvious, but the season here is still a short one and many hotels will close for months at a time.

Prosperous port: The origin and name of **Lorient** date back to the East India Company's decision in the 17th century to build a new port for its trading vessels in the wide, sheltered estuary formed by the confluence of the rivers Scorff and Blavet. Since the company's trade was exclusively in the east, the new port took the name L'Orient. It was Napoleon who made it a naval base, as it still is today.

Occupied by the Germans in 1940, the town paid a high price for its resistance to General Patton's lightning advance south from Avranches in 1944. Around 85 percent of the old buildings were destroyed. From the desolation that greeted the townsfolk when they tried to return to their homes has risen a prosperous modern town, supported by its naval dockyards, commercial port, and the third largest fishing port in France (after Boulogne and Concarneau).

It's worth getting up early to watch the trawlers unload their catch in the efficiently organised Keroman fishing harbour, active all the year round.

Many of Lorient's prosperous businessmen prefer to live in the little fishing centre of **Port Louis**, named after Louis XIII, who was responsible for developing the town in the 17th century.

It's not hard to see why: it has a good deal more character and faded charm than the commercialised Lorient.

Port Louis stands guard over the entrance to the river **Blavet**, with which it once shared a name. Since medieval times it has been a fortress; Richelieu in 1636 reinforced its defence and his sea-pounded granite citadel still greets returning sailors and fishermen, now more often than not on their way to Lorient, which has long superseded little Port Louis in importance. Even the staple sardine fleet has declined, but it is still not unusual to see giant tunny landed in the headland-sheltered harbour.

Between here and the beach lies the town, preoccupied on Saturday with its market, which straggles along the main street and fills the main square with colour and babble.

The beach comes as a very pleasant surprise. Pass through the gap in the 16th-century ramparts and there are extensive fine sands with an interesting view across the estuary to **Larmor**

Preceding pages and right: Lorient. Left, Adal Avor, Quiberon.

Plage and the **Ile de Groix**. The beach huts and cafés snap shut abruptly at the end of the school holidays; on a fine September day you could have the beach and prospect of much marine activity all to yourself.

Monotonous monoliths: Flaubert said that **Carnac** had more pages of rubbish written about it than it had standing stones—and there are more than 5,000 stones! Except for the deeply serious dolmen-fancier, the famous site can prove a disappointment.

At dusk, however, when the crowds and coaches have left and only the serried rows of megaliths and their shadows people the flat desolate scrubland, it is possible to understand a little of their power. The fact that their origins are lost in the mists of time adds to their mystery and other-worldliness. Some say they are religious symbols, others astronomical.

There are hundreds of these strange *alignements* around the surrounding countryside. The most famous are the **Ménec Lines**, over 1,000 stones, stretching for nearly a mile. The hamlet of Ménec, just two km to the northeast of Carnac, is almost surrounded by 70 of them.

For a quick view of the area and many of its megaliths, climb to the top of the St Michael tumulus, which covers several burial chambers, and on which there is an explanatory viewing table. Most of the archaeological finds—decorated vases, jewellery and weapons—from the dolmens and tumuli are now in Carnac's **Prehistorical Museum**.

Just two miles (three km) away is a very different story. Here the lines are more horizontal: human bodies stretching out on **Carnac-Plage**, a marvellous beach of fine pale sand that stretches round the vast bay.

Carnac-Plage is still being developed and the pine trees are receding under the onslaught of the smart villas and modern hotels, cashing in on the obvious potential of a beach that rivals that of La Baule. Because it is all so new, there isn't yet a lot of heart to the place, and it

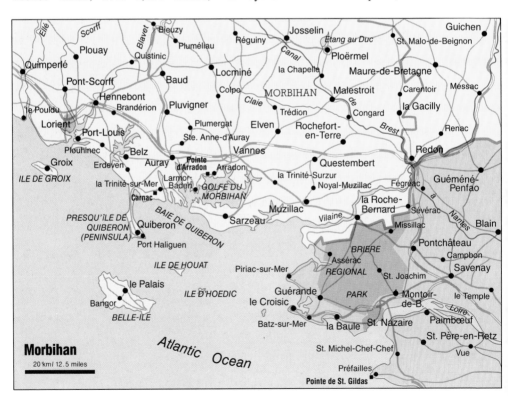

Morbihan
20 km/ 12.5 miles

lacks any strong Gallic flavour. This is obviously no deterrent, since it is one of the most popular resorts in Brittany and it would be unwise to bank on finding unbooked accommodation in high season.

La Trinité-sur-Mer, a little further east on the D186, is renowned to serious sailors as the destination of a tough ocean race, and is a favourite pull-up for all manner of boats, from the family-shabby to international-gloss. It's agreeable to stroll along the unsteady pontoons of the marina to peer down on the multinational owners and their crews, and throughout the summer the bars along the quays are alive with multi-tongued customers.

Regrettably, there are no fish restaurants around the harbour to lend local colour and atmosphere. The season is short and the town dies when the yachtsmen leave.

Perhaps its all a little artificial and expensive and not very French, but the setting on the mouth of the river Crach is splendid and there are many beautiful sheltered bays up the river begging to be explored. Take the minor roads east off the D28 for instant pleasure and perfect picnicking. The view from the new **Kérisper bridge** that spans the estuary is most photogenic.

Auray, 10 miles (16 km) to the northeast, is an enchanting ancient town, split into two distinct parts by the river Auray (sometimes called the river Loc). The little port of **St-Goustan**, once one of the busiest in Brittany, is pure picture-book, with its cobbled square and old grey stone houses, brightened with masses of flowers. Benjamin Franklin landed here in 1776 to seek French support for the American War of Independence.

Colourful parasols shade white tables at which tourists sit and write the inevitable postcards or watch local children diving off the bridge into the fast-flowing river. In summer you can take a delightful boat trip from here to the Gulf of Morbihan.

Cross the old bridge and zig-zag up the steep path through the trees to the

Carnac's aligne-ments.

Promenade du Lac for a good view of the harbour. Up here is the more down-to-earth **Auray**, with shops, market square and the 17th-century church of St Gilda—worth a visit to see the fine reredos behind the altar.

Just north of Auray is the historic battlefield where in 1364 Jean de Montfort, Oliver de Clisson and the English forces triumphed in the last battle of the War of Succession. Charles de Blois, though supported by the legendary Bertrand du Guesclin, was killed in the battle and subsequently sanctified by the Bretons.

Less than four miles inland is the great pilgrimage centre of **Ste-Anne-d'Auray**, probably the most important shrine in Brittany. Legend has it that Saint Anne was born and married in Armorica (the old name for Brittany), was widowed, travelled to Palestine and re-married, producing a daughter, Mary; when she later returned to Armorica she was visited by her grandson, Jesus.

The *pardon* of Saint Anne is on 25 and 26 July, when pilgrims come from all over France and beyond to pray to the mother of the Virgin Mary. Almost every week there is a parish pilgrimage, and thousands of devout Catholics flood into the little town and join in the processions to the elephantine 19th-century basilica, built on the spot where, in 1625, a peasant, guided by Saint Anne, unearthed a statue that had lain buried for centuries.

Apart from the historic site, there is little else to see in the town, but it is well served with hotels and restaurants to refresh the pilgrims.

Long finger: The French word for peninsula, *presqu'île* (almost an island), seems particularly apt for the **Quiberon Peninsula**, a nine-mile (14-km) strip of land that juts out from Carnac, so fragilely linked to the mainland that at one point the road is almost a causeway, with pounding ocean to the west and sheltered shallows to the east.

It's a busy road, with one or two little resorts on either side. **St Pierre Quiberon**, with its sheltered bay lined with

More sales than sails at Quiberon.

family hotels, is the only one of any size.

Port Haliguen is a yacht harbour with a modern marina. Taking advantage of the reputation for exceptionally healthy, heavily iodised air, there's a Thalassotherapy Institute—one of the first in France—at the **Pointe du Conguel**, the peninsula's most southerly tip. A fine view can be had from the Pointe of Belle Ile and the two smaller offshore islands, **Houat** and **Hoëdic**.

Walks along the wild and rugged west coast, where the waters foam and rage in the crevasses, are truly spectacular, but it's not called *La Côte Sauvage* for nothing: often the wind that has deformed the gorse bushes blows too fiercely for comfort.

Quiberon itself was once a modest fishing village, and vestiges of its past are evident still at **Port Maria**, where the sardines are landed and canned in nearby factories. From here the boats leave for Belle-Ile, the largest and most aptly-named of the Breton islands. Here, by the harbour, is the place to find inexpensive little fish restaurants; further back in the busy town, around the fine sandy beach, the atmosphere is more tourist-orientated and less good value.

The magnet in this area of Brittany is **Vannes**, 10 miles (15 km) east of Auray. You have only to look at the map to make a fair guess about its attractions. At the head of the Gulf of Morbihan, surrounded by inlets and creeks and islands, it could hardly fail to appeal. The canalised waterway probes deep into the heart of the old town, so that boats and the paraphernalia of masts and rigging and chug-chugging are an integral part of the scene.

The canal ends abruptly at a pleasant sunny square, the Place Maréchal Joffre, where there are café tables at which to sit and take stock. The prospect is one of dignified old grey houses lining the banks, whilst in the background is the medieval Porte St Vincent, leading away from the activity of the port to the shaded seclusion of the old town.

Cars are best left outside the steep narrow cobbled streets. This means

Vannes: the Old City.

that, though there are more tourists here, there are fewer fumes, and the higher you climb, the deeper the calm. The tall gabled houses lean inwards to meet their opposite numbers so that it is always restfully dark and cool.

After a spell on the beaches, the urban charms of Vannes are all the more welcome. On market days, Wednesday and Saturday, the central square, the Place des Lices, comes to life and seethes with colourful activity.

Everyone takes his camera to the House of Vannes, to photo the carved rubicond peasants, "Vannes and his wife", projecting like figureheads from the eaves. The Place Henri VI, lined with narrow timbered 16th-century houses, is no less photogenic.

The nearby cathedral of St Pierre is an extraordinary hotch-potch of styles and ideas, which is not surprising since it was started in the 13th century and not completed until the 19th. Its 13th-century tower has a modern steeple, the rotunda of the chapel is Renaissance (a rare attribute in Brittany), the transept door is Flamboyant Gothic with a few touches of Renaissance, the tombs and statues are 17th and 18th-century. The whole building is lopsided, and no wonder.

Complete the tour via the Postern Gate and the ramparts—particularly impressive in summer, when floodlighting throws the dumpy medieval towers into dramatic relief.

Another photographers' favourite is the view from the narrow bridge over the flower-filled moats to the 16th-century washhouses, with their crazy irregular roofing. They are still occupied and the lines of washing, though of anachronistic 20th-century garments, add a touch of authenticity.

The old town, neatly enclosed within its ramparts, represents only a small part of Vannes' territory, but the rest is mostly a noisy sprawl with little to offer the visitor.

Vannes is a good point to check up on the cruises around the Gulf offered by the *Vedettes Vertes* company. They vary enormously according to season and cost. The "Gastronomique" with

dinner included is excellent, but it does seem a shame to divert attention for one minute from the scenery of this unique waterscape. The *dépôt* is on the Promenade de la Rabine.

The **Golfe de Morbihan** itself is almost too pretty. On a sunny day the vast expanse of water is dotted with little boats, some purposefully busy, some with sails a-flap, negotiating between the green and intriguing islands.

Morbihan means "Little Sea" in Breton and the gulf is just that—a whole inland sea almost landlocked by the two protective arms of the Locmariaquer and Rhuys peninsulas. The micro-climate is Mediterranean in character, so that foliage is similar to that of the South of France, with palm-trees and oleanders flourishing. In fact, the predominating impression is of an enclosed little world, a little sea, totally unrelated to outside influences.

The possibilities are endless. Take any of the minor roads off the D101, west out of Vannes, and it will undoubtedly lead to a tiny harbour, a few privi-

Vannes.

leged houses, perhaps a simple hotel on the water's edge, and yet another different aspect of the Gulf.

Even as near to Vannes as **Conleau** the magic begins. But of course the beaches here (where there is a very good hotel and restuarant, camping site and windsurfing base) do get crowded at the height of the season.

A little further west a diversion down to **Arradon** brings instant reward. The **Pointe d'Arradon** is just a cluster of houses, with a dinghy harbour and good hotel; at weekends the beach is packed, but out of season and mid-week there is space to spare. At any time the walk along the water's edge in either direction is pure delight. An hour's stroll, with island succeeding island on the horizon, is likely to involve no more intrusion than perhaps a fisherman pulling up his boat or a dog out for his daily exercise.

Larmor-Baden on the tip of another south-facing promontory is a little port with a few fishing boats and an oyster cultivation centre. It has particularly

fine views across to the entrance of the Gulf.

From here you can take a boat to the **Gavrinis tumulus**, said to be "the most interesting megalithic monument in Brittany and perhaps in the world". Under the weed-covered rocky tumulus is a surprisingly spacious gallery supported by carved posts, leading to the awe-inspiring, thought-provoking burial chamber of a local grandee, his identity once known to all but now long forgotten.

At the tip of the Gulf's southern peninsula, the **Presqu'ile de Rhuys**, is a lively little fishing harbour, **Port Navalo**, whose lighthouse faces due west. It was near here that Caesar is said to have watched his fleet destroy that of the Gaulish Veneti tribe, remembered round the bay by the several hotels and restaurants named after them. Caesar, too, has his memorial: the Tumiac Tumulus here is known as Caesar's Mound.

On the peninsula's southern shore is the monastery of St-Gildas-de-Rhuys,

Fishing nets at Port Navolo.

founded by St Gildas in the sixth century. Six hundred years later Pierre Abelard arrived as abbot. Separated from his beloved Heloise, he came to try and find peace and solitude. In fact, his sojourn here was far from happy; he hated the "inaccessible shore of a rough sea" and was hated in turn by his monks on account of the scandal he had caused, and was almost successfully poisoned by them.

The former 11th-century abbey church, with remarkable Romanesque chancel, was largely re-built in the 16th and 17th centuries; the tomb of St Gildas is behind the high altar.

Further east along this same shore can still be seen the ruins of the 13th-century **Château de Suscino**, built as a summer ducal residence. The classical façade of another chateau, **Kerlévenan**, can be spotted just off the main road heading further east.

Islands of the Gulf: They say there are as many islands in the gulf as days in the year. Forty are inhabited, some are mere reefs, many are pleasantly wooded,

some have landing stages with dinghies tied up and picnickers ashore. The two biggest are the **Ile d'Arz** and the **Ile aux Moines**.

Both are connected to the mainland by ferries, and this is a cheap and versatile way of viewing the panorama. It can be combined with a stretch on the more expensive, more luxurious Vedettes Vertes, veritable palaces of pleasure steamers with excellent vision though not much aesthetic appeal. It's an oddly anachronistic sight to see the vast plate-glassed vessels bearing down over the peaceful waters.

Vannes is the departure point, but it is possible to pick one up at Locmariaquer, Port Navalo or Auray, combine a bus trip one way, and have dinner or lunch on board. The schedule is drastically cut back after the high season and it is best to make enquiries at the depot in Vannes, at the port at Auray, on the jetty at Port Navalo or at the *tabac* at Locmariaquer.

The round trip takes several hours and is quite expensive. One recommended routine is to drive to Port Blanc to catch the ferry across to the Ile aux Moines, picnic there under the pine trees before a swim from the sandy beach and then pick up the Vedette Verte for the last hour and a half of its tour. This will call in at Port Navalo and Locmariaquer and return to the island on the homeward route to Vannes. Whatever plan is adopted, a boat trip round the Gulf is an experience which shouldn't be missed.

The Ile d'Arz has a good restaurant, *L'Escale,* open from April to October, at the landing stage. The food is excellent and not as expensive as one would expect in a short-season, tourist-oriented spot. It has a few rooms from which to wave away the last departing boat as the sun goes down.

The Ile aux Moines is the most beautiful island of them all: three miles (five km) long, with mimosas, eucalyptus, fig and palm trees. There are beaches and cliffs, woods with romantic names like *Forêt d'Amour,* heaths and pines, and a steep path up to the old village from whose terrace bearings can be

Alfred Guillou's *Ramasseuse de Goëmon.*

established. Plenty of bars and crêperies obliterate hunger pangs and thirst.

The Guérande Peninsula: The diversity and contrast encapsulated within this peninsula's water-dominated bounds include features typical of Brittany, like the rocky west coast dotted with picturesque fishing villages, La Baule's sandy beaches, the delightfully situated port of La Roche-Bernard high above the wrongly-named river Vilaine. It also has some other aspects that are unique, like the marshes of La Grande Brière and the saltpans of the area just north of La Baule.

All round is a ghostly patchworked region where the men rake the grey salt from the pans, while the women skim off the white surface, before the salt is piled in monochrome heaps at the edge of the marshes. At the hamlet of **Saillé**, La Maison des Paludiers, a typical salt worker's house, is open to the public.

All the more delightful then is the surprise of **Guérande** rising unpredictable from the flat terrain like a medieval mirage. It is one of the few towns in France to have retained its ramparts intact. You can walk around their circumference, looking down on the weird chequered, moon-like landscape below. ✒

Built in the 15th century, the ramparts are punctuated by eight towers and pierced by four gateways, the most striking of which is the Porte St Michel, whose gatehouse is now a folklore museum.

Pass through its massive portals into the heart of the old town, a warren of colourful old streets, cul-de-sacs, squares and churches. Stroll from the Place du Marché au Bois, via the rue St Michel, to St Aubin.

The church of **St Aubin** was founded in A.D. 852, and rebuilt between the 4th and 16th centuries, with a bizarre exterior pulpit, flanked by two angels' heads. Look for the fascinating grotesque Romanesque carvings on the capitals inside, and a double Flamboyant Gothic west door.

It is obvious from a look at the map that Guérande must make a popular

Roche
Bernard.

excursion for those holidaymakers seeking diversion from sand and sea, and at times it seems the ramparts must bulge with the volume of tourists, but there are plenty of cafés and restaurants to offer succour to them all.

From Guérande the D99 is a pleasant road to follow to the wild **Pointe du Castelli**, with a splendid view in all direction, and on, past the signal station, to **Piriac-sur-Mer**, a small fishing village with some attractive wood-framed houses.

Much more sophisticated—and therefore not terribly Breton—is the resort of **La Baule**, "*la plus belle plage d'Europe*," they claim, and perhaps they're right. Certainly the fine sand curves for three miles (five km) round a perfect bay, enclosing water that always seems to be Mediterranean-blue. White sails and expensive power boats help the picture-postcard image.

La Baule's identity is much disputed, since the département of Loire-Atlantique is administered by the Pays de Loire region, which would like to claim La Baule's allegiance completely.

The British discovered the mild climate and sands and pines 100 years ago, and started the development of a fashionable resort. Top Parisian boutiques moved in, grand hotels and smart restaurants proliferated, the casino insisted on evening dress. Today it is still recognised as an upmarket choice, but now jeans, fast food outlets, cola dispensers and pinball machines are more in evidence than Chanel, gastronomy, Krug and chemin-de-fer.

The pine trees have retreated one by one from the prime sites near the beach, replaced by the money-spinning modern hotels and apartments. They can still be traced a block or two back, causing the roads to twist and curve attractively around them, but even the eastward extension of the town, **La Baule-les-Pins**, might soon be misappropriately named, so fast is the expansion.

Some upmarket hotels survive from the old days and, out of season (which is short, in spite of the favourable microclimate), there are attempts to fill them

La Baule.

with musical weekends and other cultural events.

At the western end of the town, at the mouth of the canal near **Le Pouligen**, is the new marina. Past Le Pouligen, the Croisic Peninsula hooks around the sheltered fishing port. The corniche road runs above the **Grotte Des Korrigans** (the cave of the goblins) to the old village of **Batz**, whose church is a landmark visible for miles in this flat inland landscape. It was in this village that Balzac wrote the novel *Beatrix*, in which he gave a vivid description of Guérande.

The old customs officers' path leads along the cliff edge from St Michel's beach, with a good view down on to the impressive rocks of **La Grande Côte**.

Le Croisic, itself is perhaps not the important port it once was, but it is still one of Brittany's most interesting fishing villages. Only a short drive from the fleshpots of La Baule, it makes a pleasant contrast in every way, the reasonably priced and impeccably fresh fish served in the dozens of little restaurants that face the harbour. At meal times, everyone crosses to this side of the road for the promenade ritual of checking the menus before the big decisions are made.

At any time of day Le Croisic is a lively little town, with much colourful activity based on its north-facing lagoon harbour, divided by three islands into several basins. Sardines and crustaceans are the port's specialities, but early risers will witness all manner of marine specimens being auctioned off in the important fish market.

Across the narrow neck of land, almost back to back with Le Croisic, is the delightful complementary little resort of **Port Lin**, with rocks and sands and good hotels. The two make a happy combination.

La Grande-Brière provides another dimension and another world—though less remote and less authentic than it used to be. Time was when the marsh folk of La Grande Brière earned their living entirely from the peat bogs and inhabited the same traditional whitewashed thatched cottages as their forefathers before them; their only means of transport was the flat-bottomed black boat tied up alongside. Nowadays the proximity and prosperity of their sprawling neighbours, La Baule and St Nazaire, has meant more attractive jobs outside, so the natives go out and the tourists pour in.

Much of the marshland has been converted to pasture by means of canalisation, but enough remains of the old eerie world of the marshes to make a trip by boat an interesting diversion, and certainly provide a striking contrast to the nearby alternatives.

You can take a boat trip from **Fédrun** in the centre, one of the best-known thatched villages, typical in that the circle of cottages all face inwards. A drive from here, via the D50 and D51, to **St Lyphard** and **St André-des-Eaux**—particularly at sundown when the shadows contrast with sharp reflections and with the water's silence—is a striking experience and leaves a lasting impression of this time-warped landscape.

Shrimp goes shrimping.

CENTRAL BRITTANY

Since the province of Brittany is endowed with a long and beautiful coastline, it isn't surprising that most of its popular attractions are found by the seaside. From earliest times, Bretons were great seafarers, so that even today the major cities of the province are on— or closely linked to—the sea. This still leaves a vast hinterland, stretching right across the country from the Atlantic coast to the frontiers of Normandy.

Here, in the heartland of Brittany, well off the beaten track, visitors will find that much of the old Breton way of life is still proceeding undisturbed, and will come to realise that, while summer tourism may now be the main source of revenue around the coast, agriculture— farming the green fields of central Brittany—is still a major source of wealth and employment in the hinterland.

This interior part of the country is well worth exploring. To see it all, the best place to begin is on the windy top of the second tallest hill in Brittany, the Ménez-Hom.

The best way to get there is through **Le Faou**, a little town at the head of the small Le Faou estuary, one of several that jut inland from the western coast. This estuary dries out completely at low tide, revealing great swathes of mud, but turns very attractive indeed if the time of high tide can be combined with sunset. Le Faou is tiny, just one main street lined with overhanging houses, though there are good views over the estuary from the terrace of the 15th-century church.

From here the road to the Ménez-Hom leads through **Châteaulin** on the River Aulne. This is a noted river for trout and salmon fishing and the creator of a long and beautiful river valley, the Vallée de l'Aulne, which runs inland as far as Châteauneuf-du-Faou. Like many other little towns hereabouts, Châteaulin was once a port, although it is just beyond the reach of the tide. The small ships which still ply around the Breton coast, though declining in num-

bers every year, usually tie up at Port Launay further downstream; but the yachts do make it to Châteaulin and tie up along the quai du Brest.

The salmon fishing, which brings hundreds of sports fishermen to Châteaulin every year, from February to July, has also declined in recent years, although catches are still comparatively good. The fishing area on the Aulne at Châteaulin lies below the tidal lock.

A good view over pretty Châteaulin and the lower reaches of the Aulne Valley can be had from the terrace of the **Chapel of Notre Dame**, which overlooks the town at the point where the river bends. This is a small, ornate chapel, with the usual representations of the Holy Family, but includes two of the Breton healing saints, St Herlot and St Mandor.

The **Ménez-Hom** is not even technically a mountain—to achieve that distinction a hill must top 2,000 ft (610 metres), and at 330 metres the Ménez-Hom barely achieves half that. It is, in

fact, a great hump of moorland, heaved up above the land overlooking the approaches to Brest, and on a clear day the views from the top, where there is a viewing platform, are quite fantastic—to Brest, Dournenez Bay, over much of Cournaille, the southern part of Finistère, and well inland across the farmlands and the valley of the Aulne far below.

The Ménez-Hom is rightly included in the great Breton National Park, the **Parc Régional d'Armorique**. This occupies much of the wilder parts of Western Brittany, including some of the offshore islands and the Montagnes d'Arrée, further inland. The park was established in 1969 and, while it permits traditional activities like forestry, fishing and farming, it guarantees the long-term protection of wildlife and plants and the preservation of ancient sites and objects, such as *menhirs*.

Turning inland, a good first stop lies at the foot of the Ménez-Hom, at the **Chapel of Ste-Marie-de-Ménez-Hom**, set in a shady grove of trees. If the chapel is shut, the key will be available in the nearby café. There has been a chapel at this spot for centuries, and the present building, though largely 18th-century, contains elements from many other eras, especially the 16th and 17th centuries when Brittany saw a religious revival. The most notable features here, apart from the calvary, are the wood-carvings in the body of the church, which include St Lawrence with his grid-iron.

Moving east into the heart of the country, the next stop along the Valley of the Aulne is at **Pleyben**, which is small but has a fine calvary and a magnificent *parish-clos*, the largest in the entire province. It is so large that it took more than a century to complete, from 1555 to 1660, and is the site of a great *pardon* on the first Sunday in August. The church is also 16th century, with much carved and painted panelling on the lives of the saints, but there are indications of an earlier church in the small Funeral Chapel, which is 15th century and was once the ossuary,

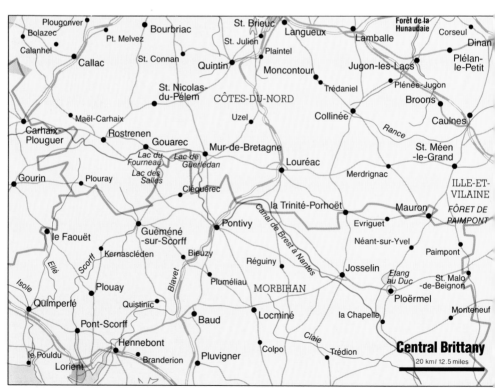

or bone-yard, for the cemetery.

At Pleyben, the **Montagnes d'Arrée** are looming up to the north, the highest range of "mountains" in Brittany, reaching up to 1,200 ft (490 metres). Like the Ménez-Hom, they are really an expanse of rolling moorland, and very attractive, especially now, when they have been endowed with a great reservoir near the Chapel of St Michel de Brasparts.

Brasparts village lies just outside the Parc Naturel, and has another smaller *parish-clos* and a calvary, both dating from the 16th century, as does the church. There are two more small *parish-clos* near here, at **Loqueffret** and **Lannédern**.

As one moves on to skirt the southern edge of the Montagnes d'Arrée, there is a little church of one of the Breton healing saints, St Herlot. He is also the patron saint of horned cattle, and therefore much revered by farmers. This church stands all alone on the moor, and has all the attractive Breton elements, including a calvary in that blue Kersanton granite, a Renaissance ossuary, and a fine oak chancel screen. The greater part of the church is built in the Gothic style, with finely pointed windows and elaborately carved choir stalls.

A few kilometres past here lies **Huelgoat**, on the River Argent, capital of the Arrée and a great walking and fishing centre. It is also well provided with woods and streams and great wind-eroded rocks. Although quite small, Huelgoat has a number of hotels and restaurants and is therefore a popular place with those visitors to Brittany who don't particularly care for the seaside.

Huelgoat's great attraction is the chance to walk into the surrounding woods and valleys, and scramble on the rocks, many of which have names. There is the **Chaos du Moulin**, (the Mill Rocks), the **Grotto du Diable** which can only be reached down a steep iron ladder, the **Virgin's Kitchen** where the rocks are said to resemble pots and pans, and the most popular of all, the **Roche Tremblant**, the Trem-

Tiles tell the tale at Huelgoat.

bling Rock which weighs over 100 tons but can be made to move—just—if shoulders are applied to a certain spot.

One of the most popular short walks in these woods is the one-hour hike to the **Cintres Rock**, which can be climbed, and the top gives great views over the little town and the surrounding countryside. Huelgoat has so many walks that the paths through the woods are never crowded, and many of the shorter ones can be combined to make day-long excursions, like the one beside the canal that was once used to take workers to the local silver mine—the name of the river, Argent, means "silver". The river's waters once drove pumps and machinery to mine the silver, until the mine petered out after World War I.

Another walker's objective might be **Artus Camp**, an historic camp site from the Greco-Roman period, about two miles (three km) on foot from the village.

From Huelgoat it is possible to continue a tour around the Montagnes d'Arrée up to the peak at the **Roc de Trévezel** (1,260 ft/384 metres). It lies close to the D785 road, but can be reached from there only on foot. This rock is in a very rugged setting and again gives great views over the surrounding countryside. It is said that from here on a clear, sharp day, you can see the spire on the Kreisker Chapel at St-Pol de Léon, many miles to the north. There is another large calvary near here, in the parish of **Commana**, and the road south towards Brasparts, which completes a circle of the Montagnes d'Arrée, passes the Chapel of St-Michel de Brasparts on a little hill, overlooking the lake.

Black Mountains: Through **Brasparts** and **Pleyben**, this road eventually arrives at **Châteauneuf-du-Faou**, another trout and salmon fishing centre, set on a hill overlooking the Aulne. Here the road east runs along beside the river for a few miles towards Carhaix-Plouguer.

This road skirts the northern edge of yet another range of moorland and hills,

The calvary at Pleyben.

the **Montagnes Noires**, the Black Mountains, which rise to 1,043 ft (326 metres) at the **Roc de Toullaëron** near Gourin, which was once a great centre for slate production.

The Montagnes Noires and the Montagnes d'Arrée form the backbone of central Brittany. But, although comprised of the same rocks—sandstone and quartz—the two ranges, if that is not too grand a term for two rolling moors, are rather different in aspect. The Montagnes d'Arrée are higher, more open and largely given over to moorland, while on the Montagnes Noires the heath is less extensive and the name seems to indicate that, once upon a time, these hills were forested. Here, as elsewhere, all those large Breton forests, mostly fir trees, have long since gone and modern re-aforestation has created great plantations which do little for the landscape.

Carhaix is quite a substantial town by the standards of the Breton hinterland, with a population of 8,000. But its principal claim to fame is as the birthplace of the soldier Theophile-Malo Corret, better known to history as La Tour d'Auvergne, who was born here in 1742 and served with distinction in the armies of Republican France and the Empire. He served first in the armies of Louis XV, and was soon noted for his bravery, but had only reached the rank of captain when he retired at 46.

Eight years later, he re-enlisted as a private to take the place of a young conscript and was soon singled out for his valour in the field. Bonaparte even offered him a safe post on the National Council, but La Tour preferred to stay with his troops. When he was finally killed on the Rhine in 1800, the entire French Army went into mourning. Carhaix is very proud of its native son and celebrates his achievements every year on 27 and 28 June.

Northeast of Carhaix the countryside becomes even wilder, but even here there are places no visitor should miss, such as the small calvary at **Lanrivain**, and the little village of **St-Nicolas de Pélem**, which lies just outside Finistère,

Spectators at Breton wedding.

back in the department of Côtes-du-Nord. St-Nicolas has a 15th-century church with fine stained glass, but the most notable feature is the carillon bell in the Ruellou Chapel, which is rung by those who need to attract the attention of the saints before praying.

From here there is a very pleasant drive through open country to **Rostrenen**, which has a shrine to a popular Breton saint, Notre Dame du Roncier, Our Lady of the Brambles. This is a good centre for exploring east or west along the line of the **Nantes-à-Brest Canal**, one of the great waterways of France. In the 10 miles (17 km) between Rostrenen and Carhaix, the canal climbs nearly 400 ft (120 metres) up a stairway of 44 locks. **Gourin**, the slate mining centre of Brittany, lies in the province's southern *département,* Morbihan, as does the next centre, Le Faouët.

Le Faouët lies in a flatter part of the country created by two rivers, the **Inam** and the **Ellé**, which flow south out of the Montagnes Noires. The village centre is, as usual, very small, with a 16th-century church and a very fine market hall from the same period. The market place contains a monument to a local hero, Corentin Carne—a very Breton name—who enlisted at the start of the Great War when he was just 15, took up flying, and was shot down over the Western Front three years later.

Le Faouët is a sleepy little place, and its great attraction is as a touring centre for the various chapels and churches in the area. It is fair to say that those who have no great interest in things religious will have a thin time of it in parts of Brittany, where many of the principal historic attractions have religious roots.

The main ones hereabouts can be reached on a circular tour, northeast first, to the Chapel of St-Barbara (**Ste-Barbe**). This is a Flamboyant Gothic building, erected on a knoll over the valley of the River Elle. The inside is rich, with glass and carvings, and there are two *pardons* here, on the last Sunday in June and on 4 December. Do not leave Ste Barbe without climbing the stairway to St-Michel's Oratory on the hill above, and ringing the little bell which calls down blessings from Heaven.

A little further on, down a side road to the right, lies another chapel dedicated to St Nicolas, with his life illustrated in a series of carved panels.

From here, head north to the restored abbey at **Langonnet**, which has retained only a 13th-century Chapter House from the original buildings.

Turning south here, down the valley of the Elle, along the D790, the road passes through Le Faouët and out to St-Fiacre, which is a 15th-century chapel and is well worth seeing for the contemporary rood screen, which dates from 1480 and shows examples of the Seven Deadly Sins.

Heading east from here, towards Pontivy, travellers will soon come to the village and church of **Kernascléden** which, like St-Fiacre, is also 15th-century, but some 30 years earlier, dating from 1450. Local legend, however, has it that they were built at the same time and may, in fact, have been built by the

Beware!

186

same masons. This church is worth selecting for a visit from the host of Breton churches available, because it has been built with great delicacy and care and contains, among other fine things, a fine fresco of the Crucifixion and a medieval Doom showing the Dance of Death and souls tormented in Hell.

Heading northeast from here, a series of quiet roads brings travellers to one of the last remaining medieval forests in Brittany, the **Forêt de Quénécan**, another area where it would pay to settle in a small hotel and devote some time to simply touring about.

A good place to do this would be in the little town of **Mur-de-Bretagne**, touring out from here into the forest, along the valley of the River Blavet, and around the great reservoir of the **Lac de Guerlédan**. Mur is a pretty little spot and was a favourite place for the painter Corot during the last century, a place of green meadows, fine oaks and stretches of water, a place where any painter would find some inspiration.

From Mur it is no distance to the vast lake at Guerlédan, which was created by damming the river at the Gorges de Blavet, and just by here the Nantes-à-Brest Canal, which traverses central Brittany and is popular with holiday craft, flows on towards Pontivy.

The Forêt de Quénécan is a marvellous place for walking, either over the heath or out to such little villages as **Les Forges-des-Salles**, which is set off by the picturesque ruins of a medieval castle, or out to any one of the smaller lakes, **Lac Fourneau** or the **Lac des Salles**.

North of the River Blavet lies another tributary river, the **Daoulas**, which flows into the main river through a steep-sided gorge. This is a beautiful part of central Brittany, ideal for people who just enjoy walking in the countryside. Those who have not yet seen enough churches and chapels can visit the ruins of the **Abbey of Bon Repos** near the Daoulas gorges, or the church at **St-Aignan**, which has a fine Tree of Jesse, a fresco illustrating the descent of Jesus Christ from his ancestors.

Lac de Guerlédan.

The Guerlédan lake and the Quénécan forest should give any visitor a day or two of sheer countryside pleasure before dropping south along the line of the Nantes-à-Brest Canal and the Blavet to the next place of any importance hereabouts, **Pontivy**, in Northern Morbihan. This town, which falls into two parts, reflects the most dramatic changes in French history.

Old Pontivy is a medieval town, built around a castle belonging to the mighty Dukes of Rohan, who ruled much of Brittany from their seat at Josselin. This castle has been repaired and is now open to the public, and the rest of old Pontivy can be inspected around the Place du Martray, a square which is lined with 15th- and 16th-century houses.

However, as a contrast which introduces the early years of the Republic, there is new Pontivy. The town supported the Republic at the start of the Revolution, and so attracted the benign attention of the First Council, Napoleon Bonaparte. He built the new town—then called Napoleonville—and so made Pontivy the commercial axis of the great Nantes-à-Brest Canal. Pontivy was called Napoleonville only for a brief time, reverting to the old name after 1815, but the straight avenues and municipal buildings make the town a distinctive relic of that early, enthusiastic Republican period.

Pontivy is another excellent touring centre, ideal for walkers or motorists, with a lot to see in the countryside round about. Many visitors head north for the Lac de Guerlédan, but the country to the south, along the River Blavet, is almost equally attractive. One pleasant place south of Pontivy is the little hillside town of **St-Nicolas-des-Eaux**, overlooking the Blavet, and it is here, for some reason, that the typical Breton roofs of slate give way to those of thatch.

Other sites to see along this part of the river are the Chapel of St-Nicodème, the Renaissance church at **Bieuzy**, and the little town of **Melrand**, which is actually little more than a village. One church which should not be missed is

Low tide at Pontivy.

188

the one at **Quelven**, between Melrand and Pontivy, which is 15th-century and stands within a group of houses and contains a statue of Our Lady of Quelven that can be opened up and reveals scenes from the life of Christ. Two other 15th-century churches lie east of Pontivy, at **Ste-Noyäle** and **Noyal-Pontivy**.

South of Pontivy lies **Baud**, at the western end of that long moor that runs away to the east to Rochefort-en-Terre, the famous and picturesque **Landes de Lanvaux**. Baud, in the valley of the River Evel, is noted locally for a curious Greek or Roman statue called the **Venus de Quinipily**, which stands near a fountain in a farmyard just off the N24 road to Hennebont.

Whatever the origins of this battered figure, it is certainly very old, and probably pre-Christian. During the Middle Ages it was frequently thrown into the river on the orders of the local bishop, but the local people, who were rather attached to it, would always fish it out again. The statue was repaired and re-cut—badly—in the 18th century, and if it ever much resembled Venus, that image has long since disappeared, but it remains a unique and curious figure.

Southeast of Pontivy, the end of central Brittany is marked by three places of distinction: the castle of Josselin, the town of Ploërmel and the Forest of Paimpont. To these one must add, between Josselin and Paimpont, the sites of the Battle of the Thirty, one of the smallest and yet bloodiest engagements of the Hundred Years War.

Mighty **Josselin**, one of France's most magnificent castles, is a place no visitor to Brittany can miss. It is one of the great attractions of Brittany, for this is the home of the Rohan family, whose motto was:

Roi ne puis
Prince ne daigne
Rohan suis."
Or, in plainer English:
"I am not King
Prince I would not stoop to be,
I am the Lord of Rohan."

The streets of Josselin.

The great castle of the Rohans over-looks the River Oust, which usually carries its reflection. It was built from about 1000 A.D. by the then Count of Porhoet, and named after his second son, Josselin. The castle was expanded and embellished continually for the next 500 years, and greatly rebuilt after England's Henry II destroyed most of it in 1168. During the Hundred Years War it was held for a long time by the Constable of France, Oliver de Clisson, who acquired the castle in 1370 by marrying the heiress, Marguerite de Rohan, who had lost her first husband, the Lord of Beaumanoir, at the Battle of the Thirty in 1351.

Oliver de Clisson lost possession of the castle in 1407, when it was given back to the Rohan family, who still live there. The castle remains a fine example of the High Medieval fortress, although it narrowly escaped total destruction by the orders of Cardinal Richelieu; he had five of the castle's nine towers pulled down in 1629.

The castle tends to overawe Josselin and those who visit it, but the town itself is well worth exploring. Apart from the castle, however, the central attraction is the **Basilica of Notre Dame du Roncier**, which was first founded in the 11th century and remodelled as recently as 1949. The bulk of the church, though, is in that Flamboyant Gothic style which becomes so familiar to the Brittany traveller. The original statue of Notre Dame du Roncier, discovered by a peasant in the year 800, was burnt by the mob in 1793, and only some fragments remain to be venerated at the annual *pardon*; it is held every year on 2 September and attracts worshippers from all over Brittany.

Inside the chapel of Notre Dame du Roncier is the tomb of Oliver de Clisson and his wife Marguerite de Rohan. Other sights connected with the *pardon* here are the Fountain of Notre Dame du Roncier, and the 11th-century **Chapel of St-Croix**, near the banks of the Oust. From here, there are good views across the river to the walls and towers of Josselin.

Josselin town.

190

Moving east from Josselin towards **Ploërmel**, the road passes the site of the Battle of the Thirty, a murderous tournament which took place on this spot in 1351 between knights and men-at-arms from the garrisons of Josselin and Ploërmel. At the time, the men of Josselin supported the cause of Blois, an ally of the Valois. The men of Ploërmel, under an English knight, Sir Richard Bamboro, held the castle for John of Montfort, a vassal of the King of England.

The French commander, Beaumanoir, sent a challenge to the English commander at Ploërmel, inviting him to bring 30 of his knights to the **Mi-Voie** oak, between the two castles, and fight there to the death. Bamboro accepted the challenge, although he had to make up the numbers with German men-at-arms, and the battle duly took place on 27 March 1351.

The *Combat du Trente* lasted most of the day and, although Beaumanoir and several of his knights were killed, and many on both sides were gravely wounded, the day ended with victory for the French. Nine Englishmen, including Bamboro, were killed, and the rest taken prisoner.

The Battle of the Thirty was a famous tournament and Froissant refers to it in his *Chronicles* as bestowing great honour on all who took part. A tall obelisk, erected in the days of Louis XVIII in the 19th century, now marks the spot and records the names of the combatants.

Ploërmel was once the seat of the de Montfort family, the medieval Dukes of Brittany. But little remains to remind visitors of the feudal time except some relics of the old walls and statues of two dukes, John II and John III, who ruled in the 13th century, in the Church of St-Armel in the town centre. There are some medieval houses in the Rue Beaumanoir, but today Ploërmel is completely overlooked by the splendours of nearby Josselin and visitors can pass on swiftly to another unusual, mystical place, the **Forêt de Paimpont**, which lies to the northeast.

Brittany shares many of the Arthu-

Josselin castle.

rian legends with England, and more particularly with Cornwall, which the coast and countryside of Brittany so greatly resembles. There are echoes of King Arthur and the Round Table in many parts of Brittany, but nowhere are they stronger than in the forest of Paimpont. It is said to be the ancient Broceliande, home of Arthur's wizard Merlin, and his deadly rival, the fairy Vivaine, or as she is better known, Morgan-le-Fay.

In fact, Paimpont is all that remains of a vast forest which once covered most of eastern Brittany. But even today, it is a remote place, with eerie silences falling in the thicker parts of the woods.

The centre of the Arthurian legend is at the fountain of **Barenton**, in the **Vallée Sans Retour**, near the castle of Trécesson, where—or so it is said—Vivaine imprisoned the magician inside a stone, where he is still entombed. The stone is certainly still there by the spring, and, if water is sprinkled upon it, Merlin will conjure up rain and thunder. This may not always work, but some local people believe in it and processions of farmers came to pour the water and invoke Merlin's help as recently as the drought-filled summer of 1935. Before that, even the Vicar of Concoret had sprinkled water on Merlin's stone after which—or so it is said—"Rain fell with such fury that we hastened to take shelter."

Those who believe in magic and can find the *perron de Merlin*, near the spring at Barenton, can try this out for themselves. **Paimpont town**, in the heart of the forest, is the best place to stay while exploring the area, but the main attraction of the town is yet another church, the 11th-century Church of St-Ann. Other attractive sights are the castle of Trécesson, which is a magnificent 15th-century castle, not open to the public, and the pretty village of **Les Forges de Paimpont**.

Paimpont Forest is so beautiful and so out of this world, that it is tempting to finish any tour of central Brittany there, but there is one final site which no tour of the Breton hinterland can reasonably miss: the **Towers of Elven**, which lie across the Landes de Lanvaux. This is the place for lovers of the medieval world, for the towers of medieval Elven—and there were once 11 of them—are marvellously evocative of the Middle Ages.

The keep of the castle still stands behind two fortified gateways and the whole place is a splendid, if ruined, example of the finest of medieval fortifications. The castle was sacked and burned by Charles VIII when he took over Brittany for the Crown in 1478.

Central Brittany is the place for those who like walking and wandering, ideal for car tours, with a feast of chapels and churches for those who like such things, and a great deal of history for people who like their travels to take them back through time, as well as forward through the countryside.

Recommendations: Essential places to visit in this part of Brittany are Josselin, Paimpont, Huelgoat (if you like walking), the valley of the Aulne and, for a breezy overview of the area, the top of the Ménez-Hom.

Peace at Paimpont.

RENNES

Rennes, capital of the province and arguably of rock music in France, is about as far as you can get in Brittany from the sea. It is uncharacteristic also in being an urban centre (of more than 200,000 people) in a predominantly rural area. In a region that attracts visitors to its fishing ports, rocky peninsulas and ancient forests, it offers something distinctly different.

Rennes' title as capital is hard to defend in a province known for its strident regionalism; the Breton culture, after all, developed very differently in various parts of Brittany. Administratively, though, Rennes' role is clear. The *Parlement de Bretagne* was established here in the 17th century, following the province's union with France in 1532, and today it is an important university town and hi-tech research centre.

Busy market: As a market town, it is a magnet for shoppers from the surrounding area. In particular, the open-air Saturday market, which fills the **Place des Lices** (Square of the Jousts) with a tapestry of multicoloured awnings, is reason enough for visiting Rennes. Despite its distance from the sea, the town seems suffused with the smell of seafood as stalls are piled high with pyramids of toppling crabs, mounds of coquilles St Jacques and line after line of oyster-packed baskets. Signs proclaiming the *pêche de nuit* point to the freshest overnight haul to reach the market.

The large rectangular square itself is dominated by some fine, late medieval houses, their crooked beams and oriel windows stretching high over the market stalls. Unfortunately, a few modern blocks add a discordant note.

A market has been held here since 1622, when an epidemic of the plague brought it within the city walls. Local farmers bring their vegetables and fruit: artichokes, shallots, leeks and cabbages. There's a wide range of apples—a reminder that Rennes is a noted cider-making region. Other stalls display cheeses, honey and brioches, and a surprising number offer Chinese food.

The Place des Lices was the site for jousting in medieval times. Legend has it that Bertrand du Guesclin, the warrior knight of the Hundred Years' War, first gained recognition here. At a joust in 1337, it is said, the young du Guesclin—supposedly an ugly, misshapen boy virtually disowned by his noble family—arrived in peasant garb, riding an old nag. On a borrowed steed and wearing borrowed armour, he astonished onlookers with his jousting skills and, when his visor was removed to reveal his identity, he won his father's approval for the first time.

The architectural interest of the Place des Lices is enhanced by the two *halles* (covered markets) in the middle of the square, 19th-century temples to commerce in steel, brick and glass. The lower of the two is the meat market, the inside all tones of red-and-white flesh—a vegetarian's nightmare. Outside, against the bottom wall, you can

Preceding pages, left and right: aspects of Rennes.

still find some outdoor *pissotières*, a fast-disappearing civic provision. The upper *halles* have been lovingly restored, their steel ornamentation painted a bright turquoise, their multi-coloured bricks freshly scrubbed.

The Place des Lices is one of four grand squares which dominate Rennes architecturally and provide useful reference points for the visitor. Two date back to medieval times; two were built in the *ancien régime* between the Middle Ages and the 1789 Revolution.

A great fire in 1720 destroyed much of the medieval centre. Observing the fine beamed houses that remain, many have cursed the carpenter whose drunken carelessness combined with wood shavings to create such a destructive blaze. Wisely, the rebuilding was executed in stone. Today, therefore, the eccentric creativity of the large medieval façades contrasts pleasingly with the refinement of granite town houses.

The town's architecture reflects evident civic pride down the centuries—as do the startling number of streets named after former mayors, their dates recorded on the blue plaques on street corners. One welcome feature of Rennes is that you're unlikely to be mown down by a vehicle while studying such ornamentations: much of the centre has been pedestrianised. Since most of the historic centre is located in a compact area north of the Vilaine river, it's easy on the shoe leather too.

The second medieval square, the **Place Sainte Anne**, is slightly northeast of the Place des Lices, towards the edge of the historic centre. It is more typical of French town squares, being given over to a tree-bordered car park with good sidewalk cafés from which to watch the world stroll by.

Medieval merchants, to make their shopfronts stand out, adopted bright decorations—a tradition followed by their modern counterparts. Number 19, a plaque reminds, was once the home of one of Rennes' most celebrated mayors, Leperdit, a man of the people and a tailor by trade. He is remembered for his emotional—if rather desperate—

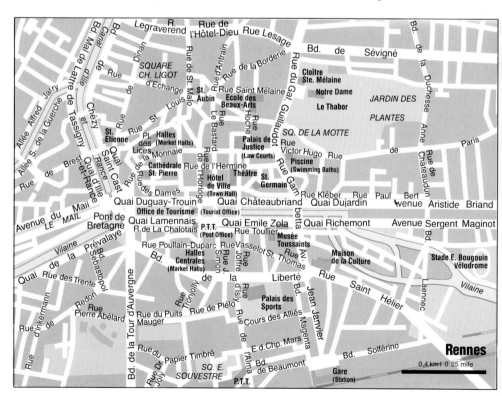

speeches, such as his calming oration to an angry, stone-throwing crowd in 1794 when the town was suffering from famine. "I cannot, like Christ, change stone into bread," he told them. "But, as for my blood, I would give it to the very last drop if it would help to feed you." He survived—as did the dark torquoise beams and vivid yellow contorted creatures that adorn them.

The best medieval streets spared by the 1720 fire radiate from the Place Sainte Anne. Behind the façades, through bulging passageways and low gateways, little courtyards open up to show jetted staircases, wooden balustrades and variations on the sharply triangular slate roofs.

Seafood and statues: To the north and east repectively, the Rue de St-Malo and the Rue St-Mélaine are packed with restaurants. **Rue de St-Malo**, now slightly seedy, has a Spanish flavour and seems to specialise in fish. The Ship-Shop fish restaurant contrasts with its gaudy yellow-beamed neighbour: it is in lovely stone, with a statue of the Virgin and Child in a niche where you'd expect to find a first-floor window.

Rue St-Mélaine specialises in crêperies—though every street in Rennes seems to have a handful. At the end of the street, the **Jardin du Thabor**, a large and beautiful garden formerly part of the abbey of St- Mélaine, overlooks much of the town, including the post-war suburbs—uninspiring treeless avenues of apartments. One 15th-century fresco remains in the church of St-Mélaine, whose cloisters have a gallery of attractive statues.

To the south of Place Sainte Anne, one can take either the **Rue St-Michel** or the short **Rue de Penhoët**. Along the latter, the Breiz ("Brittany") bookshop is well-known to students of Breton culture.

The street leads into **Rue Rallier de Baty** (really a picturesque extended square). Turn right into **Rue de Toulouse** and you are confronted with the contrast of fine stone gateways, entrances to grand *hôtels particuliers*, the

Open spaces give Rennes room to breathe.

former townhouses of the Breton parliamentarians and bourgeoisie. Appropriately enough, many of these are now given over to bank branches and lawyers' offices, the Parlement de Bretagne having been transformed into the Palais de Justice (law courts).

Left off the Rue de Toulouse is the eye-catching **"Maison du Guesclin"** on Rue St-Guillaume, with its bulging medieval frame, slate-covered side and polychrome statues over the entrance. These days it houses the tempting-looking Ti Koz restaurant.

At this point one can either continue down to the Église St-Sauveur or track back to the Rue de Toulouse and proceed left to the cathedral entrance. The **Cathedrale St-Pierre** follows the model of a Roman basilica, with a colonnaded apse. On an incense-filled Sunday morning, it is particularly atmospheric. In one of the right side-chapels is a beautiful retable, a good example of such altar panel paintings. Just opposite the cathedral entrance is the **Porte Mordelaise**, a remnant of the once imposing walls of the city.

To the right of the cathedral, follow Rue de Griffon and Rue du Chapitre on to the Place du Calvaire. Just beyond is **Rue Le Bastard**, where the winding medieval streets give way to the carefully planned vistas and wide thoroughfares of later centuries. A grand building turns out to be the most monumental and beautiful of post offices, now known as the Palais du Commerce.

Most of the medieval town is to be found along these streets, although just south of the Vilaine a few very old houses can be discovered. Running off the Place du Parlement de Bretagne is **Rue St-Georges**, perhaps Rennes' grandest medieval street. Watch out especially for the sculpted cariatyd Biblical figures in wood and the carving on the Hôtel de Moussaye at number 3. The corridors of the street hide wonderful courtyards, while decorative shop-signs line the way. Much of the pleasure of looking at medieval architecture derives from such surprising irregularities and quirkiness.

Rennes uses its festivals as a magnet to attract tourists.

By contrast, **Place du Parlement de Bretagne** and **Place de la Mairie** are models of precise planning. The Parlement de Bretagne is a confusing title, since Brittany had ceased to be an independent state when it was built in the first half of the 17th century. The Parliament was by then simply a regional government, and this political reality is reflected chamber's decoration.

The main architect came from Paris. Salomon de Brosse, known for building the Palais du Luxembourg in France's capital, designed the façade. Inside, the decoration, dating from slightly later than the building itself, is in the style of Louis XIV—*very* Louis XIV, in fact. The ceilings are gilded, garlanded and painted. The symbol of the Sun King squares up to the rays of the real sun. The coat of arms marries the fleur de lys, emblem of the French royal family, with the stylised ermine's tail, adopted by Anne de Bretagne.

In the greatest room, **La Grande Chambre du Parlement**, every square centimetre is decorated. The walls are covered with 20th-century tapestries from the Gobelins weavers, who are said to have taken 24 years to complete them. There are two main tapestries: one represents the death of du Guesclin; the other shows Anne de Bretagne's marriage to Charles VIII of France, catalyst to the union of Brittany with France when Anne's daughter Claude married the future François I.

Protruding into the chambers are two raised loggias, designed to allow ladies to follow events undisturbed. Mme de Sévigné, the noble lady whose correspondence with her daughter Mme de Grignan is a classic of French literature, came to listen to debates when she was staying at her château, Les Rochers just outside Rennes.

La Tournelle, the criminal court, is decorated in light-blue tones, with anachronistically cheeerful wispy skies depicted on the ceiling. It is still in use, and has two more loggias.

Outside, the elegant square, designed by the Parisian architect Gabriel, is of a later date. The stone balustrade around

the sunken lawn adds to the distinguished approach to the parliament. Adjoining this square is another example of grand civic architecture: the town hall's concave central bell-tower is complemented by the convex **theatre** advancing opposite it into the square. The theatre stages plays and operas and houses the town's orchestra.

These squares come to life most spectacularly in the first 10 days of July each year, during the street festival of the *Tombées de la Nuit* (Nightfalls). New Breton culture, in the form of music and theatre, has been growing in Rennes thanks to a couple of dynamic festivals established since World War II.

The *Tombées de la Nuit* transforms the town into one vast theatre, the historic centre serving as the backdrop. The organisers encourage regional creativity—though in recent years there has been an increasing international flavour, with performers from other Celtic regions. Many arts are represented: street theatre, mime, poetry, song and dance, clowning and acrobatics.

Another up-and-coming festival, held early in December at the Grand Huit (the name, "Big Eight", deriving from the peculiar shape of the building), is the *Transmusicales*. Started in 1978, this rock festival highlights regional groups, presenting them alongside international celebrities. Such big names in France as Étienne Daho, Niagra and Marc Seberg made an early impact here. As one of the organisers, Béatrice Macé, says, just as the slogan of the town's big Citroën factory is "*Mieux que Nippon, Breton*" ("Better than Japanese, Breton"), so the slogan for Rennes' music should be "*Mieux que Saxon, Breton.!*"

Every two years there is also a hi-tech *Festival des Arts Electroniques*, whose attractions have included a computerised laser display on the Vilaine. It's an indicator that technology and research are thriving in Rennes: numerous research units specialise in computers, communications, bio-industry, health and the environment.

The hi-tech approach even infiltrates

The selling tradition goes back to medieval merchants.

the town's museums. The two best, the Musée de Bretagne and the Musée des Beaux-Arts, are located centrally in the same building on the south bank of the Vilaine; you can buy a joint ticket.

The **Musée de Bretagne** encourages visitors to participate by pressing buttons to light up explanations and to set off slide shows. The museum covers Brittany's history from the prehistoric stone *alignements* onwards. It takes in the Roman conquest of Condate—the main centre of the Redones tribe, familiar to followers of the *Astérix* comic strip; the emergence of Breton culture; the transformation of Rennes into an international research centre; and the formation of the new quarter known as Rennes Atalante.

The museum tries to entertain with brain-teasing technical tests and offers some of its films with English voice-over. There's quite a variety of audio-visual extravaganza: one can move from a film of life on board a tunny-fish boat to a romantic evocation of Combourg, the château of the area's most

famous literary son, François-René de Châteaubriand.

The **Musée des Beaux-Arts** is more traditional and houses several masterpieces. The most famous is Georges de la Tour's *Le Nouveau-Né*, but there are many more individual works of interest by Veronese (*Perseus*), the École de Fontainebleau (*La Femme Entre Les Deux Ages*), and a number of Impressionist and Post-Impressionist artists.

Just outside Rennes, close to the airport and the Citroën plant, the **Ecomusée** follows the fortunes of a local farm over the past couple of centuries, presented once again with hi-tech gadgetry but also including displays of traditional farming and cider-making equipment. In the opposite direction is a **motor museum** with 70 vintage cars.

In Rennes itself, tourism is increasingly making its presence felt: half the commercial premises seem to be restaurants, and the choice between traditional Breton food and exotic foreign cuisine—such as Afghan, Lebanese and Vietnamese— induces indecision.

This international feel draws attention to Rennes' uneasy position within Brittany. It has always been somewhat on the limits of the province and well outside the *Bretagne bretonnante* (Breton-speaking Brittany) of Basse-Bretagne to the west: you will not, for instance, see women in Rennes going shopping in their coiffes.

Yet intellectually and politically the town is quite strongly Breton. The old culture is nurtured by the university and by the Centre Rennais d'Informations Bretonnes in the Place des Lices. And in the Breiz bookshop you might even bump into a purist Breton who would like to see the signposts changed from Rennes to Roazon. There's a Diwan school where the children are taught bilingually in Breton and French, and the Rennes-based *Ouest-France*, France's leading regional newspaper, publishes a regular column in Breton.

Rennes is both representative and untypical of Brittany, and a good barometer of the social and economic forces being exerted on the region as the 21st century approaches.

THE EAST

One fact the first-time visitor to Brittany finds hard to absorb is that for three-quarters of recorded time—from say, the Roman invasion until the end of the 15th century—the region was, to all intents and purposes, a separate state and not part of France at all. The degree of independence varied according to the power of the Dukes, and was never absolute, but it is a fact that the Bretons have always kept their guard up against French invaders from the east and have expressed this fact in stone with that string of fortresses and fortified towns which still march down the eastern frontier of the modern province.

In former times the island fortress of **Mont-St-Michel** was one of these, a place half-abbey, half-castle, sometimes a prison, always an obstacle against incursions from the east, until the River Couesnon (pronounced *K-way-non*), which by long tradition marks the frontier of Brittany, changed course to run round the Western walls of the island and so transferred Mont-St-Michel from Brittany to Normandy.

In Norman times, **Dol**, a few miles to the west, was another bastion of the Bretons and indeed, the Bayeux Tapestry depicts an assault on the town by Duke William and his reluctant prisoner, Harold the Saxon. Today, though the frontiers of the old Duchy of Brittany have somewhat shrunk, a number of the old fortress cities still remain almost intact, most notably Fougères, Vitré, and further south and close to the Loire, Châteaubriant.

Fougères town today is a commercial centre which turns into a traffic-jammed nightmare at least twice a day, but the castle of Fougères is magnificent, and has a military history that spans the entire era of Breton independence. Even better, it is almost intact and a fine example of the medieval fortress, with a moat and drawbridge, crenellated walls and 13 tall towers.

The castle first came to prominence in the mid-12th century, when England's Henry II decided to annexe Brittany for his second son, Geoffrey. At that time, the County of Brittany was held by Conan IV, and the castle belonged to Conan's vassal, Lord Raoul. Henry, invading Brittany with a large army, laid siege to Fougères for three months in 1166. When it surrendered, he pulled it down.

However, as soon as Henry marched away, Lord Raoul started to rebuild it, and so effectively that some of his work still stands inside the 13th-century curtain walls. These were added by a noble family from Poitou, the Lusignans, who acquired Fougères in 1220, after the Plantagenet King John had been driven out of France in 1214.

There was no lasting peace in the Middle Ages and Fougères was constantly under siege during the Hundred Years' War, when it fell to the Breton knight from Dinan, Bertrand du Guesclin. When a party of Englishmen from Normandy captured the castle in 1449, it gave King Charles VII the excuse he needed to re-open the war and led indirectly to the French victory at Formigny in 1450. This in turn led to the final expulsion of the English from Normandy and their eventual expulsion from Aquitaine.

After the Hundred Years War ended, Fougères served as a military garrison, and then, like many of these old fortresses, as a prison. In 1892, the Municipality bought it for 80,000 francs, about £9,000 or US$16,000 in today's money. It is now preserved as a fine example of a medieval fortress and is surrounded by attractive municipal gardens.

The castle stands on a loop of the **River Nançon**, which has been breached to provide water for the moat. The outer walls are complete with their 13th-century towers, some of which bear the names of military governors. One is named for Melusine, the Devil's Daughter, said to be one of the ancestors of the Plantagenets, who were known as the Devil's Brood.

The castle was once linked to the town by a connecting rampart and, although this has gone, the best overview

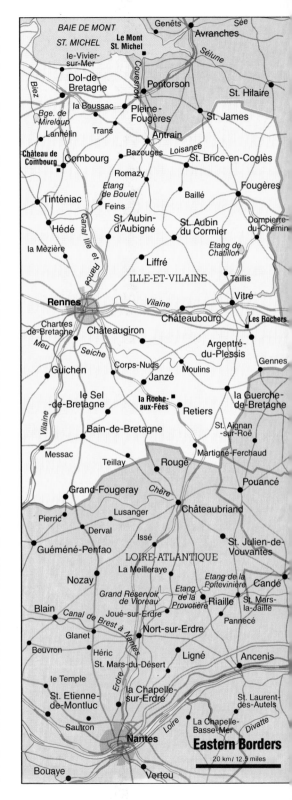

Eastern Borders
20 km / 12.5 miles

of the castle is from the town's public gardens at the Place des Arbres. Here, as elsewhere in France, however, the view is obstructed by rooftops, telephone cables and television aerials.

Inside La Haye Gate, the courtyard is wider than it was, as many of the original buildings were destroyed in the 19th century and the original keep has gone. The castle has no fewer than three lines of defensive walls, the first of which has three loop-holed towers to act as ramparts for the entire structure and offered the garrison the chance to outflank and fire down at any attackers scaling the main walls. There is a staircase to the ramparts, and a circular tour of the walls can be used to walk a complete circuit of the castle as far as the largest Melusine tower.

In fact, a better idea of the fortress of Fougères comes during a walk round the outer side of the walls and a photograph of the Surienne Tower, taken across the moat, is the classic shot of Fougères. The castle is triangular rather than circular in shape, since the de-fences were originally completed by the walls of the town.

The Raoul and Surienne Towers are particularly interesting to students of military history. They were built as gun platforms at the end of the castle's era, as a counter to field artillery brought up by any besieging force, and their walls are 22 ft (seven metres) thick. The Notre-Dame gate is flanked by two towers, one of which bears the slots to take the drawbridge. Past here the public gardens are wide enough to permit a good view back towards the full sweep of the walls and towers, running off to either flank.

The castle is the central jewel of Fougères. As such, it provides a useful break on any visit to Brittany, which must inevitably include a considerable number of churches and cathedrals. Fougères, too, has a fine church, **St Sulpice**, which lies just outside the walls of the castle and contains as one rare relic, a Papal Bull issued by the Borgia Pope, Alexander VI.

The basic style of St Sulpice is Flam-

Preceding pages, wind power by the Erdre; Fougères. Below, Fougères.

boyant Gothic, a style very popular in Brittany, though the church was built and rebuilt from the 15th to the 18th centuries. It contains a 12th-century statue of the Virgin and Child said to work miracles, although no one is quite sure how to invoke the Virgin's aid.

Castle and church apart, Fougères has an interesting old quarter around the **Place du Marchaix**, with several 16th-century houses and one other church, **St Leonard's**, which is rather older than St Sulpice's and contains several fine old paintings and modern stained glass windows. That apart, there are some good restaurants and hotels, notably the Hotel Lion d'Or and the Restaurant St Pierre, and the town, although quite small, is a busy, prosperous little place, well worth a visit, if only to see the magnificent castle.

Well-preserved: The same is true of **Vitré,** which lies 20 miles (32 km) to the south and presents a dramatic, even romantic first aspect to the visitor driving in from the north, with high walls, towers and turrets blocking the skyline. Vitré is said to be the best preserved old town in Brittany. This may be true, for it survived the Middle Ages, the introduction of cannon and all the wars since, virtually intact.

Vitré occupies a ridge overlooking the valley of the Vilaine, with the castle standing in a commanding position on the very tip, glowering across the valley below and catching every approaching eye. On the way in, stop for a good look at the castle from the little hill called **Les Tertres Noir**, just north of the city.

The castle was built all-of-a-piece in the 14th and 15th centuries, at the height of the Hundred Years' War, and had hardly been flung up by the Bretons before an English force appeared outside the walls and put it under siege. This siege was maintained on and off for several years until the exasperated Bretons, who weren't too interested in the quarrels between Valois and Plantagenet, finally paid the English mercenaries a large ransom to go away.

The area the mercenaries occupied lies below the castle and is still known as **Les Rechapt**—the *re-achat* or Repurchase. The town square has the castle as the backdrop, and a very magnificent sight it is, the castle triangular in shape, with the entrance across a deep moat guarded by two tall towers. These and the other two towers are linked by a section of curtain wall provided with a guardway from which there is a good view down into the town. The castle now contains municipal offices and the town museum, which is largely devoted to displays of local folklore and crafts.

Vitré was once completely walled and parts of the old fortifications still remain beside the main road through the town, which skirts the castle, and along the promenade which overlooks the river valley. The best way into the town, an enjoyable place to explore on foot, is up the narrow **Rue Beaudrairie**. It is now somewhat over-supplied with small shops and boutiques, but retains a distinctly medieval feel to it.

This sensation continues in the **Church of Notre Dame**, which is also from the 15th century, although it has a curious feature which dates from at least 100 years later, during the Wars of Religion. Then, Vitré belonged to the Huguenot Coligny family and was a centre of religious dissent. The Catholic priest of Notre Dame therefore knocked a hole in his church wall and built an outside pulpit, from which he could harangue the people in the streets.

Vitré is also remembered locally as the birthplace of Pierre Landais, who was born here in 1450 and rose from being a tailor to become Treasurer to Duke François II. His humble origins and evident success infuriated the nobles at the Ducal Court and they plotted to find him guilty of stealing money and works of art from the Ducal Treasury; having confessed to these crimes under torture, Landais was hanged at Nantes in 1485.

Moving south for another 14 miles (22 km), the traveller comes to the little town of **La Guerche-de-Bretagne**, originally a manor belonging to the mighty warlord Bertrand du Guesclin of Dinan, Constable of France under King Charles V. The church is medieval and

Preceding page, Vitré Castle: veteran of determined sieges. Below, farmers start young here.

quite attractive, and there are 16th-century houses in the Place de la Mairie.

But the real attraction of the town is as a touring centre for exploring the local countryside, which contains the attractive lakes at **Les Mottes**, three miles (five km) to the west, and the nearby **Roche-aux-Fées**, the Fairies' Rocks, a group of 42 megalithic stones.

Engaged couples may consult the fairies here about their prospects. To do this, they separate and walk around the stones, the man clockwise, his fiancée anti-clockwise, counting the stones. If they agree on the number, the marriage will be happy; if their counts vary by more than two, they should break off their engagement at once.

Mad jealousy: The road leads south to the town of **Châteaubriant**, the last of the three fortress cities that stand, a day's march apart, between the Channel and the Loire. Châteaubriant guards Brittany across the frontier with Anjou, and stands on the banks of the Chère.

The town was once entirely fortified but only the castle remains, and that is not intact. The castle consists of two well-separated parts, of which the older section, containing the chapel and keep, dates from the 11th century. The rest is Renaissance and dates from the time when Jean, Count of Châteaubriant, rebuilt the castle in the 16th century as a new home for his much beloved wife, Françoise. Unfortunately, the Count was madly jealous of his wife and, when she eventually succumbed to the king, François I, the Count took her back to Châteaubriant and locked her up in a dark, shuttered room with their only child. He kept them there in the dark until they died.

Apart from that part now occupied by the municipal offices, all the castle is open to visitors. It is very attractive, with a large garden occupying one corner of the grounds. The keep still stands and is linked to the medieval chapel by the remains of two curtain walls which once protected the inner bailey, in front of the keep. The apartments once occupied by the tragic Françoise are now the town museum, with a variety of folklore exhibits.

But the best part of the remaining buildings is the chapel, dedicated to St John. It was built in the 11th century with an extra pulpit added in the 15th century, when it was used to preach to the people during times of plague. Among other memorials is a beautiful 13th-century Virgin.

The unhappy history of Châteaubriant doesn't end with Count Jean and Françoise. In the last war a prison camp at Châteaubriant was used to confine those suspected of working for the Resistance. In October 1941, the German commander of the garrison of Nantes was killed in an ambush near Châteaubriant. As a reprisal, 25 men were taken from this camp and shot in a quarry a little west of the town, which now contains a memorial showing the execution posts.

The eastern border of Brittany is completed as far as the Loire by the valley of the **River Erdre**, and the flatlands and forest of the **Ancenis**, a quiet part of the province that leads down eventually to the tranquil Loire.

Wind power on the Erdre.

NANTES

Although **Nantes** is no longer the capital of Brittany, that title having long since passed to Rennes, it remains emotionally and economically an integral part of the old Duchy, even if local government reorganisation has transferred it to the province of the Western Loire.

Nantes is the largest town in Brittany and the seventh largest in France, with a population hovering near 300,000. It is a very splendid city indeed, one of the finest in provincial France, with good shops, a bustling commercial centre, docks and shipyards along the Loire, and a good deal of culture in theatres, cinemas, concert halls, museums and galleries, to which one can add alluring restaurants and the wines of Muscadet.

This was a great city of the Gauls, the Namnetes tribe, long before the Romans came. Centuries later, after the Romans had left, the native Celts put up a stout resistance against the invading Teutonic French, who swarmed into France from across the Rhine. The struggle continues to this day, at least linguistically.

Disputes between French and Breton were not finally solved politically until the Duchy of Brittany was absorbed into the realm of France in the 16th century. The Normans raided this coast in the 10th century and might well have occupied the country but for the activities of the Breton Lord of Nantes, Barbe-Torte, who drove the Normans out and then became the first Count of the Bretons.

Nantes remained the capital of the Duchy from Barbe-Torte's time until 1532, and the great castle of the Counts—later Dukes—of Brittany still dominates the centre of the town. In the late 16th century, Nantes was the scene of the signing of the celebrated Edict of Nantes by Henry of Navarre, which was signed in the castle on 13 August 1598. By this Edict, Henry put an end to the Wars of Religion, guaranteed the rights of the Protestant Huguenot citizens of France, and then took up the crown as Henri IV.

Nantes still saw plenty of strife down the years, and was once a harbour for pirates who preyed on British shipping in the Atlantic. But the next major upheaval took place at the Revolution, when the town, though staunchly Royalist, was occupied by Revolutionary troops commanded by Carrier, the Deputy for Cantal in the Auvergne. Carrier arrested Royalists by the thousand and cleared the prisons by putting the prisoners into barges which were then battened down and sunk in the Loire. All on board were drowned. For this and other crimes, Carrier was eventually guillotined. But the Revolutionary days brought hard times to Brittany, where the bulk of the country population were both Royalist and Catholic.

During World War II, the port of St Nazaire, near Nantes, was the objective of a famous 1942 raid by British Commandos, who sailed up the Loire estuary in motor-boats and an old destroyer, HMS Campbeltown, which was

Preceding pages, left and right: aspects of Nantes.

rammed into the gates of the great dry dock, the Forme Ecluse, damaging it so badly it was not repaired until 1956.

Nantes is now a major centre for ship-building and, combined with St-Nazaire, a major French sea-port. Local industries, apart from shipbuilding, include iron and steel smelting, oil re-fineries, electronics, and light industry of all kinds.

The city has always been a great trad-ing port and from the 16th to 18th cen-turies it formed one end of the infamous "Triangular Trade", which shipped trade goods to Africa where they were exchanged for slaves, then the slaves to the West Indies, where they were sold for sugar, rum and molasses. Those products were finally shipped back to Nantes and sold for vast profits in France and elsewhere. This trade was finally abolished at the Revolution and by the introduction of sugar-beet to the Loire area, where it is still a major crop.

Commerce apart, Nantes is large enough to sustain a full and lively cul-tural life and in its time has produced many famous, and some infamous, sons. Their history, with that of the town itself, can be discovered on a tour, pref-erably on foot, through the town centre, a tour which can best begin at the **Ducal Castle**.

This fine fortress was begun by the last independent duke, François II, in 1466 and work continued up to the end of the century, even after his daughter, the Duchesse Anne, was married to the King of France. It was added to during the 16th-century Wars of Religion. In the 1700s the Royal Army took over the castle as a garrison and remained in possession until 1800, when the maga-zine exploded, destroying the Tour des Espagnols and most of the northern walls. The municipality took over the castle in 1915 and, after long restora-tion, it is now a museum—or rather several museums.

The moat has been re-dredged and filled and the visitor enters across the moat and through the main gate. This castle has a central position in French and Breton history, for it was here that

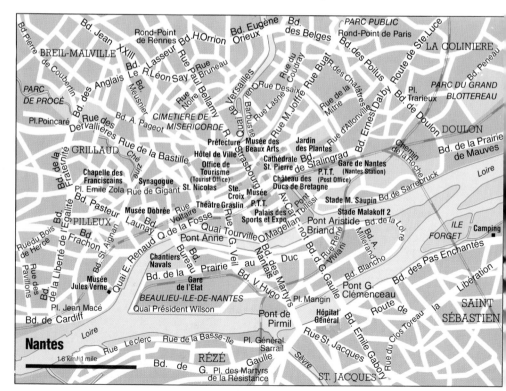

Louis XII married the Duchesse Anne, here that Henri IV signed the Edict of Nantes, and here that Gilles de Rais, the infamous "Bluebeard", was tried and burned to death on the riverbank for his fearful crimes, which included drinking human blood.

The inner courtyard was used for jousting and military exercises, and the old quarters of the Dukes provided the Governor's major palace, which now contains the Museum of Art.

Another fine building here is the **Golden Crown Tower**, and among the museums is the excellent **Maritime Museum** in the former Harness Building, which has many exhibits featuring the old trading days of Nantes and the traditional industries of Nantes and the region.

Visiting this castle could take up most of the morning. It is then no great distance to the next major attraction of the town, the **Cathedral of St Peter and St Paul**, which took 400 years to complete. The cathedral foundations were laid in 1434, and the work finally completed in 1893.

The building stone is limestone, not the usual Breton granite, but the style is familiar, that much-loved Flamboyant Gothic found in so many Breton churches. As befits the capital city of the old province, the cathedral is vast, with the vault of the nave soaring to 120 ft (36.5 metres).

Unlike many French churches, this one is light and airy and contains some fine tombs, notably one of Duke Francis and his wife Marguerite, commissioned by La Duchesse Anne in memory of her father, and carved between 1502 and 1507. The tomb was moved here after the Revolution and shows the Duke and his Duchesse reclining on a slab, surrounded by angels and the virtues, Strength, Prudence, Fidelity. The tomb niches contain "weepers" and small figures of the saints, with 16 mourners drawn from the common people. Other tombs in the church include that of Lamorcière, who led the French Colonial troops into Algeria in 1847 to defeat the Emir, Abdul-el-Krim, and is one of

the city's famous soldier sons.

This cathedral is a very fine church, which no visitor to Nantes could miss. But the town itself, other than the inevitable modern shops and office buildings, is mainly 18th and 19th century, and contains many fine examples of elegant domestic architecture.

This can be found in any of the old streets west of the castle and cathedral along the **Cours Franklin Roosevelt**, where places to head for include the **Place du Maréchal Foch**, once the Place Louis XVI. Here, in spite of the gallant Marshal's later claim, the pillar on the aisle carries a statue of the King.

Other attractive places near here are the mixture of steep streets beside the river and many fine squares. The **Place Graslin** and the **Place Royale** have especially interesting buildings.

Just off the Place Graslin runs the **Cours Cambronne**, which is lined with attractive houses and contains the warlike statue of General Cambronne. He commanded the Old Guard at the Battle of Waterloo and gave the French his famous "*mot de Cambronne*" because when *su*mmoned to surrender by the British Grenadiers, he replied simply: "*Merde!*" In later life, the gallant General declared that what he actually said was, "*La Garde meurt, mais me se rend pas.*" ("The Guard knows how to die, but has not learned how to surrender").

Down by the river, the new docks and *quais* have still not quite succeeded in pushing out or pulling down all the merchants' houses built by rich shipowners in the 18th century, but the finest of those which do survive lie along the Quai de la Fosse.

Glass-case culture: Nantes is a very pleasant city, with wide boulevards and excellent shopping of an almost Parisian elegance, but those who crave culture and have not sated a lust for museums in the Ducal Castle have many more to choose from. The **Fine Art Museum** near the Cathedral is one of the finest provincial museums in France, with work by Ingres, Georges de la Tour, Courbet and Perigini.

The city has always been a great trading port.

The **Palais Dobrée**, near the Cours Cambronne, is set beside a medieval house which once belonged to the Bishop of Nantes, although the museum itself is in a 19th-century building. Monsieur Dobrée was a famous collector of French and Flemish art from the 15th and 16th centuries, and on his death he presented both houses to the municipality.

They are now open to the public, as is the newly-restored **Natural History Museum**, which has a rich collection of local flora and fauna exhibits. All these museums, like the Ducal Castle, are open throughout the year but usually closed on Tuesdays.

Apart from the Cathedral, the other churches of Nantes are not remarkable. But two other sights are well worth seeing. They are the Botanical Gardens, the **Jardin des Plantes**, not least because they contain a statue of another famous son of Nantes, the writer Jules Verne, and the **Island of Feydeau**, which is now attached to the mainland as a result of the infilling of the northern arm of the Loire This island was once a fashionable, lively quarter and so contains a good number of fine old mansions.

Even those visitors without any great love of churches, castles or museums will find enough colour and variety in Nantes to keep them busy and happy here for several days. As is usual in provincial France, there is no lack of fine restaurants, with a further supply close at hand in the fashionable resort of **La Baule** or the quaint fishing port of **Le Croisic**.

Film buffs will enjoy a trip to **St-Marc**, where Monsieur Hulot took his Holiday. These two places would be enjoyable excursions, but three that are specifically local, are a car tour into the Muscadet wine country which lies east and south of the city, or a trip by boat up the green and pleasant valley of the **River Erdre** or along the **Sèvre-Nantaise Canal**, or as a final choice, the curious marsh of the **Brière**, to the **Ile de Fédrun** and the little walled city of **Guérande**.

'ast
'erspectives
n Nantes
Museum.

BRITTANY'S ISLANDS

Appropriately for a region whose identity depends so much on the sea, Brittany has a coastline dotted with islands. There are, in fact, more islands off the Breton coast than off any other part of maritime France.

Some, such as those which make an obstacle course of the approaches to the port of St-Malo, are scarcely more than rocks topped with a little turf. Others, such as Ile d'Ouessant and Belle Ile, are large enough to sustain complete, almost self-contained communities with their own settlements and lifestyles.

Despite this distinction, size accounts for only a small part of the variability of Brittany's islands. Accidents of geography, climate and even history have turned these Atlantic outposts into a very mixed bunch indeed. Anyone who believes that a visit to one or two of them will reveal the secrets of them all is mistaken.

Reckoning the rocks: It is sometimes said that there is a Breton island for every day of the year. Unless you count every rock with the barest vestige of plant life adhering to it, this is an exaggeration; but there are still enough to make a comprehensive tour of offshore Brittany a major undertaking. Many of the islands, however, cry out not only to be mentioned but also to be visited.

Starting in the northeast of the region at St-Malo, the first island of any significance is **Cézembre**. It is neither large nor impressive, but it has a story. During the Allies' advance into Brittany in 1944 after D-Day, a small German garrison held out there until long after units on the mainland had capitulated. Today it is impossible to look at Cézembre, which offers little in the way of cover, without wondering where the defenders sheltered as they were shelled and bombed incessantly.

An altogether gentler, more congenial place is **Ile de Bréhat**, which lies off Pointe de l'Arcouest near Paimpol. Only 10 minutes by motor launch from the shore, Bréhat consists of two islets linked by a narrow isthmus called the Pont ar Prat. Although it has an area of less than five sq. km, the island is very popular with visitors during the summer holiday season.

Its accessibility has obviously helped to put it on the tourist map, but so has its unique character founded on flowers and pink granite. The flowers thrive, thanks to pockets of adequate shelter in an otherwise exposed situation, fertile soil and, above all, a climate which remains mild thanks to the influence of the Gulf Stream. The pink granite can be seen not only on the shoreline, but also as rugged outcrops and a labyrinth of reefs stretching far out to sea.

For sailors, the expanse of rock represents a threat, but for sightseers it introduces warm colours which contrast intriguingly with the predominantly cool blues and greens of the seascape.

Bréhat is famous primarily for its flora, but on **Les Sept Iles** the fauna, in particular the seabirds, tend to steal the show. Since 1912 Les Sept Iles archipelago has been a wildlife sanctuary—a fact which shows that the French, normally so unsentimental about animals, were conservationists long before the word became fashionable. Of the islets in the group, only **Ile aux Moines** can be visited without permission, and appropriately it is the only one which shows any major signs of man's handiwork. Besides its lighthouse and in spite of its name—which translates as the Isle of Monks—Ile aux Moines has the remains of a Franciscan convent. This is one of the sights seen by visitors who make the short voyage from the pretty little port of Ploumanach, though when it was intact and active it must have been a particularly remote and forbidding place in which to serve God.

Winter swells: Certain of the Breton islands seem almost to belong to mainland towns. This is very much the case with **Ile de Batz**, which lies close enough to Roscoff to protect its harbour from the worst that the winter swells of the north Atlantic can do.

Seen from the shore, Batz looks rather bare, but the same winds which make it devoid of tree cover bring mild conditions which ensure that the island is surprisingly productive. It supports tiny fields devoted to the cultivation of early vegetables which fetch high prices on the mainland markets.

Visitors to Roscoff will also see signs of another island industry: seaweed harvesting. Small boats gather laminaria kelp from the coast of Batz and its offshore rocks and bring their dripping cargoes of brown fronds into port, where they are picked up by fleets of lorries. Some of the kelp is processed to yield alginates; some finds its way onto the land as fertiliser.

If the tip of the Brest peninsula separates the coasts of north and south Brittany, **Ile d'Ouessant**—or Ushant, as it has been called by generations of British seafarers—stands sentinel on the boundary between the Atlantic and the Channel approaches. Famed for its dangerous rock-bound coastline with 200-ft (60-metre) cliffs, dense sea fogs and rolling swells, Ile d'Ouessant lies 13 miles (20 km) from the mainland and is very much France's last outpost before the vastness of the open ocean.

In the Breton language Ouessant is known as *Enez Eussa*, and traditionally it has been a land of women. While the island's men were away at sea as crew in France's deep-sea merchant fleet, the womenfolk tended the land and their flocks of sheep and took all the decisions relating to business and the conduct of insular affairs. Modern communications and the influence of the mainland have diminished the power of Ouessant's matriarchy, but the island has still managed to retain its own special if rather rugged identity.

A glimpse of the Ile d'Ouessant of an earlier age is possible at La Maison des Techniques et Traditions Ouessantines in the village of **Niou-Huella**, not far from the small town of Lampaul. There two traditional houses of the 18th and 19th century have been preserved. They feature hand-painted furniture made from driftwood, a commodity which must once have been much in demand, given the sparse tree growth permitted by the prevailing westerly winds which

The seas off the islands are unkind to ships.

almost perpetually sweep the island.

As well as being a natural landmark for shipping, Ouessant has a formidable reputation as a wrecker of ships. For both these reasons it is the location of one of the world's most powerful lighthouses. Situated at **Créac'h** in the far west, this has a lantern which produces a beam of 250 million candle-power to help keep vessels clear of the coast and its many off-lying reefs.

A string of islets does its best to link Ile d'Ouessant with the shore. The most important is **Molène**; it supports a small community which earns a living largely by fishing for shellfish—although, as at Ile de Batz, another source of income is a seaweed harvest which provides valuable fertiliser for use on mainland crops.

Almost due south of Pointe de St-Mathieu, the westerly limit of the area known as Léon, is Pointe du Raz in Cornouaille, where, once again, the land seems reluctant to give way to the sea without a final token effort. In this case, the final effort is **Ile de Sein**, which is so flat and lies so low in the surrounding waves that severe storms threaten it with inundation.

Only five miles (eight km) offshore, Sein is a mystical place and its inhabitants, Les Sénans, of which there are fewer than 1,000, are a hardy people who survive by fishing and by cultivating small plots of land sheltered by elaborate networks of stone walls which keep out the salt-laden wind.

Bretons call Ile de Sein *Enez Sun*, and it is suggested that this helps to identify it as the Isle of the Dead, a burial place of the Druids. It is also said to be the Romans' *Insula Sena*, a mysterious island where sailors used to consult an oracle tended by nine priestesses.

As in the case of Bréhat, Sein is an island with two almost separate parts. Near the isthmus which links them is a monument to history less remote than the era of the Romans or the Druids. It commemorates 18 June 1940, when 150 Sénan men left their native isle and sailed for England to continue resistance against the invading Germans.

After Pointe du Raz only the point at

Jules
Lefran's
Belle-Ile, Le
Phare.

Penmarch remains before the Breton coastline begins to take on a gentler character which seems less determined to jut aggressively into the Atlantic. But there are still plenty of islands.

The first which one encounters after rounding the corner of Brittany during a voyage from the north are **Les Glénans**, an archipelago lying off the small resort of Beg-Meil, which, in turn, lies near the major port of Concarneau. One of the Glénans is called **Ile aux Moutons** (Sheep Isle), though it supports nothing larger than rabbits and gulls.

Another, **Penfret**, is the home of a famous sailing school, which trains everyone from novices in dinghies to ocean racing hopefuls. A third, **St-Nicolas**, has quite a good anchorage for such an exposed site and is the headquarters of a diving school. The pupils enjoy clear waters which are probably richer in undersea flora and fauna than those in any other part of France.

Less threatening: Whereas Les Glénans are essentially islets, **Ile de Groix**, which lies off Lorient, most definitely falls into the island category. It is large enough—about six sq miles (16 sq km)—to support a number of settlements, including Groix, the pretty port of Saint Nicolas and Locmaria, and has cliffs almost as high as those of Ile d'Ouessant.Groix, however, is less threatening than that landfall to the north and it has always been regarded as a very welcome sight by mariners bound for Lorient. Glad to be within reach of their home port after many weeks at sea in uncomfortable sailing vessels, East Indies traders used to say: *"Qui voit Groix, voit sa joie."* ("He who sees Groix, sees joy.")

Groix is now very much on the tourist map and can easily be reached by ferry from Lorient, but its inhabitants once depended on fishing for their livelihood. The island was the home base of a tuna fleet which sailed into Biscay and beyond to hunt its quarry.

Beautiful spot: The largest of all the Breton islands and the one with the richest history, much of it related to the years of conflict between France and England, is **Belle-Ile**. Measuring 10 miles by three (17 km by five) and with a population of almost 5,000, Belle- Ile is riven by valleys which offer shelter of a sort not found on Brittany's more exposed islands. It also has good sandy beaches, sand dunes and a rugged stretch of shoreline called the Côte Sauvage. Its settlements, which include the island capital, Le Palais, now thrive thanks largely to tourism.

Only a 40-minute ferry trip from the tip of the Quiberon peninsula, Belle-Ile, with its little white houses and its fortresses (some of them designed by the great artificer Vauban), has long been popular with visitors. It was much admired by the novelist Colette and was also a source of inspiration to other authors of distinction, including Dumas, Proust, Flaubert and Gide.

Painters, too, have been influenced by Belle-Ile, and among those who openly acknowledged their indebtedness were Monet and Matisse. The island's catalogue of artistic connections is nicely rounded off by the actress Sarah Bernhardt, who once owned a property near Poulains Point.

On a less happy note, Belle-Ile was also used as a prison. Among those briefly incarcerated there were Karl Marx and the son of the Haitian revolutionary, Toussaint-Louverture.

The nuns's store: Not far from Belle-Ile are two smaller granite isles, **Houat** and **Hoëdic**, which take their names from the Breton words for duck and duckling. They, too, can be reached from Quiberon, and Hoëdic has the odd distinction of having a shop run by nuns. This practice is a reminder of former years when the tiny communities of lay people were organised under the supervision of the church.

The Gulf of Morbihan, the sheltered "little sea" which reaches inland as far as the town of Vannes, has its own selection of islands, the largest of which are **Ile aux Moines** (another Isle of Monks) and **Ile d'Arz**. Both are very much on the summer holiday trail and the former has forested areas with romantic names—the Wood of Sighs, the, the Wood of Love—which are guaranteed to appeal to tourists.

Right, shearing time on the islands.

THE LEGENDS THAT LIVE ON

Recent reports that the activities of Arthur and his knights of the Round Table were centred in Scotland rather than in England do not alter the Breton's belief that the "events" occurred in their particular region.

First they tell how Joseph of Arimathea landed with the Holy Grail in Brittany, settling in an area now known as the Forest of Paimpont; he later vanished without trace. It was here, according to the Bretons, that Arthur and his 50 knights set out on the search for the Grail. Then they relate how Merlin the magician came to the same forest, met the fairy Viviane and lived happily ever after in the magic circle created by Viviane from which escape was feasible but not considered desirable.

Tragic love: With the arrival of the first Celts from Britain in the fifth century and the cross-immigration of the next 200 years, it is not surprising that legends, names and locations become confused and are adapted to local needs. Take the tragic love story of Tristan and Isolde, for instance. Some versions have Tristan slain by his uncle, King Mark of Cornwall, following his return with his beloved from Ireland; others claim that Tristan married and lived out his life in a castle in Brittany.

The story of the beautiful city of Is, lying off the Penmarch Peninsula in south Finistère, is purely Breton. There is the belief that Paris was named after it: *Par-is* (like-Is) because of its great beauty.

The home of King Gradlon, Is was protected by a dyke and the key to its gates was always carried by the king. His daughter, named variously Dahut or Ahés, became attracted by the Devil in the shape of a handsome young man. At the Devil's request, she stole the key, opened the gates and the sea poured into the city. Gradlon escaped on horseback with his daughter clinging to him, but a voice from heaven told him that, in order to be saved, he must ditch this evil

spirit. This he did, and the seas withdrew—but Is was completely destroyed.

Gradlon then chose Quimper as his new capital for the kingdom of Cornouaille, and his statue stands between the two towers of the cathedral. For the rest of his days, he lived a life of holiness and piety, helped by the first Bishop of Cornouaille, St Corentin. As for Dahut, she became a mermaid known as Marie-Morgane and today still lures sailors to watery graves. Things will change only when Mass is said on a Good Friday in

one of the drowned city's churches. Then the curse on Is will be lifted and Dahut will cease to be an amphibious seductress.

As for St Corentin, he is remembered for his diet, which consisted purely of the flesh of one miraculous fish. Each day he would eat half of the fish and throw the rest back into the river, only to find it restored to full size the following day. Corentin was one of the first Celtic religious leaders to move to Brittany in the fifth century and, like the others, became a saint.

As a region, Brittany has produced more than its fair share of saints. The church in Rome has recognised just a handful, al-

Preceding pages, lighthouse keeper on Ouessant, Pont du Gard, festival at Quimper. Left, Henri Royer's *Ex-voto* (1898), votive offerings to fend off evil. Above, dragon slaying, and Gradlon le Grand drowning his wife.

though many more were accepted by local bishops. In most cases, sainthood was bestowed by the local people.

Many places have their own Bluebeard legend: Brittany has also produced one of its local saints. The Bluebeard of Cornouaille, the Count of Comorre, lived in the Carncet Forest, a short distance from Quimperlé and feared the prediction that he would die at his son's hands. This led Comorre to kill his first four wives as soon as they conceived, but the fifth wife managed to save her son. On meeting him for the first time, Comorre, was struck by the family likeness, had him beheaded immediately.

Tremeur, the son, picked up his head,

century, St Anne appeared before a ploughman and asked him to rebuild a chapel which had previously existed in her name in one of the fields. After two years of searching, the ploughman found an old statue of the saint; a new church was built on the spot and the present basilica at Ste-Anne-d'Auray was created in the 19th century.

The Virgin, according to legend, was active in Brittany. At Josselin an old statue was found by a peasant and, no matter how many times he took it home, it was always back in its original place the next day. The sou dropped and a sanctuary was built on the site. The statue survived until 1793 when it was burnt. A small piece is all that remains,

Héloïse et Abailard dans la grotte de Clisson.

walked towards the family castle, and tossed a handful of soil against the building—whereupon it collapsed, burying Comorre alive. Statues of St Tremeur, as he became, show him carrying his head in his hands.

The Bretons have never been slow to associate themselves with the birth of Christianity. St Anne, mother of the Virgin Mary, was reputed to be a Breton of royal blood who took her daughter to Nazareth at the behest of angels to save her from her brutal husband. Following the birth of Christ, Anne returned to Brittany to die—but not before being visited by Christ, who created the sacred spring of Ste Anne-la-Palud. In the 17th

although it is a place of pilgrimage during the pardon days at Notre Dame du Roncier. This festival is known as the "Barkers' Pardon" following the cure in 1728 of three children suffering from epilepsy.

At Le Folgöet, a simpleton called Salaün lived in a hollow oak in a wood close by a spring. The only real words he knew or could speak were "O Lady Virgin Mary". After he died, a lily sprouted from the grave bearing the words "Ave Maria" in gold letters. The grave was opened to reveal that the lily grew

Above, the legendary lovers Abelard and Heloise visualised at Clisson.

from Salaün's mouth. This was taken as a sign for the need to build a church which was done at the end of the War of Succession in the 14th century.

Three hundred years later the church was pillaged during the Revolution. But it was saved from total destruction when 12 local farmers bought it to repair and restore.

The Bretons are on very familiar terms with their saints, where names are invoked to commemorate their lives or activities with which they have been associated. There is, for example, St Yves, the founder of the free legal-aid system which he operated at Tréguier while also sitting as magistrate; St Cornely for horses; St Herbot for oxen; and countless others who are summoned to help deal with such afflictions as rheumatism and baldness.

Yet the Bretons are not parochial in their approach to the saints. Statues of the apostles can be found in many churches and calvaries. St Michael is the saint of high places and Mount Dol, near Dol-de-Bretagne, is reputed to be the site where the archangel fought his battle with the Devil. At one stage, the Devil was thrown down so violently that he made a depression in the rock and scratched it with a claw; during another part of the battle, St Michael with a blow of his sword, made a hole in the mountain into which he tossed the Devil. But the Devil escaped to Mont-St-Michel and, with the single leap that he made from Dol, St Michael left his footprint on the rock.

Marriage customs are varied but are so deep in legend that it is almost impossible to entangle them. Why is it that custom decrees on the island of Ouessant (Ushant) that it is the girls who propose marriage to their swains? What drove the girls of Ploumanach to stick a pin into the nose of the wooden statue of St Guirec when they wanted to get married? (This, incidentally, is no longer possible: the original wooden effigy has been replaced by a granite statue.) Why should the citizens of Landerneau serenade and mock any widow who decided she was going to remarry?

Moonstruck lovers: The fairies are cited as the reason why one of the finest megalithic monuments in the region is situated at La Guerche-de-Bretagne. The Fairies' Rock comprises 42 stones of which six weigh between 40 and 45 tonnes each. Engaged couples sought the fairies' blessing on the night of a new moon. The man walked around in a clockwise direction; the girl anti-clockwise. If both counted the same number of stones, all would be well with the marriage; there was still a chance for happiness if the difference in numbers amounted to not more than two; but disparity of more than two meant that the couple would be wise to go their separate ways.

It is possible that one Sybille of Châteaubriant counted the rocks with her beloved as they lived only 18 miles (29 km) away. But their mutual happiness was short-lived. Utterly faithful to her husband, she died of joy as they embraced when he returned from a crusade in the 13th century.

Captive wife: From the same town comes an even more tragic story of a marriage. Married at 11 to a madly jealous count, Françoise de Foix was kept a virtual prisoner in her castle while her husband patrolled the grounds to make certain she met no-one else. As Françoise grew up, she developed beauty and intellect and it was not long before François I became enamoured of her. By subterfuge, they met and became lovers. But this was no "lived happily ever afterwards" story; the king found new loves and Françoise lived in these conditions a further 10 years when, it is said, her husband put her out of her misery with his sword.

In reading the legends of Brittany, one is struck by the fact that no happy medium exists: love is either eternal or there is sudden death. The philosopher-abbot Abelard could write to his Heloise: "I live in a wild country whose language I find strange and horrible; I see only savages; I take my walks on the inaccessible shores of a rough sea... (in my house) the only decorations on the doors are the footmarks of various animals—hinds, wolves, bears, wild boars or the hideous regurgitations of owl; every day brings new dangers."

It was a misfortune that Abelard was two centuries too soon to have made the pilgrimage from St-Gildas-de-Rhuya to the tiny village of St-Jean-du-Doigt near the coast north of Morlaix. There, a young man brought the miracle-working first joint of the forefinger of St John the Baptist. People suffering from eye problems still visit the village, showing that many legends are living things.

THE BRETON PARDONS

Since pagan times when Mortal and Other Worlds were regarded as coexistent, the Celtic peoples have believed themselves to have a uniquely intimate relationship with the divine. During the great festivals, supervised—as Caesar tells us—by the Druids, the gods were actually present. Indeed, they were never far away. A wayfarer might come upon one of them in the guise of a black giant or a beautiful, yet strangely sinister, woman seated in a dark corner of a hostelry.

This has bred those fervent religious attitudes found throughout the Celtic world, whether it be Scotland, Ulster, Ireland or Wales. Brittany is certainly no exception and its major manifestation is the *pardons*. So convinced are the Bretons of their significance in the divine scheme that even the elements themselves conspire to facilitate them. Hence, on the day of the *Pardon* of St Kirek at Ploumanach the tide departs from its normal pattern of ebb and flow to recoil before the saint's chapel and statue.

What it means: The name *pardon* comes from the fact that these are, above all, occasions when the devout faithful seek forgiveness of their sins, but they are also times when vows are made or fulfilled and often when miraculous cures are sought. Each of the saintly relics paraded through the streets has its own particular virtue. For example, the finger of St John the Baptist, kept in the church of St-Jean-du-Doigt in the village of that name since the 15th century, is efficacious in cases of eye-disease so that the *pardon* on the last Sunday in June attracts sufferers from all over Brittany.

However, once religious duties have been fulfilled, these are occasions for festivity, for pouring large quantities of cider down throats, for wrestling bouts and dancing.

Older Bretons will tell you sadly that the *pardons* are not what they used to be. In some places the non-religious festival has degenerated into little more than a rather tawdry funfair, while everywhere music for dancing

tends to be provided by jazz or rock groups, even by a lone accordionist. The *pardon* dances, the Ribbon Gavotte, the Tobacco and Handkerchief Gavotte and the *Dérobée*, in which the men try to steal girls from one another, are now mostly to be seen only at the great folk-cultural gatherings like the *Abadenn Veur*—a sort of Breton Eisteddfod—at Quimper every July.

But idealisation of the past can overlook that fact that the *pardons* weren't always as peaceful as they now are. That of St Servais,

regarded as potent protector of crops, annually culminated in limb-shattering battles as, to ensure themselves a bumper harvest, factions from the four dioceses of Brittany fought with clubs for possession of the saint's little wooden statue. In the end the authorities were forced to ban the *pardon*.

Diminished as they may be, the *pardons* remain a spectacle which, if the opportunity occurs, shouldn't be missed. For one thing, they are a rare chance to see the traditional headdresses and colourful costumes, the latter, like everything else, in somewhat modernised form with shorter skirts and frequently worn with fashionable shoes.

Preceding pages, a *pardon*. Left, Alfred Guillou's *L'Arrivée du Pardon de Sainte-Anne de Fouesnant à Concarneau* (1887). Above, the traditional bonnet is taken out for *pardons*.

The destination of the *pardon* pilgrims will often be a chapel used for more than 1,000 years. Some, such as the little oratory Our Lady of All Remedies, standing amid lawns and pine trees at Rumengol, are set like architectural jewels. And you may well be lucky enough to come upon elements of genuine folklore. You will almost certainly hear the nasal plaints of *biniou* (bagpipe) and *bombarde* (oboe). There are even contemporary groups who have adopted them and include pieces based on traditional airs in their repertoires.

The centrepiece of all *pardons* is the procession of hymn-singing pilgrims, men and girls bearing multicoloured banners and re-

Sunday in September, is an annual affair, but the Locronan *Grand Pardon* takes place at six-yearly intervals (1989, 1995 and so on). It is known as the *La Grande Troménie*, a corruption of the Breton *Tro Minihy*, meaning "tour of retreat". The pilgrims, drawn from all over Cornouaille, circuit the hill which marks the boundaries of the 11th-century Benedictine monastery, their progress broken by 12 halts for displays of saints and relics by each parish.

Hill climb: In those years when there is no *Grand Troménie* at Locronan, its place is taken by *La Petite Troménie* on the second Sunday in July. On these occasions participants follow the hill path which St Ronan,

ligious statues; clergy in lace-fringed surplices bearing reliquaries and monstrances. The procession usually takes place in the afternoon; but at the *Pardon* of Our Lady of Succour at Guingamp it is held at night, with the participants carrying candles to three bonfires which are lit by the bishop.

The "*Pardon* Season" is roughly from March to the end of October with most of them taking place between Easter and Michaelmas, 29 September. The biggest is the *Grand Pardon* at Le Folgoët, which is also the longest, beginning at 4 p.m. and continuing until the next day.

The Le Folgoët *Grand Pardon*, on the first

whose name is commemorated in Locronan, was said to take barefoot and fasting.

Whether *grand* or *petit*, the *pardons* invariably have a focal point. The Fouesnant *pardon* on the first Sunday after 26 July includes a feast of the apple trees—Fouesnant produces the best Brittany cider. Among the pilgrims at the *Pardon* of St Yves at Treguier on 19 May are robed lawyers as St Yves was once one of their calling. Another Le Folgoët *pardon*, that of St Christopher, on the 4th Sunday in July includes the blessing of cars. At Penhors on the first Sunday in September the congregation, after Mass, walk through the countryside to the shore where the blessing of the sea takes place. There is also a blessing of the sea at Carantec on the Sunday after 15 August and at Camaret on the first Sunday in September. All are testimony to the importance of the sea to Breton life.

Every *pardon* has its roots in a legend. That at Josselin on 8 September is named "Our Lady of the Bramble" after the ninth-century legend of a miraculous evergreen bramble bush at whose centre a wooden statue of the Virgin was found. Taken from its place it kept returning to the bush until, in the end, a chapel was built to house it. The statue was burnt during the Revolution as an object of superstition, but the few charred

fragments saved are now in a reliquary, while a new statue was made in 1868.

The Josselin *pardon* is also called the "*Pardon* of the Barking Women", recalling how a beggar woman, asking local house-wives for a drink of water, was instead set upon by dogs. She was none other than the Virgin Mary who placed a curse on the women whereby they and their descendants would howl like dogs every Whitsun.

All this Christianising notwithstanding, one can detect the archaic paganism beneath

Left and above, spectators and participants in a typical Breton *pardon*.

the surface. Saint Anne, apocryphal mother of the Blessed Virgin and the object of three *Grand Pardons* (legend makes her a Breton girl), must surely be the powerful goddess who occurs in Ireland as Dana and Anu. The Ahès venerated at the *Pardon* of Sainte Anne-la-Palud is almost certainly a Celtic marine goddess. A British traveller early this century remarked on the custom of passing children over the flames of bonfires at the Midsummer Plougastel *pardon*. This must be related to the "fire leaping" practised in the Highlands and Islands of Scotland and, among other places, at the Bonfire Night celebrations at Lewes in Sussex and is an undoubted relic of human sacrifice.

Animal rites: Nor are the antecedents of all the saints unimpeachable. St Cornély, whose *Grand Pardon* takes place at Carnac, was supposedly a third-century Pope and martyr with Breton connections. One is reminded of the Celtic horned god Cernun-nos who, like St Cornély, was associated with horned animals—his *pardon* is dedicated to cattle. The words *Carnac* and *Cornély* contain a suffix which means "horn", an element also present in the name *Cernunnos*. Evidence of a cult of extreme antiquity associated with horned animals was provided in the last century by the discovery at Kermario of a small bronze ox.

Furthermore, as the writer Keith Spence points out, the *Pardon* of St Cornély, on the second Sunday in September, almost coincides with the autumn equinox, one of the four most important dates in the pagan year.

And if there are any lingering doubts as to Cornély's origins they are surely dispelled by another festival, undoubtedly a relic of the worship of the horned Cernunnos, that of "The Deermen" which takes place at Abbot's Bromley in Staffordshire only about a week earlier. If it weren't for past changes to the calendar the two dates would coincide.

The detection of archaic vestiges underlying folklore is, of course, a very facile game which more and more people are learning to play. Perhaps we should see the *pardons* not simply in these terms nor as merely colourful local custom, but as the often extremely moving manifestations of faith by a warm, outgoing and hospitable people, and one, what is more, capable of expressing itself in other, more direct ways than through ritual and liturgy.

BRETON CUISINE

Brittany isn't a name that trips easily off the tongue when the talk turns to French culinary excellence. Sadly, the region doesn't share the fine food traditions of areas such as Périgord or even Provence, and, although those in the know realise that the best Breton cuisine deserves recognition, it is all too often eclipsed by the creamy excesses of neighbouring Normandy.

The Normans, for example, have given international menus everything from *sole normande* to Camembert. But scarcely more than a handful of Breton specialities have made a name for themselves worldwide.

The scene may sound bleak for the gourmet. However, anyone who pays too much attention to Brittany's limited reputation for good food stands to miss many worthwhile experiences. An apparent lack of big-name dishes certainly doesn't mean that the rich countryside and coastline of France's far west are devoid of either restaurants or exciting fare.

Naturally, Brittany's strongest culinary suit is seafood. Anyone who visits its harbours will instantly see that fishing is a vital part of the local economy. In the past, ports such as St- Malo, Concarneau and Lorient were made rich by offshore fishing for cod, tunny and sardines. Now the industry has a broader base, bringing an enormous variety of fish and shellfish not only to Breton tables but also to those of the rest of France. This is good news for anyone who enjoys eating: it is possible to enjoy a different fish dish every day for a month or more without repetition.

The undisputed aristocrats of the seafood restaurant are the lobster (*l'homard*) and the crawfish (*la langouste*). Caught chiefly in pots off the more rugged parts of a generally rocky coast, these crustaceans fetch high prices which fluctuate according to the season. You will often see specimens confined in tanks of seawater so that customers can choose the beast they want served with mayonnaise or *à la nage*, but their costliness means that they are ogled at more often than they are fished out and sent to the kitchen.

Preceding pages, oodles of oysters. Left, Breton breads. Right, seafood restaurants abound.

Interestingly, one method of cooking lobster and crawfish which has been adopted around the world owes its origin to Breton chefs, though they are regularly robbed of credit for their creation. Common on menus everywhere is *lobster à l'americaine*; but even restaurateurs seem unaware that the dish in question, which features a sauce of tomatoes, oil, onions, wine and brandy, should more properly be *lobster à l'armoricaine* and that it was named after Armorica, the ancient Breton's "land before the sea".

If you feel you aren't quite in the lobster league, there are plenty of cheaper alternatives which are no less delicious. Crabs, for example, come in three varieties: the brown edible crab (*le torteau*), the spiny spider crab (*l'araignée de mer*) and the tiny but tasty velvet swimming crab (*l'étrille*). All are best enjoyed straight from the shell, all go well with the home-made mayonnaise which most restaurants offer, and all are essential ingredients of a seafood platter (*les fruits de mer*), that ultimate shellfish feast.

Ranged alongside the pieces of crab on even a moderately comprehensive seafood platter will be *langoustines* (miniature pale pink lobsters which are known elsewhere as Dublin Bay prawns or scampi), *moules* (mussels), *bigorneaux* (black winkles), *paloudres* (clams), *praires* (another sort of clam with a thick, ribbed shell) and, of course, oysters, succulent bivalves which are the source not only of much pleasure but also of some controversy.

The controversy concerns which are better: the flat native oysters or the wrinkled, tear-drop shaped Portuguese oysters, with shells as flaky as *mille-feuille* pastry, which are now cultured in vast numbers in carefully tended beds (*parcs à huîtres*). Purists says that the native oysters have a more delicate flavour, but that does not stop trenchermen

With some justification, Brittany's excellent shellfish tend to be mentioned before what the English prosaically call wet fish. But don't ignore the bass (*le bar*), monkfish (*la lotte*) or skate (*la raie*) which are to be seen on fishmongers' slabs and menus throughout the region; they, too, are excellent and are also invariably fresh. Such fish can be enjoyed individually or all together (plus perhaps pollack, wrasse, mackerel, bream and conger) in *cotriade*, a seafood stew which can hold its own with the bouillabaisse of the South of France.

If the Breton coast is dominated by its fisheries and its fish cookery, the hinterland also has its characteristic culinary attrac-

from swallowing tons of the Portuguese variety (*les creuses*) each year.

Oysters are nurtured and harvested at many places in Brittany, but the place to enjoy them is in one of the waterfront restaurants in Cancale, the small port near St-Malo which is often described as the "oyster capital of the world". And if such authentic experiences appeal, you could do worse than visit another Côte d'Emeraude resort which also casts itself in the role of a world capital: Erquy. Erquy's capital status depends on its scallop fishery, so the delicacies to be tried in its restaurants are *coquilles St Jacques* in their many guises.

tions. It is not, for example, possible to travel more than a few kilometres in Brittany without seeing a sign for a *crêperie*. These small establishments, which are generally furnished and decorated in the traditional style, serve that great Breton speciality, the pancake. Called variously *crêpes* or *galettes*, these are freshly made on a griddle and are served with a wide variety of savoury and sweet fillings ranging from egg, ham and cheese to jam, fresh fruit and honey.

There is some confusion about the distinction between *crêpes* and *galettes* because of considerable local variation, but in the west at least, *galette* means a thicker, more substantial pancake. Further confusion surrounds the basic material of which the pancakes are made: in the past this was invariably buckwheat flour, but increasingly ordinary wheat flour is taking over.

There is far less confusion over what should be drunk with *crêpes* or *galettes*. Though tart, dry Muscadet and Gros Plant are produced in the Nantes area and are justifiably famous as wines which complement seafood, Brittany is essentially a cider-drinking region. Often served in rustic *faïence* mugs rather than glasses, Breton cider is available in sweet, dry, still and gassy varieties. Much of it is very good indeed, being made by methods which have

scarcely changed for hundreds of years, but some of the mass-produced product falls far short of the ideal.

In spite of the prodigious drinking feats of Asterix and his fellow cartoon character Obelix, beer no longer plays a major part in Breton life. Cervoise, the brew of the Celtic past, remains in name only; much the same fate has been shared by *chouchen*, a fermented honey mead of startling potency.

Fortunately, the same is not true of other traditional fare. It's still easy, for instance, to

Left, oysters again—indoors this time. Above, Brittany's celebrated crêpes.

find *farz breton*, a rich pudding made with wheat flour, eggs, sugar and milk and often enriched with raisins or prunes; *kig sal*, the salty bacon used in many dishes; *andouille*, a white pudding made from chitterlings; and magnificent *gros-camus* artichokes, whose spiky globes fill field after field around St-Pol- de- Léon.

You might even say that it is hard to miss one dish with a particularly noble pedigree: *Châteaubriand*, the select beef steak cut from the thickest part of the fillet. It is named after François-René de Châteaubriand, the celebrated author whose childhood home was the castle of Combourg and who is buried on the islet of Grand-Bé off St -Malo.

The sea, it seems, keeps intruding into Breton cuisine where one least expects it. Talk of lamb and one normally thinks of upland pastures—but in Brittany it is more appropriate to think of salt marshes and the sparse vegetation of coastal flood plains. Such unpromising grazing in the Marais du Dol bordering the Bay of Mont-St-Michel, around the gulf of Morbihan and on Ile d'Ouessant is the home of small flocks of hardy sheep whose meat is of exceptionally high quality. Known as *pré-salé*, the meat commands a high price and demand always outstrips supply.

The sea—and particularly the Gulf Stream—also plays its part in maintaining Brittany's mild climate. This, in turn, means that the entire region is one of the gardens of France, supplying up to 15 percent of the nation's total horticultural requirements.

St-Pol-de-Léon's artichoke crop has already been mentioned, but of equal importance are cabbages, cauliflowers and early potatoes. Huge acreages are under cultivation and a significant proportion of the region's workforce labours on the land.

Even in the case of Brittany's culinary oddities it's a question of the sea having come to the rescue in times of severe hardship. On the bleak, isolated Ile du Sein, for example, the lack of poultry used to be compensated for by the capture of seabirds. A casserole of cormorant is apparently quite acceptable if the fishiness of the flesh is suppressed with plenty of onions and wine, and the same bird, specimens of which stand like black-robed sentinels on rocks all around the coast, is said to be the basis of a good paté.

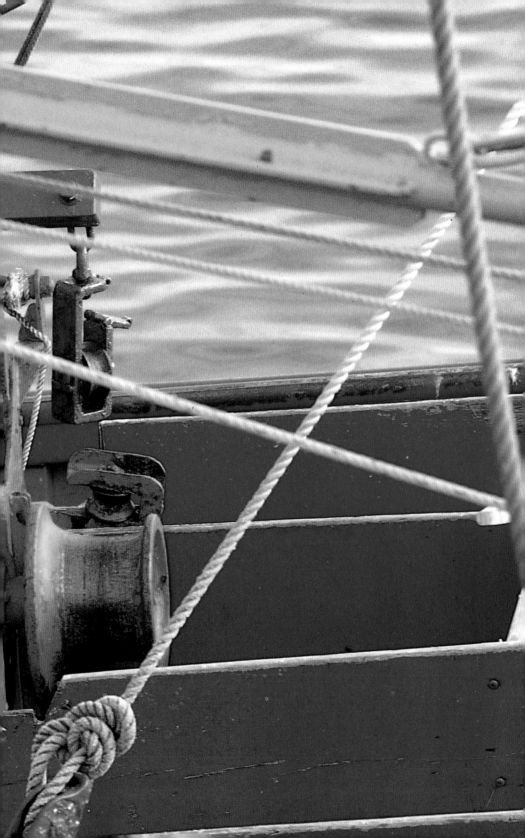

FACTS ABOUT FISHING

Visit any port in Brittany, from the major harbours such as Lorient and Douarnenez to the smallest anchorage which offers even marginal protection from the swells of the Atlantic, and you will quickly comprehend the immense importance of fishing to the region. Although the number of large vessels has decreased dramatically in the past decade, the big ports still have many trawlers capable of two-week distant-water trips and the small ones support fleets of brightly painted, sturdy wooden craft, whose bluff bows suggest that their crews are rather more than fine weather sailors.

To the layman the diversity is bewildering. But each slightly different category of vessel has its own job to do, its own method of harvesting the sea and its own quarry.

More than 12,000 Bretons earn their living directly from fishing and shore-based related industries. This means that the regional economy depends more than any other in France on what the sea can be persuaded to yield. Because Brittany can consume only a fraction of what its fleets catch, supplies of cod, mackerel, crabs and lobsters are loaded on to juggernaut lorries which thunder inland to supply the towns and cities far from the coast. In shellfish alone, the Breton fleets provide 70 percent of France's needs.

Although Breton waters are the focus of much small-scale fishing activity and hold major stocks of lobster, crab, langoustines, scallops, bass and a host of other important luxury species, the fishing grounds of the entire western Atlantic are visited by boats from the major Breton ports. St-Malo in the north, for example, still has a few trawlers which range as far afield as the Barents Sea in search of cod. The harbours of the south are the homes of wandering tunny vessels which sail far into international waters, looking for their streamlined migratory prey sometimes around the Azores, sometimes in Biscay, depending on the season.

Other craft earn their living principally in the English Channel, the Western Ap-

proaches and around the coast of the British Isles, dragging the seabed for anything that is edible but hoping to find concentrations of gastronomic delights such as monkfish (*la lotte*), turbot, hake (*le colin*) and Dover soles. Another seasonal—if declining—business is sardine fishing which starts each year in April or May.

In the nature of things, most visitors to Brittany glimpse the fishing industry only when its craft are passively tied up alongside harbour walls. The fishing processes them-

selves remain arduous routines often carried out far offshore and far from the gaze of curious onlookers. In some respects, however, even commercial fishing can be allowed to intrude entertainingly into a holiday. Fish markets of all sizes are places of entertainment as well as commerce, and to watch as catches are unloaded for auction and dispatch can be a revelation.

Broadcasting on such an event from Concarneau, the television chef Keith Floyd remarked memorably that the assorted out-of-this-world fishy bodies arranged in rank upon rank of boxes look like the *hors de combat* participants in some frightening in-

Preceding pages, gearing up for a fishing expedition. Left, patient wait. Right, all geared up for action.

ter-galactic conflict. Certainly it doesn't take much imagination to cast the penny-eyed, snaggle-toothed hake or the hideous Cheshire Cat monkfish in the role of strangers from another planet.

The fish market is a place of bizarre but fascinating corpses, but many Breton harbours are picturesque to an almost indecent degree. If, however, you can set aside postcard attributes in favour of the practicality of the places, it is interesting to find out which vessels are designed for which types of fishing. Even without becoming an instant fishing boat expert, it's easy to see how the craft with bulbous whalebacks at the bow and shelter decks covering the entire work area

Fishing may be a major commercial activity in Brittany but it is quite obvious that many members of the non-trawling, non-potting community are also determined to get in on the act. Fishing for pleasure is highly popular among Bretons.

Some of the local anglers go about their sport in a systematic way, though far more popular is the chuck-and-chance-it approach. Harbour walls and rocky promontories along the region's coastline are used as vantage points by enthusiasts who are happy to take anything which deigns to examine their bait too closely. The creature concerned might be a bass or a pollack, a pouting or a plaice, but it will often be so small that

are adapted for setting and retrieving longlines carrying thousands of baited hooks and how the open decks and capstan winches of crabbers can handle strings of 50 or more bulky shellfish pots even in the roughest conditions.

Equally, tangle-net boats are identifiable because of the drum-like haulers they carry and scallopers can be spotted by the toothed steel mesh dredges used to scour *les coquilles St Jacques* from the seabed. At Roscoff you will even see vessels equipped with hydraulic grabs which harvest seaweed for processing to yield alginates for use in making toothpaste and glue.

it ought to be returned to fight another day.

In France as a whole there seems to be only a very rudimentary understanding of what the word conservation might mean, and the immediate demands of the cooking pot universally take precedence over thoughts of the future. Even tiny and almost inedible wrasse (*les vielles*) are consigned to the catch-bag on the basis that, though they may taste like cotton wool stuffed with needles, they are nevertheless quite good enough to be ingredients of *la soupe de poisson*.

France's pragmatic attitude to angling means that there is great scope for the visiting enthusiast. Use of the correct tackle, the correct baits and, above all, the latest methods are likely to pay off handsomely. The surf beaches of the south and west and the rocky gullies and islets of the north, for instance, hold large populations of bass (*les bars*). High summer also sees the arrival of another superb fighting variety, the gilthead bream (*la daurade*), while throughout the year offshore there are congers of almost fabulous dimensions, monster ling and a bewildering variety of rays, including thornbacks and intriguingly named blondes.

The many estuaries and creeks also hold their share of fish, particularly flounders (*les flets*) and the shy grey mullet, which often congregate in huge shoals but are so hook-

shy that tiny baits and ultra-fine lines are required to secure their downfall. Every zone which has rocks, beds of the broad fronds of laminaria weed and perhaps mussel colonies has its resident wrasse.

Small, immature fish have been mentioned as the prey of the inexpert angler, but in the heavyweight division above three pounds (1.4 kg) they are worthy opponents. Catching them, however, is only part of the pleasure. Their bright colours and psychedelic patterns look as though they belong to

Left, necessary maintenance. Above, fishing house at Dinan.

the vivid world of a tropical coral reef rather than the blue-green depths of northwestern Europe.

Perhaps because of the French attitude that anything which swims is better out of the water than in, freshwater fishing in Brittany is at best average, but another pleasure awaits on the shore. The large range of tide (particularly in the north) means that various forms of low-water fishing are possible. When the tide is out, legions of locals often descend on the low-water mark armed chiefly with nets for prawning or shrimping. Watching what goes on, one is left with the impression that the pursuit is the important thing, because seldom does anyone return with a catch worthy of the name. The procedure is nevertheless taken very seriously and enjoyed hugely.

The same goes for fossicking around among the reefs and boulder banks revealed by the retreating tide. The quarry sought in the multitude of nooks and crannies will usually be edible crabs (*les torteaux*), velvet swimming crabs (*les étrilles*) and—if the gods of fishing are feeling exceptionally benevolent—the lobster (*l'homard*), although everything down to and including a sea urchin will be snapped up if it is considered remotely edible. But the main purpose of the exercise is to have fun.

Out-and-out commercialism, on the other hand, is the ruling force in those areas where the Bretons have decided to tame the sea and culture its produce. In sheltered areas from Cancale to the mouth of the Loire you will see vast tracts of the foreshore given over to oyster beds and the poles necessary for mussel culture an established part of Brittany's marine economy.

The clear, unpolluted seas of Brittany are ideal for underwater swimming, particularly when the swell abates during periods of high atmospheric pressure. Just looking at the kelp-covered submarine scenery will be enough for many, but spearfishing is allowed, although a permit to take fish in this way is required. Also required is some sort of surface float to warn passing boat traffic of the presence of a diver.

Bass and mullet are the most sought-after species and only an ignorant novice or a sadist would bother the legions of wrasse, which in some places are tame enough to be fed by hand.

HOW SAILORS CAN SURVIVE

In *The Canterbury Tales,* Chaucer's Franklyn is much exercised by the threat to navigation posed by the fiendish black rocks of Brittany. He even goes as far as having some of them abolished by magic to ensure the safe return of a key character in his story. Given access to such potent spells, modern yachtsmen would find themselves in two minds: the tangle of reefs and shoals which guard the Breton coastline certainly make it a potential graveyard for vessels of all sizes, but they also contribute greatly to its fascination as a cruising ground.

Yachtsmen also tend to be ambivalent towards the region's other navigational threats: its tidal range (well over 10 metres in the north), its fierce tidal flows (strongest between St-Malo and Les Sept Iles), its ocean swells and its impenetrable fogs. All are frequently regretted and even cursed, but all contribute to Brittany's rich and special maritime environment.

Although reefs and formidable tides are the most obvious and impressive features of the Breton coast, even a casual glance at the area's charts show that such hazards aren't the end of the story. The yachtsman's Brittany is a place of contrasts. For every rock-bound stretch of shoreline, such as those around St-Malo or Ile de Bréhat in the north and at Penmarch or Quiberon in the south, there seems to be a deep, meandering estuary or a sheltered bay. In the Golfe du Morbihan there is even what amounts to an inland sea, complete with its own archipelago of tiny islands and a labyrinth of tidal creeks.

Contrasts are again the rule when it comes to the havens available for local and visiting craft. If Brittany now has more than its fair share of modern purpose-built marinas, it also has many busy commercial harbours, such as Brest, Lorient and Concarneau, and innumerable tiny anchorages, the vast majority of which dry out at low water.

When the tide drops and the sea retreats to reveal a damp desert of shingle, sand and mud, it soon becomes obvious why so many local vessels are equipped with *les béquilles*

(literally crutches, but "drying legs" in the glossary of English nautical terms). These may not be essential for cruising in Breton waters, but they—or bilge keels or a swing keel—do make life easier and mean that otherwise inaccessible nooks and corners can suddenly be reached with ease.

Just as the Bretons take practical steps to minimise the inconvenience of their tidal range, so they have minimised the riskiness of their rock-strewn coast with a comprehensive buoyage system. It sometimes seems as

if every hazard has a sea-mark of some sort, from an elaborate tower to a bare pole, and this in itself can be bewildering for sailors accustomed to blander, more forgiving waters.

Fortunately, the French enjoy naming their reefs and the objects marking their positions, so in daylight at least, identifying them positively usually presents few problems. Be prepared for changes which remain unannounced, however. The many excellent pilot books dealing with Brittany try to keep up to date, but with so many navigational aids to keep track of the struggle is bound to be an unequal one.

Preceding pages, under full sail. Left and above, Brittany attracts sailors from all over Europe.

Other man-made additions to the seascape can be less than helpful, merely adding to the natural hazards. Brittany may be yachting territory, but long before men went to sea for pleasure they did so to earn a livelihood. Breton fishermen continue to do so in large numbers and almost all of the coast is a minefield of static fishing gear, complete with buoys and dans of all sizes and fathom upon fathom of floating rope. French yachtsmen don't appear to expend much energy complaining about these obstacles; they just avoid them with a gallic shrug, knowing that in their country at least, the serious business of wresting a living from the sea will always take precedence over pleasure.

For their part, the commercial fleets tolerate the string and canvas brigade quite affably, though they invariably and justifiably have the pick of the best moorings and will not hesitate to move yachts on if they are in the way. Perhaps more annoyingly, visitors looking for fuel also discover that the low-duty diesel oil dispensed at many commercial quaysides is very strictly reserved for use by fishermen.

The Bretons have had plenty of time to get used to visiting yachtsmen—particularly those from the United Kingdom. Brittany north of the Brest peninsula is only a day's sail away from ports in south and southwest England, so it was the natural choice when, after World War II, an upsurge in boat ownership saw more people searching for new places to explore.

North Brittany is, of course, closer than Finistère and the rest of the south but its waters are far from ideal for the novice. Those tides for which the region is famous are at their strongest and the offshore reefs are so dense in many places that the coastline has an almost limitless number of separate identities, depending on the state of the tide. Both factors make navigation difficult and there is usually no margin for error. Modern aids such as radar, echo sounders and the Decca system make life easier, though excessive reliance on them is almost as bad as sailing blind.

In the south, beyond Penmarch and its sentinel, Eckmühl light, the coastline becomes rather more forgiving, having fewer offshore hazards and gentler tidal streams. However, to get to this area from the north involves rounding the Brest peninsula and all that that can mean. Ile d'Ouessant (or Ushant as the English will have it), the Chenal du Four and the Chenal de la Helle are legendary for their Atlantic swells and dense fogs.

The former can cause the build up of very unpleasant seas indeed, and there can be frightening overfalls when the ebbing tide runs strongly against the prevailing westerlies blowing in from the open ocean. And when a small vessel dips into the deep trough between waves crests, swell can also limit visibility almost as effectively as the thickest of thick weather. Even making the sanctuary of harbour when a big swell is running may offer only the illusion of safety, for some Breton havens are so poorly protected that vessels can quite easily be damaged while lying alongside a quay.

In spite of the very real hazards of a landfall in the rocky maze of north Brittany or of the passage between Ile d'Ouessant and the mainland, the fact remains that thousands of pleasure craft make it unscathed to Breton harbours each year, though the wisest skippers make their landfall in daylight and delay their final approach if visibility is bad. The challenge of the voyage is certainly important, but so are the rewards which go with arrival. Formalities are minimal (though since 1984 all yachts visiting France must be officially registered and carry a certificate of registration), marina facilities are generally very good (French plumbers have at last cracked the secret of the hot shower) and the many pleasantly informal yacht clubs offer a warm welcome.

The clubs are also an excellent source of local advice, but even if the language barrier is no problem it's worth remembering that France has something of a tradition of enthusiastic but very amateur seamen and that possession of a striped sweater and yellow wellies doesn't automatically confer expertise.

Even the smallest ports have a choice of bars and restaurants, though yachtsmen keen to explore inland have taken to carrying folding bicycles—or even mopeds—on board their boats. Others, however, seem content to go no further than the quayside, relishing the camaraderie which exists among amateur sailors. While this is based largely on the common ground of boats and boating, a great many of the temporary immigrants occupying marina berths from St Servan to Le Croisic are English middle-class professionals at play and therefore have similar interests and attitudes.

The French, of course, are present too, many choosing La Bretagne for sailing holidays. Some cruise their own craft south from the Channel ports, others charter boats or hone their skills at a sailing school. The most famous of these is located on Les Glénans, the group of tiny islets offshore from Concarneau. In spite of its isolated location, the Centre Nautique des Glénans is one of the largest sailing schools in Europe, offering tuition in every aspect of seamanship from the basics up to ocean racing.

and rugged coasts. There is, however, another side to Breton boating: the canals.

Anyone who wants to avoid the Ushant passage but is intent on exploring Cornouaille and the rest of the south can enter the inland waterway system through the lock in the barrage across the Rance near St-Malo and navigate across country as far as St Nazaire at the mouth of the Loire, passing through Dinan, Rennes and Redon on the way. To do so requires a rather special vessel of limited draught (up to 1.1 metres for most of the system) and with maximum height of no more than 2.4 metres. Also required is the patience to negotiate some 60 locks.

For those who enjoy permanently calm

Other more modest sailing schools are cashing in on the popularity of windsurfing, aware that the thrill of standing poised between board and sail in the rôle of a piece of human rigging has enormous appeal. There is now scarcely a beach without at least a handful of windsurfers and the sleek lines and lurid sails of *les planches à voile* are, quite simply, the latest essential elements of the Breton seaside.

Brittany as a whole seems to jut aggressively into the Atlantic and sailors will always associate its name with the open sea

Down to the sea at Bénodet.

water beneath the hull there are other inland routes. These allow exits to the sea at Lorient and below La Roche-Bernard and pass through a number of major towns, including Pontivy and Josselin. Also available for the sailor who merely wants to taste inland sailing are the navigable stretches of rivers such as the Rance, the Odet and the Aulne.

An open sea more full of hazards than a book of navigational exercises, canals, estuaries and harbours for virtually every day of the year might seem like quite enough for one region. Yet there's an added bonus for the enterprising yachtsman: Brittany's islands, which cry out to be visited..

BIRDWATCHING IN BRITTANY

Around Brittany's 750 miles (1,200 km) of ragged coastline are more than 40 bird sanctuaries, nature reserves and other protected sites. As well as the renowned seacliffs, there are estuaries, creeks, mudflats, salt marshes and sand dunes. The result: outstanding birdwatching opportunities.

Yet, it would be misleading to suggest that there are no interesting birds inland. Even though most British birdwatchers by-pass Brittany and head further south in search of exotic, Mediterranean species, the Breton peninsula supports an exciting variety of birds in a diversity of habitats including freshwater lakes and marshes, reed beds, moorland, farmland and ancient woodland.

Eight of the nine reserves in Brittany, however, are on the coast and the province holds an impressive 80 percent of France's nesting seabirds. In fact, a birdwatching trip to Brittany can start even before one sets foot on French soil. From the deck of a ferry sailing towards St-Malo or Roscoff, it is possible to start logging birds well before the North Breton coast hoves into view.

Crowded skies: Gannets glide across the swell on their long, pointed wings or plummet into the water like dazzling white javelins. Puffins, guillemots and razorbills whirr past on short wings or rest, bobbing on the surface, in small groups. Kittiwakes, fulmars, skuas and shearwaters are also regularly sighted. All you need is a pair of binoculars and strong legs to brace yourself against the swaying of the boat.

The largest numbers of seabirds are to be seen in spring and summer when the breeding colonies on craggy cliffs, offshore islands and rocky stacks seethe with raucous, calling birds. The most important of these seabird colonies is Les Sept-Iles on the northern coast near Perros-Guirec. The islands, a reserve since 1912, have colonies of gannets (4,250 pairs) and puffins (300 pairs), both species here at the very southern limit of their breeding range in Europe.

In addition, guillemots, razorbills, Manx shearwaters, storm petrels, shags, fulmars,

kittiwakes and other gulls, oystercatchers, shelducks and ravens breed here. Most of the reserve is not open to the public but, in the summer, boat trips around the islands from Perros-Guirec offer good views of the birds, including the gannets.

Among the seabird colonies which have public access are Cap Fréhel, the Michel-Hervé Julien Reserve at Cap Sizun, the François Le Bail Reserve on Ile de Groix and Koh Kastell on Belle-Ile. These sanctuaries do not support such a range of seabirds as

Les Sept-Iles, lacking the gannets and puffins, but some of them in the west have breeding choughs. The best times to visit are usually between April and July; but it is wise to check locally when access is permitted.

From August onwards, other coastal sites come into their own as tired migrants from the north rest on headlands, beaches, mudflats and marshes. During both spring and autumn migration, it is possible to see spoonbill, avocet, whimbrel, curlew, sandpiper, little stint, wood sandpiper, green sandpiper, Kentish plover, gull-billed tern and black tern among other exciting migrants. It's not unusual so see an osprey

Preceding pages, birdwatching at Roscoff. Left, guillemots. Above, puffins.

hovering on broad wings above a river or marsh, its huge talons dangling, its eyes fixed on a large fish in the shallows below.

Brittany's harbours and inlets are winter quarters for thousands of birds. On the north coast, in the bays of Mont-St-Michel and Morlaix, the mudflats are dotted with rocky outcrops that provide resting places for birds when the tide is in and vantage points for birdwatchers when it is out.

Further west are the dunes of Keremma, another protected site and, to the south of Brest, there are countless little bays and creeks. At such places, in the winter months, one can hope to see a great variety of grebes, ducks, geese and waders, including avocets, turnstones, knot, purple sandpiper, bartailed and black-tailed godwits. Little egrets—graceful, snowy-white relatives of the grey heron—add spice to the scene.

Douarnenez on the west coast is one of several places where it is worth checking the gulls for interesting species such as little gull and Mediterranean gull.

The finest winter birdwatching location in Brittany—and one of the best in Europe—is the Golfe du Morbihan near Vannes, an enormous, shallow, tidal inlet with innumerable creeks, backwaters, islands, marshes and lagoons. From October onwards, magnificent views of wildfowl can be enjoyed from the roads which skirt the shoreline of the gulf, particularly on the southern side.

Timid visitors: Near Sarzeau, the Marais de Saint Armel enjoys reserve status and attracts breathtaking numbers of brent geese, wigeon and pintail. When they first arrive in October and November, the flocks tend to be rather nervous. Time and time again, sensing danger, real or imagined, they rise up in alarm until the sky is black with birds.

During winter, there are also good numbers of little egret, shelduck, shoveler and countless waders. It is also worth looking out for hen harrier, merlin or even peregrine hunting the marshes and both Bewick's and whooper swans can be seen.

By contrast, in summer, the Golfe du Morbihan can boast only a limited bird population. Little egret, garganey and Kentish plover occur in quiet watery corners alongside more common species such as shelduck, grey heron and kingfisher, while black kite and marsh harrier regularly hunt their prey over the damp margins of the gulf.

The tiny fan-tailed warbler inhabits tangles of rank grass, sharing the areas of rough vegetation with resident cirl buntings and Dartford warblers, and bluethroats may be found where scrubby bushes and trees provide sufficient cover. Several species of tern occur, including roseate and whiskered terns. The leggy elegance of the occasional black-winged stilt adds an exotic flavour.

Another place well worth a visit is the Parc Régional de Brière, just inland from St-Nazaire. This vast area of reedbed is almost impenetrable except by boat—or rather punt. However, at Ile de Fédrun near St-Joachim, it is possible to hire a punt, with a guide if you wish, and head off into the

reedbeds where otters are regularly sighted.

In summer, you can hope to see birds of prey such as marsh harrier, hen harrier, Montagu's harrier and black kite. A purple heron may be glimpsed as it moves from one part of the reedbed to another.

Unfortunately, some of the birds here are secretive and skulking species which often remain unseen in the fastness of the reedbeds, among them little bittern, night heron, Baillon's crake and spotted crake. Sometimes, the birds' calls give them away: the chink of bearded tits, the squeal of a water rail, the explosive rattle of Cetti's warbler.

During spring and summer, bitterns can be

heard booming amid the songs of various small songbirds, including Savi's, marsh and great reed warblers. In winter, many ducks and geese visit the Brière waterways. But, because of regular shooting by wildfowlers the birds tend to make themselves scarce and head for protected waters.

Brittany's other regional park, the Parc Régional d'Armorique, includes the Montagnes d'Arrée, a range of bracken- and gorse-clad hills capped by rocky summits. Although these hills rise to just 1,260 ft (384 metres), there is an illusion of a much wilder remoteness and the walker can enjoy fine views.

In summer, the open hillsides and rough

pastures hold Montagu's harrier, hobby, curlew, whinchat, wheatear, ring ouzel and red-backed shrike. Year-round residents such as buzzard, stonechat, Dartford warbler and cirl bunting are joined in winter by merlin, hen harrier and great grey shrike.

Even though Brittany has rather less woodland than other parts of France, there is enough to support a good population of woodland birds. Even in the relatively treeless west, there are picturesque wooded valleys such as Aber Wrac'h and Aber Benoît and around Huelgoat there is attrac-

Left, the pied flycatcher. Above, the kingfisher.

tive mixed woodland in gently rolling hill country where streams tumble between tall trees. Here one can find sparrowhawk, short-toed treecreeper, crested tit and crossbill, the last two, together with the resident red squirrels, suggesting the Scottish Highlands rather than Western France.

In central and eastern Brittany, there are some more extensive deciduous woods where you can walk among mature oaks, beeches and chestnuts. One such is the ancient Forest of Paimpont. Though now sadly depleted as a result of felling and commercial forestry, enough of it remains to hint at its former glory. This is a good place to search for middle spotted woodpecker and the elusive grey-headed woodpecker.

Other birds which may be found in these forests include goshawk, long-eared owl, hawfinch and summer visitors like golden oriole, hoopoe, redstart, pied flycatcher, wood warbler, melodious warbler, nightingale and honey buzzard.

Some of the Breton interior, especially in the north and west of the peninsula, is uninspiring agricultural land where only skylarks, meadow pipits and kestrels are regularly seen. However, there are some tracts of more varied farmland, particularly further south where fields, hedgerows, woodland belts and copses create a pleasing mosaic. This landscape supports a whole variety of interesting species, including hen harrier, Montagu's harrier, hobby, serin, hoopoe, corncrake, ortolan bunting, cirl bunting and wryneck.

Shooting parties: The crested lark is scarce, probably as a result of the use of intensive farming methods and chemicals. The turtle dove is also in decline, though the reason in this case is more likely to be the indiscriminate shooting of migrating birds in spring as they pass through southern France.

In the southeast of the province, especially where pines begin to predominate, the landscape assumes an almost Mediterranean character. Here, stone curlew, quail, tawny pipit, short-toed lark, woodlark and Bonelli's warbler are all possible.

Even the towns of Brittany can provide pleasant surprises. The black redstart, a rarity across the English Channel, is very common in some Breton towns and is frequently seen perching on rooftops and television aerials, its orange tail a-quiver.

TRAVEL TIPS

GETTING THERE

For travellers from the UK, Brittany is one of the most accessible regions of France.

BY AIR

Air France (see Useful Addresses) is the main agent for all flights to France, including those operated by Brittany's own airline, BritAir, which has a schedule of daily flights from London (Gatwick) to Brest, Quimper and Rennes, and also seasonal flights from Cork to Morlaix; for details, contact Air France or Britair (0293) 502044. Jersey European (Tel. (0392) 64440) has a service to Dinard from Bournemouth and Exeter via Jersey.

There are good scheduled services from the UK direct to Brittany, but travellers from other countries need to travel via Paris, or London (which may well work out cheaper). Numerous companies offer flights to these two cities; Nouvelles Frontières offer some of the most competitive fares on both scheduled and charter flights to Paris and London from the US and Canada.

Details are available from their offices at:

New York: 12 East 33rd Street, New York NY. Tel. 212 779 0600.

Los Angeles: 6363 Wilshire Boulevard, Suite 200 Los Angeles, CA 90048. Tel. 213 658 8955.

San Francisco: 209 Post Street, San Francisco, CA 94108. Tel. 415 781 4480.

Montreal: 800 Boulevard de Maisonneuve Est., Montreal, Quebec H2L 4M7. Tel. 514 288 4800.

Students and young people can normally obtain discounted charter fares through specialist travel agencies in their own countries. In the USA, try USIT, New York

Student Centre, William Sloane House YMCA, 356 West 34th Street, New York NY 10001.

From Paris, there are regular flights operated by Brit Air and France's internal airline, Air Inter and bookable through Air France, to Lorient, Rennes, Quimper, Dinard, St-Brieuc, Brest, Lannion and Nantes.

BY SEA

Several ferry services operate from the UK, Eire and the Channel Islands. All (apart from hydrofoil services) carry cars as well as foot passengers.

BRITTANY FERRIES offer the most complete service with sailings direct from Portsmouth to St-Malo and from Plymouth and Cork (Eire) to Roscoff. Alternative crossings are Portsmouth to Caen in Normandy, or by their cheaper Les Routiers service from Poole to Cherbourg (summer only). Details from The Brittany Centre, Wharf Road, Portsmouth PO2 8RU. Tel. (0705) 827701, or from Millbay Docks, Plymouth PL1 3EW. Tel. (0752) 221321.

P & O EUROPEAN FERRIES has services from Portsmouth to Le Havre and Cherbourg in Normandy. Fares and schedules from P&O, The Continental Ferry Port, Mile End, Portsmouth PO2 8QW. Tel. (0705) 827677.

IRISH FERRIES sails to Normandy with a year-round service from Rosslare to Le Havre and Cherbourg, and ferries in July and August, once a week to Le Havre from Cork. Contact them at 2/4 Merrion Row, Dublin 2. Tel. 610 511.

EMERAUDE LINES runs a ferry from Jersey in the Channel Islands to St-Malo, also from Guernsey direct on summer Sundays, or by connection with the Jersey ferry. Information from Albert Quay, St Helier, Jersey, C.I. Tel. (0534) 74458; New Jetty, White Rock, St Peter Port, Guernsey, C.I. Tel. (0481) 711414; Gare Maritime du Naye, 35400 St-Malo. Tel. 99.82.83.84.

CONDOR offers a fast hydrofoil service between St-Malo, Jersey, Guernsey and Alderney with a connecting service to Weymouth. The hydrofoils do not run from Nov. to mid-March. Details from Condor

Ltd., Passenger Dept, New Jetty, White Rock, St. Peter Port, Guernsey, C.I. Tel. (0481) 26121; Commodore Travel, PO Box 25, 28 Conway Street, St. Helier, Jersey, C.I. Tel. (0534) 71263; Morvan Fils Agent Général, Gare Maritime de la Bourse; 2 Place du Poids du Roi, 35402, St-Malo Cedex. Tel. 99.56.42.29.

CUNARD LINES New York to Southampton service sometimes puts in at Cherbourg, so if you have the time (five days at sea) and the money for a mini-cruise, contact them in the USA on 800 221 4770.

BY TRAIN

For visitors arriving from Paris, the train is a fast, efficient way to reach the region, especially with the new high-speed train (TGV), in service from Sept. 1989, bringing journey times down to two hours to Rennes and four hours to Brest. Getting across the region north to south is not so easy, and services not particularly good (see Getting Around). However, there are Paris connections to the south and west coasts (Vannes, Auray, Lorient, Quimper), and Dinard and St-Malo on the north coast.

Note that most departures leave from Paris-Montparnasse. During 1989, some trains were leaving from Montparnasse-Vaugirard because of works at the main station so allow extra time for your journey.

Tickets may be booked for through journeys from the UK including ferry travel, from any British Rail station; BR travel centres have details of continental services, or contact British Rail European Enquiries, Victoria Station, London SW1. Tel. 01 834 2345.

Some passengers can obtain discounted fares—e.g. people under 26 qualify for a Transalpino ticket to any one destination, or an Interrail ticket for one month's travel (not so useful if you just intend to stay in Brittany); holders of a senior citizen's rail pass can pay an extra £5 for a Rail Europe card which then entitles them to 50 percent reduction on fares; a Family Rail Europe card is available for £5 for family groups of a minimum of three and maximum of eight people, which can be used to purchase cheaper tickets. Details of all these tickets can be obtained from British Rail European Enquiries, as above.

You can also request information and book tickets through the SNCF (French Railways Ltd), French Railways House, 179 Piccadilly, London W1V 0BA. Tel. 01-491 7622 and at 610 Fifth Avenue, New York, NY 10020. Tel. 212 582 2110.

BY COACH

Eurolines European coach services operate two services from London to either Roscoff or St-Malo, but do not go any further inland into Brittany. However, booking this way takes care of the ferry reservation too, and National Express coaches have connections with the London departures from most major towns in the UK. For details contact National Express, The Coach Travel Centre, 13 Regent Street, London SW1Y 4LR. Tel. 01-439 9368.

BY CAR

Brittany is an ideal destination for motorists from the UK—roll off the ferry and you're there. There are no motorways in the region, but good fast "N" roads. If speed is not of the essence, follow the green holiday route signs to your destination—these form part of a national network of *bison futé* routes to avoid traffic congestion at peak periods. The first weekend in August is usually the worst time to travel, so avoid it if you can. For further details about driving in France, see Getting Around.

TRAVEL ESSENTIALS

VISAS & PASSPORTS

All visitors to Brittany need a valid passport; in addition, visitors from the USA, Canada, Australia and New Zealand (and in fact anywhere outside the EEC), require a current visa. These are available from the French consulate in your country and last for either 90 days or three years, and are valid from the date of issue. If you intend to stay in France for more than 90 days at any one time, then a *carte de séjour* must be obtained (again from the French consulate)—this also applies to EEC members.

MONEY MATTERS

The Franc is divided into 100 centimes—a five-centime piece being the smallest coin and the F500 note the highest denomination bill.

Banks displaying the *Change* sign will change foreign currency and usually at the best rates (you will need to produce your passport in any transaction). If possible avoid hotels or other independent bureaux which may charge a high commission. It is becoming easier all the time to pay by credit card—Visa (or Carte Bleue) is the most common and is even accepted in many supermarkets. Access (Mastercharge/Eurocard) and American Express are also accepted in some establishments.

Eurocheques, used in conjunction with a cheque card, drawn directly on your own bank account, can be used just like a cheque in the UK and are commonly accepted. Apply for these, or if you prefer, travelers'

cheques, from your own bank, allowing a couple of weeks before your departure.

The main British banks are now introducing "payment" cards which may be used abroad, to debit your British current account directly. These are not credit cards, but may become the most efficient way of paying for purchases and settling bills.

ANIMAL QUARANTINE

It is not advisable to take animals to France from the UK because of the six-month quarantine required by the British authorities on your return. However, if you do wish to take a pet to Brittany you need to have either a vaccination certificate for rabies, or a certificate to show that your country has been free of the disease for three years. No animal under three months of age can be taken into the country. For further information, contact the French Consulate in your country.

CUSTOMS

All personal effects may be imported without formality (including bicycles and sports equipment). It is forbidden to bring into the country any narcotics, pirated books, weapons and spiritous liquors which do not conform to French legislation. Certain items (e.g. alcoholic drinks, tobacco, perfume) are limited as to the amount you may take in, and these amounts vary for those coming from the European Community, other European countries or outside Europe.

For example, visitors coming from another EEC country can bring in 300 cigarettes, four litres of table wine and 1.5 litres of spirits; visitors from outside Europe are allowed 400 cigarettes, two litres of wine and one litre of spirits.

GETTING ACQUAINTED

GOVERNMENT & ECONOMY

For years the French put up with a very centralised form of government, but under the Socialists (1981-86) the Paris-appointed *préfets* lost much of their power as the individual *départements* (or counties) gained their own directly elected assemblies for the first time, giving them far more financial and administrative autonomy. Each *département* still has a *préfet*, but the role is now much more advisory. The *préfec*-Côtes-du-Nord; Quimper in Finistère; Rennes (also the regional capital) in Ille-et-Vilaine; and Vannes in Morbihan. These offices handle most matters concerned with the social welfare of their citizens.

Each *département* is divided into a number of disparately-sized communes whose district councils control a town, village or group of villages under the direction of the local mayor. Communes are now responsible for most local planning and environmental matters.Decisions relating to tourism and culture are mostly dealt with at regional level, while the state still controls education, the health service and security.

The economy in Brittany has obviously had a boost in recent years from the development of tourism, making coastal areas less dependent on declining profits from fishing. However, tourism is not the only thriving industry: Rennes has been an important centre for printing for more than a century; Citroën established itself in the region over 20 years ago and more recently Brittany has developed a reputation for excellence in the hi-tech field, particularly communications—Ille-et-Vilaine was the first *département* to have the Minitel system—the tele-phone/computer-linked telephone information service.

Agriculture remains an important earner in the region: nearly three-quarters of the nation's cauliflowers and artichokes come from Brittany. Indeed, it was because of a farming co-operative, set up by farmer Alex Gourvennec, needing to export to Britain, that Brittany Ferries was launched and rapidly the freight service developed to carry passengers and cars and become one of the region's most important companies.

GEOGRAPHY & CLIMATE

Out on a 150-mile (250-km) peninsula, it is self-evident that Brittany is primarily a coastal region. Indeed, its Celtic name was *Armor*—country of the sea. Its coastline stretches for practically 650 miles (1,000 km), from the so-called Emerald Coast with famous resorts such as Dinard and Cancale, across the channel coast of Côtes-du-Nord, around the beautiful, rugged Finistère coast with its many rocky promontories to the southernmost Atlantic coast of Morbihan whose fine sandy beaches and inlets are ideal for water sports. Dotted around the coast are a series of windswept islands: Belle-Isle-en-Mer is the largest and most visited.

The Celtic name for inland Brittany was *Argoat*, meaning woodland, as at that time the region was heavily forested. Now, however, the woods have given way to moorland (not unlike that of Scotland), and a fairly varied countryside. In the northeast, the Parc Naturel d'Armorique was created in the late 1960s to protect the local environment and wildlife. In the south, two areas of particular interest border the region of the Western Loire: the Brière Nature Park is in fact a vast, drained peat bog, where some of the local people still make a living from the peat and reeds; and the Guérande Salt Marshes (now only minimally panned for salt), famous for its lamb.

The climate is a maritime one—be prepared for strong breezes from the sea—similar to Cornwall, but usually more reliable for sunshine, The average temperature in July and August is around 70°F, 20°C, so lightweight clothes are all that is needed, with a sweater or jacket to keep off the winds. The French are fairly informal about dress, so do not feel you have to dress up for restaurants. Winter brings frosts, but not, in general, snow.

TIME ZONES

For almost all the year, Brittany, like the rest of France, is one hour behind Greenwich Mean Time, so if it is noon in Brittany, it is 1 p.m. in London, 6 a.m. in New York and Toronto and 9 p.m. in Melbourne.

CULTURE & CUSTOMS

It is impossible today to separate Brittany from its Celtic heritage, which can be discerned in every aspect of its culture and customs: religious observances, costumes, architecture, music and of course the language—particularly apparent to the visitor in place names. The ideal way for visitors to acquaint themselves with the Breton traditions is to attend one of the major festivals when musicians and dancers from all over the region gather in traditonal costumes to play traditional music on original instruments such as the *binou*—a type of bagpipe. Some of the best of these festivals (including some more modern ones) are listed in the Culture Plus section under Live Arts.

Apart from the festivals, the major traditional spectacle in Brittany is the *pardon*. Once a serious religious affair, when the faithful folk of Brittany used to follow a statue of their own particular saint through the village streets to church, there to ask forgiveness for their sins, the *pardons* are now more secular in outlook and a tourist attraction in their own right. Some of the major *pardons* are listed below.

Breton *pardons*
Arranged alphabetically by location
Bubry: 4th Sunday in July
Camaret: 1st Sunday in September

Carantec: 3rd Sunday in July & Sunday after 15 August
Carnac: 2nd Sunday in September
Fouesnant: Sunday after 26 July
Guincamp: Eve of 1st Sunday in July
Hennebont: Last Sunday in September
Josselin: 8 September
Le Faouet: Last Sunday in June & 4 December
Le Folgoet: 4th Sunday in July & 1st Sunday in September
Locronan: 2nd Sunday in July
Montcontour: Whit Sunday
Notre-Dame-du-Crann Chapel: Trinity Sunday (1st Sunday after Whitsun)
Notre-Dame-de-Tronoen: 3rd Sunday in September
Penhors: 1st Sunday in September
Perros-Guirec: 15 August
Persquen: 3rd Sunday in July
Ploerdut: Sunday after 15 August
Plouguerneau: Last Sunday in June & last Sunday in September
Quelven: 15 August
Quintin: 2nd Sunday in May
Rumengol: Trinity Sunday (1st Sunday after Whitsun)
Ste-Anne-d'Auray: 26 July
Ste-Anne-la-Palud: Sunday after 15 August
St Herbot: Ascension Day (normally mid-May)
St-Jean-du-Doigt: Last Sunday in June
St-Tugen: Sunday before St John's Day (24 June)
Treguier: 19 May

Arranged by date
Ascension Day (normally mid-May): St. Herbot
2nd Sunday in May: Quintin
Saturday to Whit Sunday: Montcontour
Whit Sunday: Carantec
19 May: Treguier
Trinity Sunday (1st Sunday after Whitsun): Notre-Dame-du-Crann Chapel; Rumengol
Sunday before St. John's Day (24 June): St.-Tugen
Last Sunday in June: Le Faouet; Plouguerneau; St-Jean-du-Doigt
Eve of 1st Sunday in July: Guincamp
2nd Sunday in July: Locronan
4th Sunday in July: Le Folgoet
26 July: Ste.-Anne-d'Auray
4th Sunday in July: Bubry

3rd Sunday in July: Carantec
3rd Sunday in July: Persquen
Sunday after 26 July: Fouesnant
15 August: Perros-Guirec; Quelven
Sunday after 15 August: Carantec; Ploerdut; Ste.-Anne-la-Palud
1st Sunday in September: Camaret; Le Folgoet; Penhors
8 September: Josselin
2nd Sunday in September: Carnac
3rd Sunday in September: Notre-Dame-de-Tronoen
Last Sunday in September: Hennebont; Plouguerneau
4 December: Le Faouet

LANGUAGE

French is the *lingua franca* of the region, but in recent years there has been a backlash against the enforced suppression of the Breton language by the French authorities. While there are only a small number of native Breton speakers, mostly in the west of the region, there has been a resurgence of interest recently in keeping the language alive. In particular, the Union for the Defence of the Breton Language has campaigned for it to be taught in schools and there is a Chair of Celtic Language at the University of Rennes.

Breton is made up of four dialects: the Trégorrois, the Léonard, the Cornouaillais and the Vannetais, this last being substantially different to the others.

Welsh speakers will find much in common with their own language, particularly in place names which often have similar prefixes and suffixes. The common ones listed below may help to identify the roots of some place names—e.g. Mor-bihan is small sea.

bihan small
braz large
coat, *goat*, *hoat* wood
ker village, hamlet or house
lann and *loc*, *log* consecrated ground (often a church)
men stone
mor sea
pl, *pleu*, *ploë*, *plou*, *plé* parish (often followed by name of local saint, e.g. *Ploërmel* St. Armel's parish).

WEIGHTS & MEASURES

The metric system is used in France for all weights and measures, although you may encounter old-fashioned terms such as *livre* (roughly one pound weight—500 grams) still used by small shopkeepers.

For quick and easy conversion remember that one inch is roughly 2.5 cm, one metre roughly equivalent to a yard, 4 oz is just over 100 g and a kilo is just over two lbs. As a kilometre is five-eighths of a mile, a handy reckoning while travelling is to remember that 80 km = 50 miles; 40 km = 25 miles. Accurate conversions are given below:

Weight
100 grammes (g) = 3.5 oz
500 grammes = 1.1 lb
1 kilo (kg) = 2.2 lb
Length
1 centimetre (cm) = 0.39 in
1 metre (m) = 1.094 yard
1 kilometre (km) = 0.62 mile
Liquid
1 litre (l) = 2.113 pints
1 litre = 0.22 Imp gallon; 0.26 US gallon
10 litres = 2.2 Imp gallons; 2.6 US gallons

TEMPERATURE

Temperatures are always given in Celsius (centigrade). For conversion to fahrenheit, see below:
  0° C = 32° F
 10° C = 50° F
 15° C = 59° F
 20° C = 68° F
 25° C = 77° F
 30° C = 86° F

ELECTRICITY

Electricity is generally cheaper than in the UK. However, even with the the benefit of the tidal power factory on the Rance, currents can be slightly variable. The current is generally 220/230 volts, but still 110 in some areas.

BUSINESS HOURS & HOLIDAYS

Office workers normally start early—8.30 a.m. is not uncommon, but often stay at their desks until 6 p.m. or later. This is partly to make up for the long lunch hours which are still a tradition in Brittany (from noon or 12.30 until 2 p.m.).

A list of major public holidays is given below. It is common practice, if a public holiday falls on a Thursday or Tuesday for French businesses to "*faire le pont*" (literally bridge the gap) and have the Friday or Monday as a holiday too. Details of closures should be posted outside banks etc. a few days before the event but it is easy to be caught out, especially on Assumption Day in August, which is not a holiday in the UK.

New Year's Day (1 Jan); Easter Monday (but not Good Friday); Labour Day (Mon closest to 1 May); Ascension Day; Whit Monday (Pentecost); Bastille Day (14 July); Assumption Day (15 Aug); All Saints' Day—Toussaint (1 Nov); Armistice Day (11 Nov); Christmas Day (25 Dec, but not Boxing Day).

COMMUNICATIONS

POSTAL SERVICES

Post Offices—Postes or PTTs (pronounced *pay-tay-tay*) are generally open Mon-Fri 9-12; 2-5 and Sat 9-12 (opening hours are posted outside). Inside major post offices, individual counters are marked for different requirements—if you just need stamps, go to the window marked *timbres*. If you need to send an urgent letter overseas, ask for it to be sent *par exprès*, or through the Chronopost system which is faster, but expensive.

Although France does not have a system of sub-post offices, stamps are often available at tobacconists (*tabacs*) and other shops selling postcards and greetings cards. Letters within France and most of the European Community go for F2.40 for up to 20g, (F2.50 for the UK and Ireland). Airmail to the USA is F4.05 for letters up to 5g.

Telegrams can be sent during post office hours or by telephone (24-hours); to send a telegram in English dial 16-1 42.33.21.11.

For a small fee, you can arrange for mail to be kept *poste restante* at any post office, addressed to Poste Restante, Poste Centrale (for main post office), then the town post code and name, eg. 35000 Rennes. A passport is required when collecting mail.

Many post offices have coin-in-slot photocopying machines.

Telex, Minitel information service and fax facilities are available in the main post office in most major towns.

The French telephone system has undergone a drastic overhaul in the past 20 years, and from being one of the worst in the world is now one of the best. That is not to say that you can be guaranteed to find telephone boxes (*cabines publiques*) that are always operational, but most are. Telephone numbers have been rationalised to eight figures, given in sets of two, eg. 99.44.63.21., the only codes necessary are for Paris (16-1) or overseas.

International calls can be made from most public booths, but it is often easier to use a booth in a post office—you have to ask at the counter to use the phone, then go back to the counter to settle the bill—the only unnerving thing is that you do not have any record of how much you are spending whilst on the phone.

Coin-operated phones take most coins and a recent innovation is the card phone, displaying the *Télécarte* sign. Cards are available from post offices, railway stations, some cafés and *tabacs*.

If you use a phone (not a public call box) in a café, shop or restaurant you are likely to be surcharged.

To make an international call, lift the receiver, insert the money (if necessary), dial 19, wait for the tone to change, then dial the country code (see below), followed by the number (omitting any initial 0).

International dialling codes:

Australia 61
Canada 1
Ireland 353
UK 44
USA 1

Useful numbers: operator services 13

Directory enquiries 12 (NB numbers will be given in pairs of figures, unless you ask for them to be given *chiffre par chiffre*—singly).

If you need to make a phone call in rural areas, or small villages with no public phone, look out for the blue plaque saying "*telephone publique*" on private houses. This means the owner is officially required to allow you to use the phone and charge the normal amount for the call.

You cannot reverse charges (call collect) within France but you can to countries which will accept such calls. Go through the operator and ask to make a PCV (*pay-say-vay*) call.

Regional newspapers, containing national and international as well as local news, have a far higher standing in France than in the UK and are often read in preference to the national dailies such as *Le Monde* (the most highly regarded of the serious papers), *Libération* and *Le Figaro*. In fact, Brittany's major regional daily, *Ouest-France*, has the largest circulation of any in France. This and the *Télégramme*, the other morning paper, are worth buying for listings of local events, such as *pardons*, festivals and nightlife. English-language papers, notably *The Times* and the *International Herald Tribune* are available in larger towns and cities of the region.

The Centre Commun d'Etudes de Télédiffusion et Télécommunications (CCETT) is situated in Rennes and so one would expect television to be fairly well deveoped in the region. In fact Rennes was the first city to have cable television, and the département of Ille-et-Vilaine the first to try out the Minitel (telephone-computer linked information system). On a more mundane level, viewers in Brittany can receive the two main national channels: TF1 (commercial) and Antenne 2 (state-owned but largely financed by advertising); as well as FR3 which offers regional programmes.

France Inter is the main national radio station (1892m long wave), it broadcasts English-language news twice a day in summer (generally 9 a.m. and 4 p.m.). BBC Radio Four and the World Service can also normally be received in Brittany.

EMERGENCIES

Sensible precautions regarding personal possessions is all that should really be necessary when visiting Brittany. Petty crime exists here as elsewhere but is not a serious problem. Drivers should follow the rules of the road and always drive sensibly. Heavy on-the-spot fines are given for traffic offences, such as speeding and drivers can be stopped and breathalysed during spot checks. Police are fairly visible on the main routes of France during the summer months.

To report a crime or loss of belongings, visit the local *gendarmerie* or *commisariat de police*. Telephone numbers are given at the front of local directories, or in an emergency, dial 117. If you lose a passport, report first to the police, then to the nearest consulate (see Useful Addresses). If you have the misfortune to be detained by the police for any reason, ask to telephone the nearest consulate for a member of the staff to come to your assistance.

HEALTH

Before leaving for France, check with the Department of Health that you qualify for subsidised treatment under the EEC (most British nationals do) and acquire from them the form Elll. Alternatively, arrange private medical insurance, as should all non-EEC citizens. The Elll does not cover the full cost of any treatment so you may find it worthwhile to take out private insurance too. The International Association for Medical Assistance to Travelers (IAMAT) publishes for its members a directory of English-speaking doctors abroad. Contact IAMAT at 736 Center St., Lewiston NY 14092, USA or 1268 St, Claire Ave W., Toronto M6E 1B9, Canada.

For minor ailments it may be worth consulting a *pharmacie* (recognisable by its green cross sign), who have wider "prescribing" powers than chemists in the UK or USA. They are also helpful in cases of snake or insect bites and identifying fungi! If you need to see a doctor, expect to pay around F80 for a simple consultation, plus a pharmacist's fee for whatever prescription is issued. The doctor will provide a *feuille des soins* which you need to keep to claim back the majority of the cost (around 75 percent) under the EEC agreement. You have to attach to the *feuille* the little sticker (*vignette*) from any medecine prescribed to enable you to claim for that too. Refunds have to be obtained from the local *Caisse Primaire* (ask the doctor or pharmacist for the address).

In cases of medical emergency, either dial 15 for an ambulance or call the Service d'Aide Médicale d'Urgence (SAMU) which exists in most large towns and cities—numbers are given at the front of telephone directories, at time of going to press, they are as follows:

Côtes du Nord (St-Brieuc) 96.94.40.15.
Finistère (Brest) 98.46.11.33.
Ille-et-Vilaine (Rennes) 99.59.16.16.
Morbihan (Vannes) 97.54.22.11.

The standard of treatment in Brittany's hospitals is generally high, and you should be able to find someone who speaks English to help you. Show the hospital doctor or authorities your Elll and you will be billed (once you are back home usually), for approximately 80 percent of the cost of treatment.

GETTING AROUND

MAPS

A first essential in touring any part of France is a good map. The Institute Géographique National is the French equivalent of the British Ordnance Survey and their maps are excellent; those covering Brittany are listed below:

Red Series (1:250,000, 1 cm to 2.5 km) sheet 105 covers the whole of Brittany including Nantes.

Green Series (1:100,000 (1 cm to 1 km) corresponds roughly to the individual départements—sheet nos. 13, 14, 15 and 16.

Also available are the highly detailed 1:50,000 and 1:25,000 scales.

The Michelin regional map sheet no. 230 covers Brittany at a scale of 1:200,000 (1 cm to 2 km). Michelin also publish town plans, as do Blay, but local tourist offices often give away their own free town plans.

In the UK, McCarta of 122 King's Cross Road, London WC1X 9DS, Tel. 01-278 8276 is the best source for all general and specialist maps (eg walking and waterways, see below). They also offer a mail-order service—their French map catalogue is available on request. Also in London is Stanfords Map Shop, 12 Long Acre, Covent Garden WC2. Tel. 01-836 1321. In Brittany, most good bookshops should have a range of maps, but they can often be bought more cheaply in hypermarkets or service stations.

DOMESTIC TRAVEL

Unless you are staying in one place or just visiting cities, some form of private trans-

port will be necessary in rural Brittany. Car hire is very expensive, but bikes are fairly readily available (most railway stations have them for hire at around F50 per day). Bikes can be carried free of charge on buses and some trains (*Autotrains*), on other, faster services you will have to pay. Travelling by bike and bus or train can be an excellent way of touring the Brittany countryside, and relieves you of some of the legwork. Cycling holidays run in conjuction with French Railways (SNCF) are organised by A.B.R.I. (see Useful Addresses).

Bus and rail stations are often found together and details of routes and timetables are generally available free of charge. If you intend to travel extensively by train it may be worth obtaining one of the rail passes available before leaving home (see Getting There).

These tickets can be used on any journey, otherwise individual tickets need to be purchased, but check on any discounts available, e.g. the *Carte Couple* for married couples travelling together on off-peak services. Children under four travel free, from four to twelve for half-fare. All tickets have to be put through the orange machines at the stations to validate them before boarding the train. These machines are marked *compostez votre billet*.

DRIVING

Driving in rural Brittany can be an absolute pleasure after the chaos and congestion in other parts of France and in Britain. Those used to driving on the left generally don't take long to get used to driving on the right; but particular care needs to be taken if, for example, you cross the road to use a service station—it's very easy to come out and automatically drive on the left, especially if there's no other traffic around. British, US, Canadian and Australian licences are all valid in France and you should always carry your car's registration document and valid insurance (third party is the absolute minimum, but a green card—available from your insurance company—is strongly recommended).

Additional insurance cover, which can

include a get-you-home service, is offered by a number of organisations including the British and American Automobile Associations and Europ-Assistance, 252 High Street, Croydon CR0 1NF. Tel. 0l-680 1234; in the US: Europ Assistance Worldwide Services Inc, ll33 15th Street, Suite 400, Washington DC 20005. Tel. 202 347 7113.

RULES OF THE ROAD

The use of seat belts (front and rear if fitted) and crash helmets for motorcyclists is compulsory. Priority is given to traffic approaching from the right, except where otherwise indicated by any of the following signs:

STOP

cedez le passage give way.

vous n' avez pas la priorité you do not have right of way.

passsage protégé no right of way.

This is an important rule to remember, especially in towns; on main roads, the major route will normally have priority. Speed limits are as follows 130 kph (80 mph) on motorways; 110 kph (68 mph) on dual carriageways; 90 kph (56 mph) on other roads except in towns where the limit is 60 kph (37 mph). On-the-spot fines can be levied for speeding.

Nearly all motorways (*autoroutes*) are toll roads, so you will need to have some cash with you. However, the only autoroute in Brittany is the one from Paris which stops before Rennes. Autoroutes are designated "A" roads, national highways "N" roads, "D" roads are usually well maintained, while "C" or local roads, may not always be so.

You must carry a red triangle to place 50 metres behind the car in case of a breakdown or accident. In an accident or emergency, call the police (dial 17) or use the free emergency telephones (every two km) on motorways. It is useful to carry an European Accident Statement Form (obtainable from your insurance company) which will simplify matters in the case of an accident.

For information about current road conditions, telephone the regional Highway Information centre at Rennes: 99.32.33.33.

CAR HIRE

Hiring a car is an expensive business in France, partly because of the high VAT (TVA) rate—33 percent on luxury items. Some fly/drive deals work out reasonably well if you're only going for a short visit— Air France for instance do a weekend fly drive trip to Nantes. It can be cheaper to arrange hire in the UK or USA before leaving for France. Offices of the major car hire companies are listed below:

AVIS
Brest: 3 boulevard des Français Libres. Tel. 98.44.63.02.
Dinard: Aéroport de Pleurtit. Tel. 99.46.25.20.
Lorient: 14 boulevard Leclerc. Tel. 97.21.00.12.
Quimper: 8 avenue de la Gare. Tel. 98.90.31.34.
St-Brieuc: 2 boulevard Clemenceau. Tel. 96.33.44.14.
St-Malo: Gare Maritime du Naye. Tel. 99.81.73.24.

BUDGET
Central reservation: freephone 05.10.00.01; also offices at
Brest: 1 rue Georges Didailler. Tel. 98.41.70.60.
Rennes: 11 rue de la Santé. Tel. 9.65.13.21.

EUROPCAR
Auray: 38 rue Jean-Jaurès. Tel. 97.24.23.33.
Brest: 43 rue Voltaire. Tel. 98.44.66.88.
Dinard: Aéroport de Pleurtit. Tel. 99.46.75.70.
Lannion: 10 avenue de Général de Gaulle. Tel. 96.37.02.l7.
Morlaix: rue des Lavoirs. Tel. 98.62.11.94
Pontivy: 10 rue Quinivet. Tel. 97.25.07.26.
Quiberon: avenue du Généeral de Gaulle. Tel. 97.50.07.42.
Quimper: 12 rue de Concarneau. Tel. 98.90.00.68.
Rennes: 56 avenue du Mail, Rennes. Tel. 99.59.50.50.
St-Brieuc: 11 boulevard Charner. Tel. 96.94.45.45.
St-Malo: 16 boulevard des Talards. Tel. 99.56.75.17.

Vannes: 46 avenue Victor Hugo. Tel. 97.42.43.43.

HERTZ
Brest: 14 rue Colbert. Tel. 98.80.11.51.
Guingamp: boulevard de la Marne. Tel. 96.43.74.71.
Lannion: 6 quai de Viarmes. Tel. 96.37.09.95.
Rennes: 10 avenue du Mail. Tel. 99.54.26.52.
St-Brieuc: 53 rue de la Gare. Tel. 96.94.25.89.
St-Malo: 48 boulevard de la République. Tel. 99.56.3161.

INTERRENT
Brest: rue Colbert. Tel. 98.43.15.39.
Lorient: 19bis boulevard Svob. Tel. 97.64.22.47.
Rennes: 31 aveune L. Barthou. Tel. 99.31.57.33.
St-Malo: 81 rue Ville Pépin. Tel. 99.81.64.03.
Vitré: 46 boulevard Chateaubriand. Tel. 99.75.03.49.

INLAND WATERWAYS

There can be few more relaxing ways of exploring rural France than cruising at a snail's pace along its inland waterways, and Brittany is especially well endowed in this respect with some 600 km of navigable rivers and canals. The main ones are the Nantes-Brest canal, the Aulne and the Blavet. Many companies hire fully equipped craft from early spring to late autumn. Some companies offering boat hire and all-in-holidays are listed below.

Chemins Nautiques Bretons, Le Port Lyvet, La Vicomté-sur-Rances, 22690 Pleudihen. Tel. 96.83.28.71 (English spoken).

Blue Line Cruisers, Freepost PO Box 1000, Croydon CR9 6ES. Tel. (0883) 40721.

Hoseasons Holidays Abroad, A42 Sunway House, Lowestoft, Suffolk NR32 3LT. Tel. (0502) 501501.

SFV Holidays, Summer House, Hearnes Road, Summertown, Oxford. Tel. (0865) 57738—represents seven canal companies in Brittany.

Waterways guides and other information are available from the Comité des Canaux Bretons at A.B.R.I. (see Useful Addresses). There is also an excellent guide published in French/English by ECM called *Brittany Rivers and Canals* (£9.65) which gives technical and navigational information along with mooring points, where to buy food and tourist attractions on or near the waterway. The guide is available in the UK from McCarta (see Maps).

An alternative to a canal crusing holiday, but maybe one less suited to families with young children is to hire a canoe and either camp or stay in hotels. Holidays such as these are offered by the Loisirs Accueil services of the tourist authorities (see useful addresses) or by private companies such as VVF, 5 Worlds End Lane, Green Street Green, Orpington, Kent BR6 6AA. Tel. 0689 62904. The A.B.R.I. organisation (see Useful Addresses) can also provide information on canoeing and kayaks.

RAMBLERS

Brittany offers excellent opportunities for walkers, whether for a complete walking holiday, or just for a day's outing. There is a network of long-distance footpaths (*Sentiers de Grandes Randonnées* or *GR*) covering the whole of France; in Brittany these are mainly inland, but some stretches cover the coast, for instance part of the GR34 goes from Mont-St-Michel to St-Malo and then follows the splendid Granit Rose coast as far as Lannion. Inland there are a some good round trips, eg the Tour des Chouans (for which Vitré would be a good starting point) and the Tour des Monts d'Arrée (the region's highest hills) which takes in the *enclos paroissiaux* (the parish closes, noted for their elaborate church architecture).

The Fédération Française de la Randonnée Pédestre (FFRP) based at 8 avenue Marceau, 75008 Paris. Tel. 1.723.62.32. publishes *Topoguides* (guide books incorporating IGN 1:50,000 scale maps) to all France's footpaths but they are in French.

Two new publications from Robertston-McCarta are: *Coastal Walks—St-Malo to Roscoff*, and *Walks in Brittany* which covers inland routes. The guides will include information about accommodation along the way. All the above are available in the UK from McCarta (see Maps), or in Brittany, *Topoguides* are available from A.B.R.I.(see useful addresses) and good bookshops. A.B.R.I. also offers walking holidays in conjunction with SNCF (with a 30 percent reduction on rail fares).

The local representatives of the French Ramblers Association (FFRP) can be contacted at the following addresses:

Brittany region: Comité de Bretagne de la FFRP. 14 boulevard Beaumont, 35000 Rennes. Tel. 99.30.55.15 (Wed afternoon or Sat morning).

Côtes-du-Nord: OT/SI Gare Routière, boulevard Rousseau, BP 448, 22000 St-Brieuc.

Finistère: M Chevalier, Coatufal, 29290 St-Renan.

Ille-et-Vilaine: 14 boulevard Beaumont, 35100 Rennes.

Morbihan: Mairie, BP 14, 56150 Baud.

If you want to join a group of hikers, the following organisations arrange walks which visitors to the region are welcome to join:

A.B.R.I. (see useful addresses)

Henchou Koz, c/o Mme Garrec, 13 Cité St-Cado, Ploumilliau, 22300 Lannion.

Association Populaire pour l'Inventaire, l'Etude et le Développement des sentiers, c/o M Vichard, 8 rue G.-de Maupassant, 29200 Brest.

Association de défense des usagers des chemins piétonniers et de la nature, c/o M Ollivier, 3 rue des Hurlières, 35210 Châtillon-en-Vendelais.

Randonneurs Gallos, c/o M Guisnel, 16 rue André-Désilles, 35000 Rennes.

Sentiers Nature de Gévézé, 4 rue des Fauvettes, Gévézé, 35850 Romillé.

Eveil et Connaissance, Languidic Randonnée, BP 13, 56440 Languidic.

HITCHHIKING

With sensible precautions, hitchhiking can be an interesting and inexpensive way to get around Brittany. Would-be hitchhikers may be discouraged by the difficulty of getting a lift out of the channel ports, so it may be worth taking a bus or train for the first leg of your journey. Hitching is forbidden on motorways, but you can wait on slip roads or at toll booths. Allostop is a nationwide organisation which aims to connect hikers with drivers (you pay a registration fee and a contribution towards the petrol). Telephone numbers are: Paris (1) 42.46.00.66; Rennes 99.30.98.87; Nantes 40.89.04.85.

WHERE TO STAY

Finding the accommodation you require in Brittany depends very much on whether you are travelling "on spec", staying where the fancy takes you, or whether you wish to have everything booked in advance of departure. Both are of course feasible, the former more fun maybe, but not necessarily with a young family in tow, and not at the height of August when *la toute France* (and everyone else come to that) is *en vacances*.

HOTELS

There are over one thousand hotels in the Brittany region, so to single out just a few for recommendation would seem to be fairly pointless; instead, a few facts (and some opinions) to make the choosing and booking easier.

All French hotels are classified (by a simple star-rating system), by the national Ministry of Tourism. One-star hotels are plain, but fairly comfortable, while four-star (L) are *grande luxe* with prices to match. The system has several advantages, not least that if you budget to stay in one or two-star hotels you can expect to pay around the same kind of price for your room each night.

Hotels are required to show their menus outside the hotel and details of room prices should be visible in reception and on the back of individual room doors. It is possible for a hotel to have a one-star rating, with a two-star restaurant. This is great if you're more interested in your food than the odd bit of fading wallpaper or eccentric plumbing.

When booking a room, you should normally be taken to see it before agreeing to take it; if it doesn't suit you, ask to be shown another (this may sound odd advice, but rooms can vary enormously within the same building).

Prices are charged per room (supplements may be charged for additional beds, cots etc.). A double room in a single-star hotel may cost as little as F80, in a two-star the average is more likely to be Fl50-l80. Do not be surprised if you're asked when booking if you wish to dine (preference should not, but may in fact, be given to hungry customers, as there is not a lot of profit in letting rooms alone), also the simple request, "*On peut dîner ce soir?*" will confirm that the hotel's restaurant is open (many are closed on Sun and Mon evenings).

Lists of hotels in the region can be obtained from French Government Tourist offices, who can also supply the invaluable (free) *Logis et Auberges de France* guide (also available from their Paris HQ, see below). This is an association of family-run hotels who aim to offer a friendly welcome and good local cuisine. In more than a dozen years of travelling in France, the present writer has only once been disappointed in a Logis hotel—and that was only because they served tinned peas! Use the guide while travelling, or to choose and reserve in advance a resort hotel (in which case a deposit or *arrhes*, will be required).

If you are not restricted by a budget and want to stay at the very best hotels in Brittany, try those in the Relais et Châteaux chain (see below)—there are seven in Brittany with rooms from F360 upwards. If you're stuck for somewhere to stay, always try the local tourist office (*syndicat d'initiative*) where the service will vary from simply providing a list of hotels to booking one for you.

The following organisations are hotel chains or associations which will make your bookings for you:

Brittany Hotels, Le Jarrier, St-Herblain, 44150 Ancenis. Tel. 40.96.00.03.

Minotels France Accueil, 85 rue du Dessous-des-Berges, 75013 Paris. Tel. (1) 45.83.04.22; overseas offices: UK: France Accueil Hotels (UK) Ltd., 10 Salisbury Hollow, Edington, Westbury, Wiltshire BA13 4PF. Tel. (0380) 830125. US: Extra Value Travel Inc., 689 S. Collier Boulevard, USA Marco Island, 33937 Florida. Tel. (813) 394.33.84—toll free (800) 336.46.68.

Climat de France, BP 93, 91943 Les Ulis

Cedex. Central reservations: tel. freephone 05.11.22.11.

France Accueil, Hôtel Bellevue, 20 rue des Calcuots, 22730 Trégastel-Plage. Tel. 96.23.88.18.

Relais et Châteaux of Brittany, Château-Hôtel de Locguénolé, 56700 Hennebont. Tel. 97.76.29.04.

Logis et Auberges de France, 23 rue Jean-Mermoz, 75008 Paris. Tel. (1) 359.91.99. (no central booking office—book direct with owners).

Hotels Abroad, 5 World's End Lane, Green Street Green, Orpington, Kent BR6 6AA. Tel. (0689) 57838.

BED & BREAKFAST

Apart from members of the Fédération Nationale des Gîtes Ruraux de France, who have always offered a few *chambres d' hôtes* (guest rooms), the notion of bed and breakfast, so well established in the UK, is a recent one in France. It has always been so easy to find good, cheap hotels in France that there has been less need for this kind of accommodation.

Now, however, visitors to the country are more keen to get to know the local people and enjoy their hospitality. This is the idea behind Café-Couette, a private association of more than 400 (over 40 in Brittany) host members who offer guest rooms (and sometimes evening meals), on a bed and breakfast basis. To make a booking, you have first to become a member (£12 per person/£30 per family), then you will receive the latest Café-Couette guide along with details of how to book and current prices (ranging in 1989 from £12.50 to £25 per person per night).

Café-Couette: Bed and Breakfast (France), PO Box 66, Henley-on-Thames, Oxon RG9 1XS. Tel. (0491) 578803. The company are also happy to handle bookings from the USA, Canada and Australia.

A luxurious version of the Café-Couette idea is offered by Châteaux et Manoirs de Bretagne, where you can stay as a private guest in some of the finest country houses in Brittany. For details contact the Brittany Chamber of Commerce in London (see Useful Addresses).

B & B Abroad, part of the Hotels Abroad organisation (see above) also offer a bed and breakfast service which can include ferry bookings if desired. Their brochure currently lists nine homes in Brittany.

SELF-CATERING

France offers what is probably the best network of self-catering holiday cottages anywhere in Europe. The Fédération des Gîtes Ruraux de France was set up some 30 years ago with the main aim of restoring rural properties (by means of offering grants to owners) on the condition that these properties would then be let as cheap holiday homes for the less-well off town and city dwellers. These impoverished urban holidaymakers can mostly now afford to laze on the Mediterranean, while the *gîtes* have become the rural idylls of the middle-class English. Brittany has a terrific selection of *gîtes* (literally, a place to lay one's head), and unusually for rural properties, a fair smattering of these are on the coast. They range from very simple farm cottages to grand manor houses and even the odd château.

The properties are all inspected by the Relais Départemental (the county office of the national federation) and given an "*épi*" (ear of corn) classification. The *gîtes* are completely self-catering (in many cases expect to supply your own bedlinen), but most have owners living nearby who will tell you where to buy local produce (and if on a farm, often provide it). One salutary note—many of these cottages are on farms, and as such, are surrounded by wildlife so if you are squeamish about the odd mouse in the kitchen, stay in an hotel.

However, the properties should be and generally are, kept clean and in good order. Most are rather off the beaten track and a car, or at least a bicycle is usually essential. Bicycles can often be hired locally or even from *gîte* owners. Car hire is horribly expensive, but some fly/drive packages still make this a relatively inexpensive way to visit Brittany, as *gîtes* can cost as little as Fl000 a week for the whole house.

Many companies now offer "package

tours" to *gîtes* and other self-catering properties, which include ferry travel and other
services. A few are listed below, see also the
small ads in the Sunday press. *Gîtes* do get
very heavily booked in high season, so start
the process in the New Year. If you prefer to
deal directly with France, the Relais Départemental will send you a list of all the *gîtes* in
their *département*. Alternatively, you can
book through the London booking office:
Gîtes de France, 178 Picadilly, W1V 9DB.
Tel. 01 493 3480—for a £3 membership you
have the choice of 250 *gîtes* in Brittany; or
buy the *French Farm and Village Holiday
Guide*, price £4.95 (Farm Holiday Guides,
Seedhill, Paisley PA1 1JN), available in the
US from Hunter Publishing Inc., 300 Rari-
tan Center, Parkway, Edison, N.J. 08818,
price $12.95. This book lists around 70 *gîtes*
in Brittany with full details for the independent traveller of how to book (sample letters
in French are given).

The main ferry companies also offer *gîte*
holidays in association with the Gîtes de
France office in London—apply to the ferry
companies for their brochures.

Relais des Gîtes Ruraux;

Côtes-du-Nord: 28 boulevard Hérault,
22000 St-Brieuc. Tel. 96.61.82.79.

Finistère: Maison de l'Agriculture, Stang
Vihan, B.P. 504, 29109 Quimper. Tel.
98.95.75.30.

Ille-et-Vilaine and Morbihan, write to
Loisirs Accueil addresses (see Useful Addresses).

"Package" Holiday Operators:

Vacances en Campagne, Bignor, nr Pul-
borough, W. Sussex RH20 1QD. Tel.
(07987) 433. Overseas agents—USA: Mr
Carl Stewart, 153 West 13th Street, New
York, NY 10011; Canada: Mr Douglas
McKay, European Villas, 27 Gordon Rose
Crescent, Richmond Hill, Toronto, Ontario
L4C 8R9; Australia: Mr Peter Monie, 11
Laver Street, Kew, Victoria 3101.

Vacances, 28 Gold Street, Saffron
Walden, Essex CB10 1EJ. Tel. (0799)
25101. Do not have overseas agents but have
handled bookings from Villas International,
71 West 23rd Street, New York, NY10010,
and will deal with overseas queries direct.

Starvillas Ltd., 25 High Street, Chester-
ton, Cambridge CB2 1ND. Tel. (0223)
311990. Handles bookings from overseas.

CAMPING

Brittany, with more sites than any other
region of France, is an ideal base for campers, especially for UK visitors who do not
fancy a long haul south with heavily laden
car or caravan in tow. The majority of Brittany's 11,000 official sites are located along
the region's long coastline, with particular
concentrations around popular destinations
such as Dinard, the Quiberon peninsula,
Bénodet and Carnac.

As with hotels, the sites get heavily
booked in high season, so advance booking
is well worth considering, either directly
with the site, or through the Centrale de
Reservation run for the Brittany tourist
board by Camping Plus, 69 Westbourne
Grove, London W2 4UJ. Tel. 01-792 1944,
who can confirm bookings immediately as
they have an allocation of pitches on all the
official sites.

Camp sites, like hotels have official clas-
sifications from one-star (minimal comfort,
water points, showers and sinks) to four-star
luxury sites which allow more space to each
pitch, and offer above-average facilities,
often including a restaurant or takeway
food, games areas and even swimming-
pools. The majority of sites are two-star.
Average prices are around F20 per family
per night at a one-star site, to around F140 at
a four-star.

If you really like to get back to nature, and
are unimpressed by the modern trappings of
hot water and electric power, look out for
camp-sites designated *Aire naturelle de
camping* where facilities will be absolutely
minimal and prices to match. These have a
maximum of 25 pitches so offer the opportunity to stay away from some of the more
commerical sites which can be huge.

Some farms offer "official" sites too
under the auspices of the Fédération Nationale des Gîtes Ruraux—these are designated
Camping à la ferme, and again facilities are
usually limited but farmers are only allowed
to have six pitches and if you are lucky you
will get to know and enjoy the farm life and
some of its produce.

Packaged camping holidays are becoming more and more popular with British
holidaymakers and are ideal for overseas

visitors too, as all the camping paraphernalia is provided on the site—you only have to take your normal luggage. Many companies now offer these type of holidays, mostly with ferry travel in the all-in price.

Like other package tours, the companies have couriers on the sites to help with any problems. It is interesting to note that where such companies have taken over sections of existing sites, facilities have improved to meet the demands of their customers and so benefit all campers. Be warned though that some of the sites are very large, so might not suit those who wish to get away from it all.

For a list of Brittany's campsites, write to Camping Plus (see above), the regional tourist office (see Useful Addresses), or enquire at the French Government Tourist Office in your country. A selection of the package operators is listed below, for others check the Sunday press.

Canvas Holidays, Bull Plain, Hertford, Herts. SG14 1DY. Tel. (0992) 553535—one of the first in the field.

Eurocamp, Edmundson House, Tatton Street, Knutsford, Cheshire WA16 6BG. Tel. (0565) 3844—25 sites in Brittany.

Carefree Camping, 126 Hempstead Road, King's Langley, Herts WD4 8AL. Tel. (09277) 61311.

Brittany Ferries, The Brittany Centre, Wharf Road, Portsmouth PO2 8RU. Tel. (0705) 751708.

YOUTH HOSTELS

Holders of accredited Youth Hostel Association cards may stay in any of Brittany's hostels which are in fact run by two separate organisations; Fédération Unie des Auberges de Jeunesse (FUAJ), 27 rue Pajol, 75018 Paris. Tel. (1) 42.41.59.00, which is affiliated to the International Youth Hostel Federation, and by the Ligue Francaise pour les auberges de jeunesse (LFAJ), 83 rue de Rennes, 75006 Paris. Tel. (1) 45.49.11.73.

The British YHA publishes the *International Youth Hostel Handbook*, Vol I (revised each March), which includes all the hostels in Brittany, price £4 by post from Youth Hostel Association, 14 Southampton Street, London WC2E 7H7. Tel. (01) 836

8541. They will also handle membership queries.

In the USA apply to the American Youth Hostel Inc, PO Box 37613, Washington DC 29 hostels, write to the Association Bretonne des Auberges de Jeunesse, 41 rue Victor-Schoelcher, 56100 Lorient. Tel. 97.37.11.65.

Gîtes d'Etape offer hostel accommodation and are popular with ramblers and horse riders (some offer stabling). All official *gîtes d'étape* come under the auspices of the Relais Départementaux des Gîtes Ruraux (for addresses see self-catering above). Prices are similar to youth hostels (around F20 per night for basic accommodation), but you do not have to be member of any organisation to use them.

FOOD DIGEST

Every region of France has its own specialities and delicacies, but those of Brittany tend to be rather overlooked by most food "experts", which is a great shame. While Brittany may not be considered France's gastronomic capital, the food here is just as good (and good value) as elsewhere in the country—with some extra bonuses such as the wonderful seafood and the Breton speciality—*crêpes* and *galettes.*

It is still traditional in Brittany to have a big meal at lunchtime and if indeed you have the appetite to do so, then start looking for a restaurant at ll.45 a.m. because the good ones fill up quickly. All restaurants display their menus outside and all will offer a *prix fixe* (fixed price) menu as well as *à la carte.* Look for the handwritten menus that are obviously changed daily, then you will be assured of the freshest produce and probably the most inventive cuisine. *Prix fixe* menus often offer superb value—three or even four courses from around F60. Some menus include wine (*vin compris*) and although this is usually the cheapest house wine it is often quite drinkable.

Brittany offers more opportunities than most of France for a light meal at lunchtime because of the abundance of *crêperies*—a simple buckwheat *galette* (savoury pancake) comes with a variety of delicious fillings—cheese, seafood, mushrooms, ham—and will probably keep most people going until dinnertime for less than F20. You do have to have an iron will however to resist the delicious sweet *crêpes* with fillings of chocolate, strawberry or apple, laced possibly with chantilly cream.

If the weather is just too good to sit in a restaurant then splendid picnics can be concocted without any effort, by a visit to the baker for fresh bread, the *fromagerie* for delicious camembert, the *charcuterie* for ready-prepared quiches, patés, various salads, cooked chicken quarters and other delights, topped off with a bottle of cool muscadet and fresh peaches. Remember, though, to get all this organised before the long lunchtime close-down at noon.

A trip to Brittany is hardly complete without a visit to a good seafood restaurant—and they are not hard to find! A *plateau de fruits de mer* (seafood platter) generally comes on a great metal dish, totally dominating the table. The shellfish has come out of the sea only hours earlier; two people will share a crab each, piles of shrimps, prawns and langoustines in their shells, a generous portion of oysters (the French eat them first), mussels, cockles, whelks and winkles all laid out on crushed ice and decorated with seaweed. It is not so much a meal as an entertainment, with pins to prise the whelks and cockles out of their shells and strong crackers to open the crabs which in Brittany are never dressed, but arrive just as they've left the boiling pot a short while before. Other typically Breton seafood dishes include mussels (not served *marinières* as in the rest of France, but simmered in cider and finished with cream); *cotriade*—fish soup; *homard à l'Armoricaine* (the correctly spelt version of the popular *homard à l'Américaine*)—lobster in a delicious sauce of wine, brandy, garlic, shallots and tomato.

Meat dishes often borrow recipes from neighbouring Normandy, so *escalopes à la normande,* for example, is commonly seen—veal fillets in a creamy sauce with maybe the addition of some calvados and mushrooms. One truly regional meat dish though is the *gigot pré-salé,* roast lamb from herds raised on the region's flat salt marshes.

Brittany is one of the few regions in France not to have its own viticulture. Dry, crisp white muscadet which is an excellent accompaniment to seafood is the closest thing to a local wine, coming as it does from the Nantes area which most Bretons still consider to be part of Brittany anyway. Otherwise, all restaurants will have a selection of the country's wines.

But, just as a pint of beer helps a ploughman's lunch go down in an English pub, so Brittany cider is the best thing to drink with some of the local dishes—particularly savoury pancakes. Cider really is the local brew of the region—do not be surprised when it is served from a jug into a large teacup, in traditional style. After your meal, try a digestif of Calvados—apple brandy produced in Brittany and Normandy.

TIPPING

Most restaurant bills will include a service charge, but if in doubt ask—*"Le service, est-il compris?"*. In any case, it is common to leave a small additional tip if for the waiter or waitress if service has been good. Please remember to address waiters as *"Monsieur"*—never *"garçon"* and waitresses as *"Mademoiselle"* or *"Madame"* (according to age).

WHERE TO EAT

If you want to try a meal in really different surroundings, and are not of a queasy disposition, you can take a gastronomic cruise on a floating restaurant—for example, the *Chateaubriand*. This boat leaves for lunch and evening meals from the Port de la Richardais, near the barrage on the Rance river and cruises around the bays of Dinard and St-Malo while you dine. Three menus are offered from around F180 to F240, which includes the price of the cruise. For more information contact Société Maritime de la Rance, BP 27, 35780 La Richardais. Tel. 99.46.44.44. If you prefer to stay firmly on *terra firma*, then you will have no difficulty in finding a restaurant within your budget and to suit your taste. Bear in mind that nearly all restaurants (including those in hotels) are closed on Mondays, and many also on Sunday nights.

In rural areas, seek out a *ferme-auberge*, but build up a good appetite first. *Fermes-auberges* are usually on working farms and offer a fixed-price meal, usually with little choice, but all home-cooked there and then, using local produce—often from the farm itself. Portions are usually suited to farmhands' appetites and wine may be included in the very reasonable price. These are not restaurants, but family homes where you will be made to feel like a guest, not a visitor. Local *syndicat d'initiatives* can provide lists of *fermes-auberges* in your locality and you normally have to book in advance, as meals are prepared as required. Most provide lunches only.

If you want to try the finest in Brittany cuisine, make a booking at one of the following restaurants—many of these have earned praise from Gault-Millau and Michelin which shows in the prices, but some also provide set menus at around F100.

Côtes-du-Nord

Auberge Grand'Maison, 1 rue Léon-le-Cerf, 22530 MUR-DE-BRETAGNE. Tel. 96.28.5110.
Avaugour, 1 place du Champ-Clos, 22100 DINAN. Tel. 96.39.07.49.
Chez Crouzil, 22130 PLANCOET. Tel. 96.84.10.24.
La Cotriade, Port de Piegu, 22370 PLENEUF-VAL-ANDRE. Tel. 96.72.20.26.
L'Escurial, boulevard de la Mer, 22430 ERQUY. Tel. 96.72.31.56.
Manoir de Lan Kerellec, Allée de Lan Kerellec, 22560 TREBEURDEN. Tel. 96.23.50.09.
Le Quatre Saisons, 61 Chemin des Courses, 22000 St-BRIEUC. Tel. 96.33.20.38.
La Vieille Tour, 75 rue de la Tour, 22190 PLERIN. Tel. 96.33.10.30.

Finistère

L'Auberge de la Pomme d'Api, 49 rue Verderel, 29250 St-POL-DE-LEON. Tel. 98.69.04.36.
Auberge de Kerveoc'h, route de Kervéoc'h, 29100 DOUARNENEZ. Tel. 98.92.07.58.
Bourhis, 3 place de la Gare, 29140 ROSPORDEN. Tel. 98.59.23.89.
Le Chasse Marée, 4 venelle du Pain-Cuit, 29000 QUIMPER. Tel. 98.53.69.09.
Le Cheval d'Orgueil, 49 rue du Mur, 29210 MORLAIX. Tel. 98.88.08.62.
Le Frère Jacques, 15bis rue de Lyon, 29200 BREST. Tel. 98.44.38.65.
Le Galion, 15 rue St-Guénolé de la "Ville Close", 29110 CONCARNEAU. Tel. 98.97.30.16.

Les Moulins du Duc, 29116 MOELAN-SUR-MER. Tel. 98.39.60.73.

La Touline, 29211 ROSCOFF. Tel. 98.61.20.50.

Ille-et-Vilaine

Hôtel du Château, 1 place Chateaubriand, 35270 COMBOURG. Tel. 99.73.00.38.

Restaurant des Parcs, 35120 CHER-RUEIX. Tel. 99.48.82.26.

Morbihan

Château de Locguenolé, route de Port-Louis, 56700 HENNEBONT. Tel. 97.76.29.40.

Lann-Roz, 56340 CARNAC.

Le Lys, 51 rue du Maréchal-Leclerc, 56000 Vannes. Tel. 97.47.29.30.

Le Pic'Assiette, 2 boulevard, Franchet-d'Esperey, 56100 LORIENT. Tel. 97.2118.29.

La Sterne, 56400 AURAY.

THINGS TO DO

ARMOR OR ARGOAT

What you see or do in Brittany will depend very much on your own circumstances; families will tend to spend a lot of time at seaside resorts, whilst older or independent travellers may prefer to travel inland to the cities and historic sights.

For the former, it is important to remember that the Breton coast is not the Med—for a start it never has the excessive temperatures of the south, and the breeze usually means that you will want to keep active on the beach. Also the resorts are, on the whole not very highly developed, but are good for families as they do not get too crowded and most have beach clubs or play facilities for children.

Possibly the best resorts for families are Quiberon (but beware of heavy traffic at weekends along sole entry road), Carnac and St-Bénodet (not too commercial), Le Val-André (one of Brittany's larger resorts) and Concarneau which also has a large fishing port.

The most glamorous resort of all is not strictly in Brittany: La Baule on the south coast is popular with the French at weekends—being closer to Paris than the Med, and thus has some excellent restaurants as well as other attractions. Perros-Guirec also has a good nightlife and boasts one of the best beaches in the region.

It has to be said that Brittany could not be the first choice for real city-lovers—for a start, many of the region's older towns and quarters were bombed flat during the war, but there are some notable exceptions.

Dinan, for instance, is a delightful fortified town of old houses and cobbled streets; Vannes too escaped the worst ravages of the war and has a charming town centre and port area; St-Malo on the other hand is worth a visit to see how faithfully its *Ville Close* (walled city) was rebuilt in heavy grey stone, after the war.

Concarneau still boasts its original *Ville Close* which dates back to the 13th century. As a port of entry Roscoff is often overlooked in the rush to get on, but this medieval town is worth a second look.

Locronan has some fine Renaissance buildings, while Rochefort-en-Terre, in its sylvan setting, has some wonderful (and expensive) antique shops. At Tréguier, do not miss the superb Cathedral of St-Tugdual, nor the Locmaria quarter in Quimper, famous for its ceramics workshops. The ancient centre of Rennes is a delight, but the urban sprawl which surrounds it is a necessary evil.

Most visitors will probably want to take a trip out of the region to visit its former capital, Nantes. The Breton people are still very upset by the administrative "blunder" of the 1960s that made Nantes part of a "new region", commonly known as Pays de la Loire. However, this fine city and busy port with its château, cathedral and many other sights, is well worth a detour.

PLACES OF INTEREST

The listing below covers a variety of different activities: technical visits, bird and nature reserves, parks and gardens (of which there are an abundance in Finistère). Please see Useful Addresses for further information about bird-watching and nature conservation. Please note that this is just a selection of the huge variety of things to see and do in the region—fuller details are given in the booklet *Détours Bretagne*, produced by the Comité Régional de Tourisme.

The awe-inspiring fortified abbey at Mont-St-Michel is one site (although strictly in Normandy) that most visitors will wish to see. However, like many very famous sites, a visit can often be marred by the excess of tacky souvenirs and other people! Go out of season if at all possible.

Côtes du Nord

LAMBALLE National Stud (haras)—one of the largest in France breeding thoroughbreds, as well as farm horses, open mid-July to mid-Feb (out of season on request). Free entrance. Tel. 96.3100.40.

PLEUMEUR-BODOU Planetarium—permanent exhibitions. Nearby is the radôme des Télécommunications (radar station) which is also open to the public Apr-Oct. The Centre Ornithologique de l'Ile Grande nearby has a permanent exhibition and was the first such centre to use live video links of bird colonies, open daily. Tel. 96.91.91.40.

TREGOMEUR Parc Zoologique du Moulin de Richard—10 hectares of woods with animals roaming freely. Tel. 96.79.01.07.

Finistère

BREST Conservatoire Botanique, 52 allée du Bot—collection of threatened species from all over the world, open daily. Tel. 98.02.63.14. Océanopolis, rue de Kerbriant, Port de plaisance du Moulin Blanc—an exciting new centre (opened in 1989), where you can discover the wildlife which exists 100 metres under the sea.

CAP SIZUN-GOULIEN Bird reserve—mostly nesting and migratory colonies, on Mon and Thu mornings in July and August, tours are taken for close-up views; otherwise open daily mid-March to end-Aug. Tel. 98.70.13.53.

COMBRIT Parc Botanique de Cornouaille—one of the best in France with over 3,500 species over seven hectares. Tel. 98.56.64.93.

LAZ Parc de Loisirs de Laz—leisure park with mini-golf, amusements and 550-metre luge run. Tel. 98.26.82.47.

LOCQUIREC Parc de Loisirs de Tregamor—leisure park with mini-golf and children's amusements including pony rides. Tel. 98.67.40.06.

MENEZ MEUR-HANVEC Parc d'Armorique, near Daoulas—animal park open daily June-Sept, otherwise Wed. and Sun. Tel. 98.21.90.69.

ST-GOAZEC Parc de Trévarez—floral gardens, open every afternoon April-Sept (July and Aug. opens at 11 a.m.), weekends only Oct-Mar. Tel. 98.26.82.79.

ILE-DE-BATZ Jardin Colonial—the warm gulf stream is perfect for the cultivation of the exotic plants at this garden which has just undergone a complete overhaul. Tel. 98.61.76.76.

Ille-et-Vilaine

DINARD-ST-BRIAC Barrage de la Rance—the world's first tidal power factory; free tourist visits in English (technical tour on request), open all year, 8.30 a.m. to 8 p.m.

IFFENDIC Base de Loisirs de Trémelin—lake, amusements, mini-golf, animal park and horse-riding. Tel. 99.09.70.40.

PLEUGUENEC Parc et Château de la Bourbonsais—animal park and gardens, also visits to the château, open every afternoon. Tel. 99.60.40.07.

RENNES Jardins du Thabor—10 hectares of gardens in the town centre, open daily.

Morbihan

GOLFE DU MORBIHAN—inland sea with more than 365 tiny islands, a handful of which are inhabited. Of particular interest are the Ile de Groix for its mineralogical deposits (permanent exhibition); Hoedic where there is an exhibition at Fort d'Hoedic, and Ile d'Houat, with its cliffs and golden dunes.

MUZILLAC Parc Zoologique du Château de Branféré, le Guerno—with some animals at large, open daily from Easter to Nov. Tel. 97.42.94.66.

PLOERMEL Etang au Duc—bird reserve.

PONT SCORFF Kerruisseau—zoo and permanent exhibition of local fauna, open daily Easter to end-Oct. then weekends, Mon, Tue. only. Tel. 97.32.60.86.

SENE Réserve Naturelle de Falguérec—bird reserve, open daily ex. Mon. July and Aug.

VANNES Parc du Golfe—opening in 1989, a new park recreating an equatorial environment, principally for the breeding of tropical butterflies (over 500 species).

LIGHTHOUSES

Brittany's coastline is dotted with lighthouses (*phares*), several of which are open to the public, including le Phare Ile Vierge at Plouguerneau—with 392 steps to climb, it is the highest in Europe. Ask at the local *syndicat d'initiative*, for information and make an appointment with the keeper.

THALASSOTHERAPY

The British, in general, do not share the European fascination with cures and treatments of various kinds, but a trip to Brittany may encourage you to try one of France's most natural remedies for all kinds of aches and pains (including rheumatism and arthritis). We all know sea air does us good, but thalassotherapy combines this with treatment by seawater and seaweed. To give it a try, contact the regional tourist office for the list of seven marine hydrotherapy centres in Brittany, most of which have English-speaking staff.

Culture Plus

Brittany's culture goes back further than the Celtic heritage with which it is mostly associated. Some of the region's fascinating early history can be witnessed still today in the neolithic remains which cover the countryside, especially in southern Brittany around the Gulf of Morbihan. These stone monuments fall into two main categories:

Menhirs are single standing stones which may be found alone or grouped in circles (*cromlechs*) or arranged in lines;

Dolmens are table stones—slabs of stone laid across upright stone supports to mark the tombs of the neolithic nobility. Particularly fine examples of these megalithic monuments can be seen at Carnac and Erdeven (Morbihan), on the island of Er Lannic (Gulf of Morbihan), at St Just (Ille-et-Vilaine) and Camaret-sur-Mer (Finistère). Perhaps the most famous *dolmens* are to be seen at Locmariaquer (Morbihan) and at the Barnenez cairn at Plouezoc'h (Finistère).

MUSEUMS & ART GALLERIES

Most museums charge an entrance fee—expect to pay an average of F10 per person (reductions usually given for children, the elderly and students—on production of a card). Remember, like everything else in France, museums close for lunch—normally from noon till 2.30 p.m.; practically all are closed on public holidays. Opening times given below should be accurate, but may be subject to change.

Côtes du Nord

DINAN Musée du Château—in Duchess Anne's castle: local history, Breton cos-tumes. Tel. 96.39.45.20. Musée de l'Oiseau: stuffed birds, aviary and gardens. Tel. 96.39.22.43. Both museums open daily (afternoons only Nov-Feb, closed Tue p.m. except summer).

LA CHEZE Musée de l'Outil, Centre Culturel des Métiers: old tools and implements. Tel. 96.26.63.16. Open daily (closed mornings and Mon. Oct.-May).

LAMBALLE Musée Mathurin Méheut, Place du Martray: major collection of works by Breton artists. Tel. 96.31.05.38. Open Mon-Sat, 1 June-15 Sept.

PAIMPOL Musée de la Mer: the sea—its history and evolution. Tel. 96.20.80.15. Open daily April to mid-Sept.

PLEDELIAC Ferme de St. Esprit des Bois: reconstruction of an early 20th-century Breton farm. Tel. 96.3114.67. Open every afternoon 1 July-30 Sept, and Sunday afternoon only Easter-1 Nov.

PLEUDIHEN-SUR-RANCE Musée de la pomme et du cidre: cider with tastings. Tel. 96.83.20.78.

St-BRIEUC Musée Municipal: county museum, regular exhibitions. Tel. 96.61.29.33. Open Tue-Sun.

TREGASTEL Aquarium de la Côte de Granit Rose: Breton fauna and exotic fish set amongst the rocks. Tel. 96.23.88.67. Open May weekends; June, Sept, Oct afternoons; July, Aug, all day.

TREGUIER Musée Ernest Renan: birthplace of famous Breton writer. Tel. 96.92.45.63. Open daily ex. Tue Easter-Sept.

Finistère

BREST Musée des Beaux-Arts, 22 rue Emile-Zola: 16th-18th century French/Italian painting; Pont-Aven school; 19th-20th century Breton paintings. Tel. 98.44.66.27. Open daily ex. Tue and Sun morning. Artothèque, Bibliothèque municipale, 22 rue Traverse: modern paintings, photographs, engravings, in the public library. tel.

98.46.35.90. Open Wed. and Sat. Musée Naval, in the castle: naval museum.

COMBRIT Musée des Mécaniques Musiques, on D44 Pont l'Abbé-Bénodet road: a one-man museum of mechanical musical instruments. Tel. 98.56.36.03. Every afternoon 15 June-15 Sept or ring for an appointment.

CONCARNEAU Musée de la Pêche: fishing museum in the walled town. Tel. 98.97.10.20. Plus Marinarium. Tel. 98.97.06.59.

DOUARNENEZ Musée du Bateau: all about boats. Tel. 98.92.65.20.

LANDERNEAU Centre Culturel, Manoir Jehan de Keranden, rue Jehan Bazin. Regular contemporary art exhibitions and workshops. Tel. 98.21.61.50. Open daily ex. Sun, Mon morning.

MORLAIX Musée des Jacobins, rue des Vignes: European art (16th-19th century; 19th-century Breton paintings. Tel. 98.88.68.88. Open daily ex. Sun and Tue.

PONT-AVEN Musée des Beaux-Arts: fine arts—20 galleries, regular exhibitions. Tel. 98.06.14.43. Temporary exhibits of the Pont-Aven school, initiated by Gauguin, can be seen at the town hill whilst a permanent centre is being set up.

PONT-L'ABBE Musée Bigouden: costumes. Tel. 98.87.24.44. Guided visits June-Sept, closed Sun.

QUIMPER Musée des Beaux-Arts, 10 place St-Corentin: fine arts. Tel. 98.95.45.20. Open daily ex. Tue. Musée Départemental Breton, rue du Roi Gradlon: county museum. Tel. 98.95.21.60. Musée de la Faïence, route de Bénodet: pottery. Tel. 98.90.09.36. Galerie Artem, 16 rue Ste-Catherine: contemporary works of mainly young artists—photography, painting and sculpture. Tel. 98.87.74.57. Open daily ex. Sun Oct-June.

ROSCOFF Aquarium Charles Perez. Tel. 98.69.72.30. Open end-Mar to end-Oct.

ST-GUENOLE-PENMARCH Musée Préhistorique Finistérien: local prehistoric exhibits. Tel. 98.58.60.35. Open daily ex. Tue and Sun morning, June-Sept; other times by arrangement.

Ille-et-Vilaine

BAGUER-MORVAN Musée de la Paysannerie: aspects of rural life. Tel. 99.48.04.04. Open daily May-Sept.

CESSON-SEVIGNE (near Rennes) Musée automobile de Bretagne: 70 cars, as well as bicycles and other early forms of transport. Tel. 99.62.00.17. Open daily.

DINARD Musée de la Mer, 17 ave Georges V: the sea. Tel. 99.46.13.90. Open Whitsun to mid-Sept. Musée du Pays de Dinard, Villa Eugénie: local museum. Tel. 99.46.81.05. Open Easter-11 Nov.

DOL-DE-BRETAGNE Musée Historique, place de la Cathédrale: local history and sculpture. Open daily ex. Tue Easter to end-Sept. (open Tue July-Aug.).

FOUGERES Musée de la Chaussure, in the castle: dedicated to footwear. Tel. 99.99.18.98. Open daily (closed Jan). Musée de la Villéon, 51 rue Nationale: half-timbered house containing works of impressionist painter, Emmanuel de la Villéon. Tel. 99.99.18.98. Open daily Easter to end-Aug., otherwise weekends and school holidays.

MONTFORT-SUR-MEU Eco-Musée d'Art et Traditions Populaires: rural arts and traditions, including costumes. Tel. 99.09.31.81. Open daily ex. Mon, Sun morning June-Sept; otherwise Tue-Fri.

QUEBRIAC Musée Internationale de la Faune, Les Brulons: 300 stuffed animals in "naturalistic" settings. Tel. 99.68.10.22. Open daily Easter to end-Oct.

RENNES Musée des Beaux-Arts, 20 quai Emile-Zola: regional collection of fine arts from 15th-20th century. Tel. 99.79.44.16. Open daily ex. Tue. Galerie Jaques Callot, Le Grand Huit, 1 rue St-Helier: four or five exhibitions a year of artists of international standing. Tel. 99.37.35.33. Daily ex. Mon.

St-MALO Musée d'Histoire de la Ville, in the castle: town's history from slave trade and piracy to Nazi occupation. Tel. 99.56 41.36. Open daily ex. Tue. Musée Quic-en-Groigne, in the castle: waxworks. Tel. 99.40.80.26. Open daily Apr-Sept. Aquarium et Exotarium. Tel. 99.40.91.86. Open daily (until 11pm June-Sept). Musée International du Long-Cours et des Caps-Horniers, Tour Solidor, St-Servan: dedicated to ocean sailing. Tel. 99.56.26.68. Open daily June-Sept and Easter holidays, otherwise every afternoon ex. Tue (closed Jan). Musée de la Poupée, 13 rue de Toulouse: 300 dolls. Tel. 99.44.67.40. Open daily ex. Thu. mid-Apr. to mid-Nov.

TINTENIAC Musée de l'Outil et des Métiers: skills and tools of local crafts of yesteryear. Tel. 99.68.02.03. Daily July-Sept.

Morbihan

BIGNAN Domaine de Kerguehennec: 18th-century château dedicated to promotion of modern art; regular exhibitions. Tel. 97.20.21.19. Open daily Apr-Oct.

BELLE-ILE Musée Acadien: relating to French Canada. Tel. 97.52.84.17. Belle-Ile-Le-Palais: Musée de la Citadelle Vauban. Tel. 97.31.84.17.

CARNAC Musée Miln-le-Rouzic: prehistoric archaeology. Tel. 97.52.22.04. Open daily.

LE FAOUET Musée du Faouët: figurative paintings of the 19th-20th century. Tel. 97.23.07.68. Open daily July-Aug.

JOSSELIN Musée des Poupées, 3 rue des Trente: dolls. Tel. 97.22.36.45.

LORIENT Galerie Espace l'Orient, 13 rue Beauvais: modern art. Tel. 97.21.78.73. Open Mon-Sat afternoon. Musée de la Mer, Maison de la Mer, Quai Rohan: sea museum. Tel. 97.84.87.37. Open daily ex. Tue.

PORT-LOUIS Musée de la Citadelle: encompasses two museums, one of naval weaponry, one dedicated to the Compagnie des Indes, set up in the early 18th century to trade with the Indies. Tel. 97.82.19.13. Open daily ex. Tue. (closed 1 Nov-15 Dec.).

St-MARCEL Musée Régional d'Histoire de l'Occupation et de Resistance en Bretagne: recalls wartime occupation and resistance. Tel. 97.75.17.41.

VANNES Musée des Beaux-Arts, rue des Halles: local and international artists (Corot, Goya, Delacroix). Tel. 97.42.59.56. Open daily. Musée Préhistorique, Château Gaillard, rue Noë. Tel. 97.42.59.80. Open daily ex. Sun and public holidays. Aquarium, la Ferme des Marais. Tel. 97.42.74.93.

LIVE ARTS

Artistic expression in Brittany embraces the traditional (and to a great extent) Celtic festivals and performances which are listed below, as well as more modern theatre and musical spectacles. Most theatrical offerings are produced on a provincial or local basis, but Brittany also benefits from national tours of the Paris-based ballet and opera companies.

Côtes-du-Nord

DINAN Festival Musical—modern and classical music in an historic setting, mid-July. Includes international competition of Celtic harp. Tel. 99.54.20.20. Fête des Remparts—medieval festival in the old town, Oct.

GUINGAMP La St Loup—festival of Breton dance, mid-Aug.

LAMBALLE Festival folklorique des Ajoncs d'Or—traditional festival, second Sun in July.

LANNION Festival d'orgue et Musique Spirituelle—organ festival Fridays in July and August.

PERROS-GUIREC Fête des Hortensias, mid-Aug.

PLOEZAL-RUNAN Festival de la Roche-Jague—exhibitions and cultural events, June-Sept.

St-BRIEUC Le mai Breton—traditional festival in May.

Finistère

CHATEAUNEUF-DU-FAOU Festival des Danses et Traditions Populaires: international event, mid-August. Tel. 98.81.80.10.

CONCARNEAU Fêtes des Filets Bleus—originally a festival to bless the fishermen's nets, now a major folk festival, third Sunday in Aug.

PLOMODIERN Fête du Menez-Hom, 15 Aug.

PLOZEVET Festival International de Folklore, end-July. Tel. 98.95.20.67.

PONT-L'ABBE Fête des Brodeuses, second Sun in Aug.

QUIMPER Festival de Cornouaille—major Breton festival, over 140 events and 4,000 people taking part in a week-long extravaganza, last week in July. Tel. 98.55.53.53.

Ille-et-Vilaine

BAIN-SUR-OST Son-et-lumière of history of Redon and the origins of Brittany, throughout July.

BECHEREL Festival de Théâtre, Danse et Musique, mid-July. Tel. 99.31.55.33.

DINARD Fête de la Jeunesse et de la Mer—"the youth and the sea", late Aug.

HEDE Festival de Théâtre, Musique, Danse, mid-Aug.

MONTERFIL Grand Concours de musique gallèse—music competition, mid-June.

REDON La Bogue d'Or—(Golden Husk) festival, October.

RENNES Festival of traditional arts, late April. Tombées de la Nuit—(literally Nightfall), the main summer event in the city, a week of Breton music, theatre and dance, late June/early July.

ST-MALO Fête folklorique du Clos Poulet—traditional event in July.

Festival de la Musique Sacrée—religious music, July-Aug. Tel. 99.56.51.28.

Morbihan

CARNAC Grande Fête des Menhirs, third Sun in Aug.

ELVEN Lancelot du Lac—*son-et-lumière* spectacle of the legend of King Arthur, Fri and Sat mid-July to end-Aug. Tel. 97.53.52.79.

LIZIO Fête des Artisans, mid-Aug.

LORIENT Festival Interceltique—major international festival of Celtic art and traditions, first two weeks in Aug.

VANNES Journées mediévales de Vannes—medieval spectacle retelling the arrival of Anne of Brittany in Vannes, more than 600 costumes, plus troubadours, tournaments and medieval music, early July. Festival du Jazz, early Aug. Tel. 97.54.18.22.

ARCHITECTURE

On a dull day in Brittany, the towns and villages take on a rather sombre appearance, due to the abundance of grey granite—the main building material used in the region. However, in summer sun, the long, low country cottages, particularly those which have retained their traditional thatched roofs and are wreathed in geraniums are a delight to the eye.

Brittany does not possess a lot of grand architecture—its best cathedrals are to be found in Tréguier, Dol-de-Bretagne, St-Pol-de-Léon and Quimper—but there is an unusual style of religious architecture which is unique to the region: *les enclos paroissiaux* (parish close). From the 15th to 17th century it became common practice for parishes to embellish their churchyards with flamboyant decoration. Much rivalry went on between parishes and the more wealthy the community, the more elaborate became the churchyard. The best preserved examples can be visited in the Léon area of Finistère: St-Thégonnec is one of the most complete, whilst its main rival Guimiliau is also superb. Other good examples include St-Servais, Lampaul-Guimiliau and Pencran.

Manor houses, traditionally built around a courtyard, are more commonly seen in Brittany than grand châteaux. However, some châteaux and other interesting buildings are open to the public, some of the best are listed below.

Côtes-du-Nord

DINAN Château de la Duchesse Anne (see museums).

ERQUY Château de Bienassis: one of the last fortified châteaux built in France. Tel. 96.72.22.03. Open June to mid-Sept. daily ex. Sun and public holidays.

LANVELLEC Château de Rosanbo: 14th century; rooms have original Louis XIII and XIV furnishings; gardens designed by Le Nôtre (France's Capability Brown). Tel. 96.35.18.77. Open Sat, Sun mid-Apr to end-Sept; daily in July and Aug.

PLEDELIAC Château de La Hunaudaye: fortified château of 14th-15th century. Tel. 96.34.18.47. Open Easter to end-Sept. (Sun and daily in July and Aug).

PLENEE-JUGON Abbaye de Boquen: Cistercian abbey founded in 1137. Guided visits Tue-Sat 2-4.30p.m. in July and Aug.

PLOEZAL Château de la Roche-Jagu: half manor house, half fortified château, overlooking the Trieux estuary. Children's amusements. Tel. 96.95.62.35. Open all year, guided visits Apr to mid-Sept.

QUINTIN Château de Quintin: houses a museum and restaurant, also in the park is the 18th-century pavilion—the only part of the proposed "new" château to be completed. Tel. 96.74.94.79. Open daily Apr-Oct, otherwise Sat-Sun only.

TONQUEDEC Château de Tonquedec: ruined château dominating the Léguer valley; tours around the site in horse-drawn carriage available. Open June-Aug.

Finistère

CARANTEC Château du Taureau, built in 1542 to defend Morlaix from the English. Later served as a prison. Visits organised through the *syndicat d'initiative*. Tel. 98.67.00.43.

DAOULAS Abbaye de Daoulas: 12th-century cloisters, "miraculous fountain" of druidic origin and 16th-century oratory; the garden has 200 species of medicinal plants. Tel. 98.25.84.39. Open daily.

PLOUZEVEDE Château de Kerjean, St-Vougay: Renaissance château and park, summer exhibitions and spectacles. Tel. 98.69.93.69. Open every afternoon ex. Tue and public holidays.

ST-GOAZEC Château de Trevarez: Built around 1900 of granite and brick, this fine house stands in a rhodendron park and also operates an experimental farm. Tel. 98.26.82.79. Open daily (ex. Tue) Apr-Oct, otherwise Sat., Sun and public holidays.

SIBIRIL Château de Kérouzéré: an example of 15th-century military architecture. Tel. 98.29.96.05. Visits by appointment, July to mid-Sept.

Ille-et-Vilaine

BAZOUGES-LA-PEROUSE Château de la Balue: home of the Chouans (Breton royalists during the Revolution); exhibition of gardens of the world. Tel. 99.97.45.78. Open daily, ex. Tue, mid-Apr to mid-Oct.

BECHEREL Château de Caradeuc: "the Versailles of Brittany"; park open all year. Tel. 99.66.77.76.

COMBOURG Château de Combourg: sombre and imposing medieval château where the writer Chateaubriant spent his youth and is remembered. Tel. 99.73.22.95. Guided tours Mar-Nov daily ex. Tue.

FOUGERES Château de Fougères: with its 13 towers still intact, this is one of the most impressive and best preserved examples of medieval military architecture in Europe. Open daily all year ex. Jan. (see also Museums)

LES IFFS Château de Montmuran: rebuilt in the 12th-14th centuries, the castle has connections with one of Brittany's greatest heroes, Bertrand Duguesclin who was knighted and later married there. Open every afternoon Easter to end-Oct., otherwise Sat., Sun only.

MONTAUBAN-DE-BRETAGNE Château Montauban: feudal castle with horseshoe-shaped keep; display of armour. Tel. 99.06.40.21. Open every afternoon June-Sept.

PLEUGUENEUC Château de la Bourbansais: l6th-century castle (see Places of Interest).

St-MALO Château de la Chipaudière (see museums); Manoir de Limoeleu: 15th-century manor house of Jacques Cartier. Tel. 99.40.97.73. Open Wed-Sun, Jun-Sept.

VITRE Château de Vitré: another fine example of medieval military architecture—illuminated in summer. Tel. 99.75.04.54. Open daily Apr-Sept (but closed Tue until July); open Wed, Thu, Fri Oct-March. Château des Rochers-Sévigné: favourite home in Brittany of Madame de Sévigné and mentioned in her famous "Letters". Gardens designed by Le Nôtre. Tel. 99.96.76.51. Open daily ex. mid-Nov to mid-Feb.

Morbihan

BEGANNE Château de Léhéllec: this granite house is typical of the area and was a refuge for Chouans during the Revolution. Tel. 99.91.81.14. Open evey afternoon, ex. Tue., July-Aug.

BIGNAN Château de Kerguéhénnec: built at the beginning of the 18th-century for one of the founders of the Compagnie des Indes, the château is now a centre for contemporary art (see Museums).

ELVEN Château de Largoët: only two towers now remain of this 14th-century edifice, but these form an impressive backdrop for the *son et lumière* spectacles in summer. Tel. 97.53.35.96. Open daily.

JOSSELIN Château du Duc de Rohan: one of the finest châteaux in the region, also houses the Rohan family's collection of dolls (see Museums).

PONTIVY Château des Rohan, rue du Général de Gaulle: the fortified castle of one of Brittany's most important families has survived well the many attempts to destroy it. Tel. 97.25.12.93.

ROCHEFORT-EN-TERRE Château de Rochefort: overlooking the delightful medieval town and the surrounding Gueuzon valley, the castle now houses a museum. Tel. 97.43.81.78. Open Sat, Sun in Apr-May and daily June-Sept.

ROHAN Abbaye Notre Dame de Timadeuc, Bréhan: 19th-century Cistercian abbey where it is possible to attend the Gregorian chants. Tel. 97.51.50.29. Open daily.

SARZEAU Château de Suscinio: oppulent building commenced in the 13th century, vandalised during the Revolution. Currently being restored. Tel. 97.41.82.37. Open Tue, Sat, Sun Oct-Mar; daily Apr-Sept.

THEIX Château du Plessis Josso: a mix of styles with a fine Louis XIII style pavillion. Tel. 97.43.16.16. Open daily mid-July to end-Aug.

VANNES Château Gaillard: 15th-century manor house, now a museum of prehistory. Tel. 97.42.59.80.

NIGHTLIFE

A glamorous nightlife is not what most people seek when choosing Brittany as a holiday area. However, there is plenty to do in the evenings, providing you stick to the holiday resorts or major towns such as Rennes. The cafés and bars, with their unrestricted licensing hours, are the main meeting place for young and old alike—you will quickly find the ones that suit you. Most resorts have nightclubs or discothèques of varying quality.

Casinos often offer more than the opportunity of losing all your holiday money in one throw—the Palais d'Emeraude at Dinard, for instance, also has a theatre, restaurant and nightclub. If you do intend to gamble, take your passport with you—you may be asked to show it.

Cinemas and theatres mostly start their programmes around 9 p.m. to allow customers to dine first.

Generally, however, Brittany is not the place for night owls—in inland areas (especially small towns and villages) you will find that most bars and restaurants close relatively early, even in high season.

SHOPPING

Over the past couple of decades most major towns in the region have made the sensible decision to keep the town centre for small boutiques and individual shops. Many of these areas are pedestrianised and so rather attractive (although beware—some cars ignore the *voie piétonnée* signs). The large supermarkets, hypermarkets, furniture stores and do-it-yourself outlets are grouped on the outskirts of the town, mostly designated as a *Centre Commercial*. This laudable intent is however, somewhat marred by the horrendous design of some of these centres—groups of garish functional buildings which make the town's outskirts very unattractive—St-Brieuc is a case in point.

These centres are fine for bulk shopping for self-catering or for finding a good selection of wine to take home at reasonable prices, but otherwise the town centres are far more interesting. In tourist areas, every other shop sells Breton sweaters and traditional lace—these are of variable quality but good examples make fine souvenirs. Maritime artefacts also abound—prints, ships in bottles, model boats, etc.

Just about every town has a weekly market. Even if you do not wish to buy produce they are irresistible. On the coast seafood stalls are a sight to behold, while inland the huge market at Rennes on Saturday morning has a vast selection of fruit, vegetables, flowers, cheeses and other produce. Other particularly atttractive markets include Vannes (Wednesday and Saturday mornings) and Auray (Monday morning). In Finistère, Quimper, famous for its china, has a covered market (*marché couvert*).

Try to plan excursions for market days and you will get an extra bonus—visit St-Cast on Monday, Dinan on Thursday and Guingamp on Friday.

Children in particular will often enjoy

visiting a livestock market, which are very common in the area. Also fascinating are the *Criées* which take place in Finistère. When the fishing boats land the catch is sold early in the morning on the quayside by auction. *Criées* can be witnessed at the following ports (enquire at the *syndicat d'initiative* for details): Audierne, Concarneau, Douarnenez, Le Guilvinec, Lesconil, Loctudy and St-Guénolé.

PRACTICAL INFORMATION

Food shops, especially bakers, tend to open early; boutiques and department stores open from 9 a.m., but often not until 10 a.m.. In town centres, just about everything closes from noon until 2 p.m. or later, although out-of-town hypermarkets are often open all day. Most shops stay open until at least 6.30 or 7 p.m., and later in resorts in summer. Most are closed Monday mornings and large stores generally all day. If you want to buy a picnic lunch, remember to buy everything you need before midday. The delicatessens (*charcuterie*) have mouthwatering ready-prepared dishes, which make picnicking a delight.

On most purchases, the price includes TVA (VAT or purchase tax). The base rate is currently 18.6 percent, but this can be as high as 33 percent on luxury items. Foreign visitors are entitled to claim back TVA paid and may be worth doing if you spend more than F500 in one place.

Most large stores and hypermarkets have information bureaux where you can obtain a refund form. This must be completed to show (with the goods purchased) to customs officers on leaving the country (pack the items separately for ease of access). Then mail the form back to the retailer who will refund the TVA in a month or two. Certain items purchased (eg antiques) may need special customs clearance. The Direction Générale des Douanes in Paris (Tel. 16-1.42.60.35.90) operates an information service.

If you have a complaint about any purchase, return it in the first place to the shop as soon as possible. In the case of any serious dispute, contact the Direction Départementale de la Concurrence et de la Consommation et de la Répression des Fraudes (see telephone directory for number).

CLOTHING

Most shops are happy to let you try clothes on (*essayer*) before buying. Children's clothes sizes, in particular, are rather on the small side compared with British and US age ranges. The charts below will help you find the right size to try:

Women

Dresses, Suits, & Coats							
Dresses,	France	38	40	42	44	46	48
Suits, &	UK	30	32	34	36	38	40
Coats	USA	8	10	12	14	16	18
Blouses,	France	28	40	42	44	46	48
Pullovers	UK, USA	30	32	34	36	38	40
	France	36	37	38	39	40	40
Shoes	UK	3	4	5	6	7	8
	USA	3	6	7	7.5	8	9
Stockings	France	1	2	3	4	5	
	UK, USA	8.5	9	9.5	10	10.5	

Men

Suits, Sweaters, & Coats							
Suits,	France	32	34	36	38	40	42
Sweaters,	UK	33	34	35	36	37	38
& Coats	USA	42	44	46	48	51	54
	France	41	42	43	44	45	46
Shoes	UK	8	9	10	11	12	13
	USA	8	8.5	9.5	10	10.5	11
Socks	France	39-40	40-41	42	42-43	43-44	
	UK, USA	10	10.5	11	11.5	12	
Hats	France	53	54	55	56	57	58	59
	UK, USA	6⅝	6¾	6⅞	6⅞	7	7⅛	7¼

SPORTS

Whatever sport you wish to pursue, you are likely to find opportunities to do so in Brittany. Naturally, water sports abound, but also, maybe surprisingly, the region has become one the best equipped in France for golf. Most medium-sized towns have swimming-pools and even small villages often have a tennis court (you may have to become a temporary member to use it—enquire at the local *syndicat d'initiative* or *mairie*—town hall).

The *syndicat d'initiative* will also provide details of all sporting activities in the locality, general information is given below.

WATER SPORTS

Wind-surfing is possibly the main water sport practised around Brittany's extensive coastline. Although it can be expensive to hire equipment (boards—*planches à voile*—are roughly F150 per day to hire, and tuition around F150 per hour), it is still less costly than yachting, and is a good sport both for novices who can get some practice in the sheltered coves or for experienced surfers who tackle the open Atlantic. The best beaches for all standards lie along the south coast from Audierne to Concarneau. Pointe de la Torche near Pont l'Abbé in Finistère offers the most challenging conditions and indeed it is here that the French hold their round of the world series windsurfing championships. Most coastal resorts have wind-surfing schools. Some camp-sites, especially those offering "all-in" holidays have facilities and tuition available.

Brittany has almost 40 harbours, offering full facilities for yachtsmen (and women) and many more where mooring is safe, but facilities limited. Yachting clubs are as common here as tennis clubs in the English provinces, but for a list of harbours, and yachting schools write to the tourist office at Rennes (see Useful Addresses) or to La Ligue Haute-Bretagne, 1 rue des Fours à Chaux, 35260 Cancale (for details of Ille-et-Vilaine and Côtes-du-Nord); and La Ligue Armor, 2 cours de la Bôve, 56100 Lorient (for Morbihan and Finistère).

If yachting is a little beyond your means but you still want to get onto the sea, plenty of resorts will hire boats (motor or rowing). Make sure all on board can swim and that children are provided with lifejackets. Most resorts have a 72-ft (22-metre) fairway at right angles to the coastline so that boats may beach safely. At Cancale in Côtes-du-Nord trips (including fishing trips) are offered in a beautiful many-sailed *bisquine*, a faithful copy of a former Breton fishing vessel. Trips are run by the Association la Bisquine Cancalaise, tel. (Mairie) 99.89.77.87.

Water-skiing is popular too and tuition available; for a list of facilities, write to the Ligue de Bretagne de Ski Nautique, BP 99, 49303 Cholet.

Underwater diving offers a different perspective of Brittany's coastline—apart from submarine species, some fascinating sites can be observed, such as the Er Lannic cromlech in the Golfe du Morbihan. For a list of diving clubs, which mostly have their own compressors or facilities for filling tanks, write to the Comité Régional Bretagne-Normandie de la Fédération Française d'étude des sports sous-marins, 78, rue Ferdinand-Buisson, 44600 St-Nazaire. There are decompression chambers at Brest and Lorient in case of accident. Please note a licence is required for underwater fishing—apply to the nearest Bureau des Affaires Maritimes (see telephone book for address).

Many of the region's long, unspoilt beaches are great fun for enthusiasts of sand buggies (*char à voile*)—for details of hire, write to the Ligue Régionale de Char à Voile, 26bis, rue Belle-Fontaine, 56100 Lorient.

Amenities for canoeing are not confined to inland waterways (for information, see Getting Around), exciting possibilities, including *kayak de surf* and *kayak polo* (team game) are offered for experienced canoeists by the Ligue de Bretagne de canoë-kayak, as well as instruction for beginners. Many activities, including "package" holidays with accommodation, are organised by A.B.R.I. (see useful addresses).

More information can be obtained from:
M C. Hunaut, Président du Comité Régional de Canoë-Kayak, Ponthoën, Servel, 22300 Lannion.

Comité Départemental de Canoë-kayak du Finistère, 5 rue de la Vallée, 22360 Langueux.

CYCLING

Cycling could almost be considered as France's national pastime, with innumerable clubs—not least in Brittany. To take your own *vélo* is easy—carried free on most ferries and trains—or you can rent cycles for a reasonable cost; main railway stations usually have them for hire. Otherwise, try bicycle retailers/repairers or ask at the local tourist office.

Some youth hostels rent cycles and also arrange tours with accommodation in hostels or under canvas. Other cycling holidays are arranged by A.B.R.I. and the Loisirs Accueil services in the individual *départements* (see useful addresses). Some tour operators also offer "package" holidays, in the UK try Triskell Cycle Tours, 35 Langland Drive, Northway, Sedgley DY3 3TH. Tel. (09(73) 78255.

In accordance with the national passion for cycling there is a tradition of Sunday cycle trips organised by local clubs. Many of these welcome guests (who have to provide their own bikes); for details contact:
Comité Départemental de Cyclotourisme (Côtes-du-Nord), 11 bis rue des Cheminots, 22000 St-Brieuc. Tel. 96.33.67.59.

For Finistère: M Meaude, 5 lot. de Bellevue, 56250 St-Nolff.

HORSE-RIDING

In rural Brittany you will come across plenty of riding schools (*centres équestres*) where you can hire horses by the hour or join in a hack. The Association Régionale du Tourisme Equestre en Bretagne has a programme to preserve the "Breton Ways" for horse-riders. They can provide an extensive network of routes and useful addresses. Write to A.R.T.E.B., 8 rue de la Carrière, 56120 Josselin. Tel. 97.22.22.62. Riding holidays, and tours with horse-drawn caravans are offered by some of the Loisirs Accueil services—in particular in Ille-et-Vilaine (see Useful Addresses).

GOLF

In recent years, golf has caught on in a big way in France and Brittany now has ten 18-hole courses, some nine-hole courses and pitch and putt courses which are ideal for families. For the serious golfer, who can expect to pay around F150 for green fees (this is for the whole day), the following 18-hole courses all offer good facilities:

Côtes-du-Nord

Golf des Ajoncs d'Or, Etables-sur-Mer, 22920 Lantic. Tel. 96.71.90.74.—municipal course of high standard, 6230 metres, par 72.

Boisgelin, Pléhédel. Tel. 96.22.31.24.—in the parkland of Château Coatguelen, open April-Dec, 2356 metres, par 32.

Golf de St. Samson, 22670 Pleumeur-Bodou. Tel. 96.23.87.34.—not easy to find, four km from Trégastel, 5692 metres, par 72.

Finistère

Iroise, Landerneau. Tel. 98.21.68.49—public course with children's play area, closed Tue., 6213 metres, par 72.

L'Odet, Clohars Fouesnant, Benodet. Tel. 98.57.26.16.—new course, fees vary according to season, 6207 metres, par 72.

Ille-et-Vilaine

Golf de la Freslonnière, le Rheu, 35000 Rennes. Tel. 99.60.84.09—opening Spring 1989.

Golf de Dinard—St.Briac, 35800 Dinard. Tel. 99.88.32.07—one of the oldest courses in France, 5197 metres, par 69.

St. Malo, Le Tronchet. Tel. 99.58.96.69 —championship standard course, 5708 metres, par 71.

Morbihan

Golf de St. Laurent, Ploëmel, 56400 Auray. Tel. 97.56.85.18—deceptively tricky course, self-catering accommodation available, 6040 metres, par 72.

Golf de Sauzon, Belle-Ile-en-Mer (by boat from Quiberon). Tel. 97.31.64.65— course being increased to 18 holes for 1989; club house in Sarah Bernhardt's ancient farm.

SPECTATOR SPORTS

The sea again provides ample opportunities for those who prefer to sit back and watch others do the work on the sporting scene. Many sailing events take place through the summer; some of the main ones are listed below:

Côtes-du-Nord

LEZARDRIEUX Grand Prix Mononautique—early July.

St-QUAY-PORTRIEUX Championnat international de pêche de mer—sea fishing competition with quayside sale of catches, late June.

TREGASTEL 24 heures de la voile—Le Mans with sails, mid to end-Aug.

Finistère

BREST Grand Prix des Multicoques— multi-hulled craft, late April; European wind-surfing championships, mid-May; Yole Cup, Oct.

CONCARNEAU Festival des Vieilles coques—display of old seafaring equip-ment, mid-July.

DOUARNENEZ Atlantic Challenge— international sailing race and boat show, mid-Aug. Tel. 98.92.89.30.

OUESSANT Tour du Finistère à la voile—sailing race, early Aug.

Morbihan

CARNAC Epreuve par CAT—largest gathering of catamarans in France, end-April. LORIENT Course de Lorient-Gijon—sailing race, starts towards the end of June. Tel. 97.21.07.84.

VANNES Tour de France à la voile— competitors in the round France sailing race stop off for a day in late July.

BRETON SPORTS

"Trial of strength" sports days, similar to those held in the north of England and Scotland, are also a tradition in Brittany. The most commonly seen nowadays is Breton wrestling, and a major competition is held every year in Belle-Isle-en-Terre. But other sports are also being revived, such as discus throwing, tossing the caber and *tire-bâton* where two contestants try to lift each other using a pole. Enquire at the nearest *syndicat d'initiative* about these local events.

OTHER SPORTING EVENTS

Equestrian events take place throughout the summer in particular at St-Malo, Dinard, Questembert and Lorient. St-Malo and Dinard are also among the towns hosting tennis tournaments. Golfing prizes are played for at the region's main courses, including Dinard, St-Malo and Rennes.

SPECIAL INFORMATION

DOING BUSINESS

It is good business practice, even if you are not a fluent French speaker yourself, to initiate business dealings with a well-constructed letter (in French). But who do you contact? *La Bretagne Economique* is a monthly publication with business advertising and features on the region's enterprises. The Chambre de Commerce et d'Industrie in Rennes at 2 avenue de la Préfecture, 35042 cedex. Tel. 99.33.66.66. offers some useful services to foreign executives: its Bureau d'information sur les entreprises has details of all local business; the Centre de formalités des entreprises assists with the paperwork of conducting your affairs; the department of Commerce extérieur exists mainly to encourage foreign business (tel. 99.33.66.50).

The new Chambre de Commerce building, on the south side of the town also has conference rooms available for hire which may be useful as Brittany's hotels are more geared to tourism than the needs of the business community—the facilities of the modern chains, such as Novotel or Sofitel may suit a business executive better than a rural retreat—although one of the joys of doing business in Brittany must surely be to sample some of its culinary delights and relaxed atmosphere after a day's work.

The following towns also have conference facilities available; for further information contact the Comité Régional du Tourisme (see useful addresses):

Côtes-du-Nord: Perros-Guirec, Trégastel, St-Brieuc.

Finistère: Brest.

Ille-et-Vilaine: Dinard, Rennes, St-Malo.

Morbihan: Lorient, Quiberon, Pontivy, Vannes.

The addressses of the region's other main Chambres de Commerce are given below:

Côtes du Nord: rue de Guernesey, 22000 St-BRIEUC. Tel. 96.94.20.94.

Finistère: Place du l9e R.I. BP 126, 29268 BREST Cedex. Tel. 98.44.14.40; 14 place des Otages BP 6, 29210 MORLAIX. Tel. 98.88.61.74; 145 avenue Keradennec, BP 410, 29330 QUIMPER. Tel. 98.98.29.29.

Morbihan: 21 quai des Indes BP l47, 56101 LORIENT Cedex. Tel. 97.02.40.00.

Ille-et-Vilaine: 5O rue Nationale BP 1061, 35301 FOUGERES Cedex. Tel. 99.99.04.89; 33 avenue Louis-Martin BP 185, 35409 St-MALO Cedex. Tel. 99.56.60.02.

Interpreters can be hired from the following companies:

Gaëlle Guides Service, 13 rue Pont-aux-Foulons, 35000 Rennes. Tel. 99.35.00.09.

Tombelaine, BP 2ll, 35302 Fougères Cedex. Tel. 99.94.29.40.

Bretagne Buissonière, La Villeneuve, 56400 Auray. Tel. 97.56.27.91.

Association Lagad-Tourisme, Office de Tourisme, Place des Otages, 29210 Morlaix. Tel. 98.62.14.94.

CHILDREN

In Brittany, as elsewhere in France, children are treated as people, not just nuisances. It is pleasant to be able to take them into restaurants (even in the evening) without heads being turned in horror at the invasion. It has to be said however, that French children, being accustomed to eating out from an early age, are on the whole well behaved in restaurants so it helps if one's own offspring are able to understand that they can't run wild.Although many resort restaurants offer a children's menu for around F25, it is unnecessary to order a complete meal for young children: set menus often give ample enough portions for you to share with toddlers. For older children, an omelette (with or without the *frites*) will almost always be supplied, even if it does not appear on the menu.

Most hotels have family rooms so children do not have to be separated from parents and a cot (*lit bébé*) can usually be provided for a small supplement, although it is a good idea to check availability if booking in advance.

In other respects, children are well provided for. Many seaside resorts have supervised beach clubs where parents can safely leave their young ones (for a small fee) to take part in various activities.

It is fairly common for French children to take holidays away from their parents in *colonies de vacances* (holiday camps or villages). This idea is fairly well developed in the USA and becoming more so in the UK. This type of holiday offers children a wide range of activities, horseriding, water or other sports and some organisations offer holidays on working farms (eg the Ille-et-Vilaine Loisirs Accueil—see useful addresses). It has advantages too, for parents who can perhaps have a touring holiday without a car full of bored children. Contact the companies and organisations below for more details.

Loisirs de France, 30 rue Godot-de-Mauroy, 75009 Paris. Tel. (1) 47.42.51.81.—has two centres at Carantec in Finistère and St-Cast in Côtes-du-Nord.

Vacances-Loisirs, 12 rue 8 mai 1945, 75101 Paris. Tel. (1) 42.06.19.56.

Union Française des Centres de Vacances Bretagne (U.F.C.V.), 16 rue de la Santé, 35000 Rennes. Tel. 99.67.21.02.

GAYS

Gay organisations and social centres are pretty thin on the ground in Brittany. The local papers *Ouest-France* and *Télégramme* may list clubs, otherwise the national *Gai Pied Guide* (published in French, but available in the UK), is the most reliable guide. If you need urgent help or information, try the Paris-based gay switchboard (SOS Homosexualité), tel. 16.1-46.27.49.36) where there are English-speakers; please note this service is only active Wednesday and Fridays from 6 p.m. until midnight.

DISABLED

Most disabled travellers will be keen to book accommodation in Brittany rather than arriving "on spec". The region's official list of hotels (available from the FGTO or the Brittany tourist office—see useful addresses) includes the international wheelchair symbol to indicate which have rooms suitable for disabled people, but the facilities may vary widely, so do check before booking if you have particular needs. A guide, *Où Ferons Nous Etape* (in French only) lists accommodation, throughout France, suitable for the disabled, including wheelchair users. It is available (for F40 by post) from the Association des Paralysés de France, 17 boulevard August-Blanqui, 75013, Paris.

The Royal Association for Disability and Rehabilitation (RADAR), 25 Mortimer Street, London W1N 8AB. Tel. 01-637 5400, has some useful information for tourists, including a guide book, *Access in Brittany*, which was researched by a group of young disabled people. Note, however, that this was published in 1978, so facts need to be checked.

France's sister organisation, Comité National Français de Liaison pour la Réadaption des Handicapés (CNFLRH), is based at 38 boulevard Raspail, 75007 Paris. Tel. (1-45.48.90.13). They offer a good information service for disabled visitors to France and publish a free guide in French/English entitled *Touristes Quand Même* which gives information about access at airports, stations, tourist sites, restaurants, etc. as well as where to hire wheelchairs and other aids. The guide covers the three Breton *départements* of Côtes-du-Nord, Finistère and Morbihan but not Ille-et-Vilaine. They also have a list available (for F10) of hotel chains which have suitable accommodation for handicapped travellers (request the list for the provinces, a separate one covers Paris). This list was however compiled in 1982, so it may be best to contact the hotel chains directly for information. Wheelchairs and other equipment can be hired from Ouest Medicap Service, 21 rue Marcel-Proust, St-Brieuc. Tel. 96.78.12.77.

There is a holiday centre at Beg-Meil which is adapted to cope with physically handicapped guests and offers a central restaurant, entertainment and cultural facilities. For more information, contact Renouveau, Service Diffusion, 2 rue Trésorie, 73023 Chambéry Cedex. Tel. 79.70.37.72. Some gîtes ruraux in Côtes-du-Nord are equipped for handicapped guests (see Where to Stay).

Brittany Ferries offers free passage for cars of registered disabled travellers on all their routes (except Plymouth-Santander). Most major railway stations in Brittany have facilities for disabled people with good access. A free guide—*Guide pratique du voyageur, à l'intention des personnes à mobilité réduite* (in French only) is available at major stations or by post from SNCF, BP 234.09, 754536 Paris Cedex 09. A similar guide is published for motorway travel—*Guide des autoroutes à l'usage des personnes à mobilité réduite*—available free from Ministère des Transports, Direction des Routes, Service du Contrôle des Autoroutes, BP 70, 69672 Bron Cedex. Some towns in Brittany organise special transport for handicapped people—enquire at the town hall (*mairie*) of the town you wish to visit. Information about air and sea travel is also available in a guide (new edition due March 1989), entitled *Door-to-Door*. For a free copy write to Department of Transport, *Door-to-Door Guide*, Freepost, Victoria Road, South Ruislip, Middlesex HA4 0NZ who can also provide copies on cassette for the vision-impaired. In the USA, the following organisations offer services to disabled travellers:

Federation of the Handicapped, 211 West 14th Street, New York, NY 10011—leads tours for its members.

Travel Information Service, Moss Rehabilitation Hospital, 12th St. and Tabor Rd., Philadelphia, PA 19141—has general information for would-be travellers.

Wings on Wheels, c/o Evergreen Travel Service, 19505L 44th Avenue West, Lynnwood, WA 98036—private company organising travel for the disabled.

STUDENTS

Anyone under the age of 26 can benefit from cut-price travel to Brittany and rail cards for getting around the region—for details see Getting There.

If you wish to have a prolonged stay in the region, it may be worth finding out about an exchange visit or study holiday. Several organisations exist to provide information or arrange such visits. In the UK, the Central Bureau for Educational Visits and Exchanges, Seymour Mews House, Seymour Mews, London W1H 9PE produces three books; *Working Holidays* (although opportunities in Brittany are limited); *Home from Home* (a wealth of useful information about staying with a French family) and *Study Holidays* (details of language courses which include some in Brittany). In Brittany itself, try the Union Française des Centres de Vacances (UFCV), 16 rue de la Santé, 35000 Rennes. Tel. 99.67.21.02 who organise cultural, leisure and sporting holidays and activities for young people.

Organisations in the USA include the Council on International Educational Exchange (CIEE), 205 E. 42nd Street, New York, NY 10017 (Tel. 212 6611414)—a wide range of services, including travel; American Council for International Studies Inc., 19 Bay State Road, Bost, Mass. 02215 (Tel. 617 236 2051); AFS International/Intercultural Programs Inc., 313 East 43rd Street, New York, N.Y. 10017 (Tel. 212 949 4242); Youth for Understanding International Exchange, 3501 Newark Street, NW, Washington DC 20016 (Tel. 202 966 6800) and Nacel Cultural Exchanges, Board of Trade Building, Suite 528, 301 West First Street, Duluth, Minn. 55802 (Tel. 218 727 8202).

Once in Brittany, students will find a valid student identity card is useful in obtaining discounts on all sorts of activities. including admission to museums and galleries, cinema, theatre, etc. If you do not happen to have your I.D. card with you, reductions may sometimes be allowed by proving your status with a passport.

The Centre d'Information et Documentation de Jeunesse, based at 101 quai Branly, 75015 Paris. Tel. (1) 45.66.40.20 is a national organisation which disseminates information pertaining to youth and student activities. There is an office in Rennes at 6 cours des Alliés, tel. 99.31.47.48 which is open to the public—its notice board can be a useful source for accommodation and events.

For individual holidays, the cheapest way to stay is generally under canvas, or in a hostel, but if communal living does not appeal, then there are plenty of one-star hotels where you can find very reasonably-priced, simple rooms. See Where to Stay.

FURTHER READING

Ardagh, John. *France Today*. London: Secker and Warburg. Up-to-date, hefty tome on modern France.

Balzac, Honoré de. *The Chouans*. London: Penguin Classics. Historical novel of the Breton Royalists.

Burl, Aubrey. *Megalithic Brittany*. London: Thames and Hudson. Over 350 ancient sites and monuments.

Cole, Robert. *A Traveller's History of France*. London: The Windrush Press. Slim volume for background reading.

Hamilton, Ronald. *A Holiday History of France*. London: The Hogarth Press. Illustrated guide to history and architecture.

Zeldin, Theodore. *The French*. New York: Random House. How the French live today.

USEFUL ADDRESSES

In Paris:
Air France, 119 Champs Elysées, 75000 Paris. Tel. 1-42.99.23.64.

Maison de la Bretagne, Centre Commercial Maine-Montparnasse, 17 rue de l'Arrivée BP 1006, 75737 Paris Cedex 15. Tel. 1-45.38.73.15.

In Brittany:
A.B.R.I. 3 rue des Portes-Mordelaises, 35000 Rennes. Tel. 99.31.59.44.

Air France, 7 rue de Bertrand, 35000 Rennes. Tel. 99.63.09.09.

Association Bretagne-Irlande, Monsieur Polig Monjarret, Lan Langroez, 56270 Ploemeur. Tel. 97.86.33.73.—to promote Irish/Breton links.

Association Bretagne-Pays de Galles, c/o Institut Culturel de Bretagne, 13 rue de Belfort, BP 66A, 35031 Rennes Cedex. Tel. 99.38.89.88.—to promote Celtic ties with Wales.

Association Bretagne-Trans América, La Maison Pour Tous, Place du Rumel, BP 34, 56110 Gourin. Tel. 97.23.47.46—promotes international relations.

Comité Régional du Tourisme, 3 rue d'Espagne, B.P. 4175, 35041 Rennes, Cedex. Tel. 99.50.11.15.

Institut Franco-Américain, 7 Quai Chateaubriand, BP 2599, 3509 Rennes Cedex. Tel. 99.79.20.57

Ligue Française pour la protection des Oiseaux (LPO), La Corderie Royale, BP 263, 17305 Rochefort.

Société pour l'étude et la protection de la nature en Bretagne, 186 rue Anatole-France, BP 32, 29276 Brest.

Cotes du Nord:
Comité Départemental du Tourisme, 1 rue Chateaubriand, 22000 St-Brieuc. Tel. 96.61.66.70.

Centrale de Réservation Loisirs Accueil, 5 rue Baratoux, BP 556, 22010 St-Brieuc. Tel. 96.62.12.40.

Finistère:
Comité Déepartemental du Tourisme, 34 rue de Douarnenez, 29000 Quimper. Tel. 98.53.72.72.

Accueil Rural, Maison de l'Agriculture, Stang Vihan, BP 504, 29109 Quimper. Tel. 98.95.75.30 (for *gîtes* etc.).

Ille-et-Vilaine:
Comité Déepartemental du Tourisme, Préfecture, 1 rue Martenot, 35032 Rennes Cedex. Tel. 99.02.97.43.

Centrale de Réservation Loisirs Accueil en Haute-Bretagne, 1 rue Martenot, 35000 Rennes. Tel. 99.02.97.42.

Morbihan:
Comité Departemental du Tourisme, Préfecture, BP 400, 56009 Vannes Cedex. Tel. 97.54.06.56.Service de Réservation Loisirs-Accueil, as above. Tel. 97.42.61.60.

Relais des Gîtes Ruraux, 2 rue du Chateau, 56403 Auray Cedex. Tel. 97.56.48.12.

In the UK and Eire:
Air France, 158 New Bond Street, London W1Y OAY. Tel. 01-499 9511; 38 Patrick Street, Cork, Eire. Tel. (21) 24331.

Sophie Goodfellow, Brittany Chamber of Commerce, 69 Cannon Street, London EC4N 5AB.

Consulat Général de France, College House, 29/31 Wrights Lane, London W8 5SH. Tel. 01-937 1202.

French Government Tourist Office, 178 Piccadilly, London W1V 9DB.

In the USA and Canada:
Air France, 666, Fifth Avenue, NEW YORK NY 10019. Tel. 212 247 0100; 8501 Wilshire Boulevard, Beverly Hills, Los Angeles, Ca. Tel. 213 614 0999; 979 Ouest boulevard de Maisonneuve, Montreal. Tel. 514 284 2825; 151 Bloor Street West, Suite 600. Tel. 922 5024.

French Government Tourist Office, 610 Fifth Avenue, New York, NY 10020; 9401 Wilshire Boulevard, Beverley Hills, Los Angeles Ca 90212. 645 North Michigan Avenue, Suite 630, Chicago, Illinois 60611; World Trade Center, 103-2050 Stemmons

Freeway, Dallas, Texas 75258; 360 Post Street, San Francisco, Ca 94108.

French Government Tourist Office, Suite 490, Tour Esso, 1981 Av McGill Collège, Montreal H3A 3W9, Quebec; Suite 2405, 1 Dundas Street, Toronto M5G 1Z3 Ontario.

EMBASSIES & CONSULATES

In most cases, the nearest consular services are in Paris.

American Embassy, 2 avenue Gabriel, 75382 Paris, Cedex 08. Tel. 16-1.42.96.12.02.

Australian Embassy, 4 rue Jean-Rey, 75015 Paris. Tel. 16-1. 45.75.62.00.

British Consulate (Honorary Consul), "La Hulotte", 8 avenue de la Libération, 35800 Dinard. Tel. 99.46.26.64.

British Embassy, 35 rue du Faubourg-St-Honoré, 75008 Paris. Tel. 16-1.42.66.91.42.

Canadian Embassy, 35 avenue Montaigne, 75008 Paris. Tel. 16-1.47.23.01.01.

Irish Embassy, 12 avenue Foch, 75116 Paris. Tel. 16-100.20.87.

ART/PHOTO CREDITS

INDEX

M, N

O, P